A Path to Follow...

Reflections of a student at Gobind Sadan

A Path to Follow...

Reflections of a student at Gobind Sadan

Ralph Singh

Sterling Paperbacks

STERLING PAPERBACKS
An imprint of
Sterling Publishers (P) Ltd.
A-59, Okhla Industrial Area, Phase-II,
New Delhi-110020.
Tel: 26387070, 26386209; Fax: 91-11-26383788
E-mail: sterlingpublishers@airtelbroadband.in
ghai@nde.vsnl.net.in
www.sterlingpublishers.com

A Path to Follow: Reflections of a student at Gobind Sadan
© 2008, Ralph Singh
ISBN 978 81 207 3793 8

The author invites readers to visit the book's companion site at:
www.ExploringSpirituality.org
or write to info@exploringspirituality.org
to read the latest updates, and join the conversation.

Back cover photo: *Jean Armour Polly*

*All other photos except as noted are property of Ralph and Joginder Kaur Family Trust,
taken by either Ralph or Joginder*

Printed and Published by Sterling Publishers Pvt. Ltd.,
New Delhi-110 020.

DEDICATION

To His Holiness Baba Virsa Singh,
that this small tribute to the love of God
which you have filled me with can spread just a little of Your
Light in the darkness.

And to all my classmates who have already passed their course,
to those who are with me today, and to those who are yet to come.
And to the great ones of my generation.
You were always just a "beat" ahead.

Our Goal

Many people seek enlightenment – merging with God. But the goal of a student at Gobind Sadan is first to learn to become a halfway decent human being. Maharaj ji often says:

"A good person possesses many great qualities. First become a good human being." In the process, God gathers you up in His Infinite Love.

Lagay chalo

"Just keep moving along the path. He'll never disappoint you."

Aram nal chalo

"Take your time, go step by step."

"You face East and He sends you to the West."
"Whatever God wants will ultimately happen."

Guru Granth Sahib

Foreword

He has listened to silence for hours. He has sensed the day dawning and ebbing away. He has watched the few blades of grass in his compound, Gobind Sadan, turning green season after season. He has felt days converting into weeks, months, and years.

Ralph Singh, an American who has embraced Sikhism, has gone through this cycle for years in search of faith. His experiences with truth are real and he narrates his fears and frustrations in this book. I find that his search has been meaningful. He has been able to overcome disbelief and doubts and has arrived at a solid platform of commitment. He believes that the important thing is to rise above yourself and this can be done by reciting, *Nam*, God's Holy Name. He makes no secret of his wanderings and sufferings. Indeed, he has gone through the valley of the shadow before reaching the Sunlit mountain tops.

Ralph is lucky because he met Baba Virsa Singh and spent years in Gobind Sadan under his wings till he breathed his last. It is the message of Baba Virsa Singh that Ralph interprets in his book and it is the message of Babaji that inspires him. He has his mission cut out for the rest of his life, to strengthen pluralism which Babaji practiced and preached.

Ralph's narration of truth sets one thinking that time, like a river, flows relentlessly. Or, is time only standing water? Decades or centuries are only ripples. What do changes around us mean? What is progress? Material or moral. How is it measured? Is it all only an illusion.

Ralph's book shows that he has sought answers to such questions for many years and wonder if there is any single answer. Sages through the ages have tried to dins a key to the riddles of life. Several religions have supplied answers to some of the questions raised in the minds of human beings. Man is divine enough to delve into the intricacies of life. Has Ralph found what it means?

My own feeling is that there must be a purpose for which the whole world is working. I have clung to this faith. I have not been able to comprehend what it is all about but faith helps. It is like a peg on which you can hang all your doubts and fears.

However fleeting, life has a meaning. Perhaps one life is part of a series of life. Death is only one turning of the endless wheel of life. As the Purana says: "Life is transitory. So are the youth and wealth of a man. Wives, children, friends and relations are but passing shadows of life. Only virtue and good deed endure; the rest is but changeful like a wave of the ocean. This is the law of life."

As Romain Rolland says in his book, *Jean Christopher*, man must die for a child to be born like the day which must consume itself in the darkness of night for a new dawn. An individual must be born again and again. So must a human being or self. This is a journey from the horrible to the sublime. It does not end the search.

Still, it helps one bear one's sorrows. It tells on how to live and gives assurance in the presence of death. I feel it is not the life that is important but the way in which you lead it. Ethical living is more endearing than the God. After all, agnosticism or atheism too is a faith in the sense that it is based on some belief that there should be a scientific proof for the Almighty.

Confucius, probably the greatest of Chinese sages, did not teach of God as such. Instead, he taught a system of good conduct. He told us, it is not the life that matters but the way you live. Ralph has felt life, followed its message in the *Nam*.

I am proud that I have known a person like him.

Kuldip Nayar

Preface

I am nothing special. I like to think of myself as an ordinary person who continues to have extraordinary experiences. And, I have determined that whatever has happened to me had nothing to do with me as a person anyway. Whatever I have learned or experienced is all His Grace. As I write, there are countless people around the world in whom His Voice is calling, and to who He appears.

Special can be a trap. And I have fallen into it many times. It is only through His kindness and all forgiving nature have I been able to crawl out and learn to stand and walk again. For when we feel we are special we are in fact no better and perhaps far worse than the simple creatures that live in the earth we tread upon and trample every day. They go about their business with none of our vices, none of our endless quest to be something in our own right. Our only true existence is being part of Him and finding our place of service in His order.

Our only saving grace is our potential to recognize and follow the Light within. The only thing special in us is the Guru, the Voice within, the "form" of God and the One who can lead us to God. For me it is the one they call *Sarawan wale* or just Maharaj ji.

To me, His is the Voice of God and all the saints and prophets who came in God's name. He embodies all Truth. He is all love.

I know because when I asked to hear the Voice of God it was His Voice that spoke to me.

When I sat in meditation at the sacred fire as I was directed to, it was His form that arose out of Jesus and Guru Gobind Singh as they ascended they merged into Him.

No one ever used His name. It was only Maharaj ji. I didn't even know His name. It didn't matter. He was the One to lead me to God, and for some special reason, which I will never understand, I was led to Him.

For we are all orphans born into this world to surrogate parents. No matter how kind our parents are and how much love and luxuries they shower upon us we are ever longing for something else, something intangible. Something is missing that we ourselves can't identify. But in the midst of all the noise of the world we long to hear One Voice. In the midst of all the glitter and beauty, there is One Face we want to see yet we may not even know what it looks like. Surrounded by the wonders of the material world, wanting for nothing, there is a gaping hole inside us which hungers to be filled.

So often events unfold which allow us to find Him, our True Father. He may send a brother or sister to lead us to Him. To some He appears as He did to me. But somehow or another He finds us and finds a way to bring us home. And when we finally meet Him and are ushered into His presence there is no mistaking it. All that we have hoped and yearned for is suddenly standing or sitting before us and the joy of Homecoming is beyond description.

For me my earliest recollections are as a little boy. Suffice it to say that from childhood I had been guided by a Voice and a sound which I could never share with anyone for I myself did not know from where it came.

24 December, 2007   *Ralph Singh*
                                                        Gobind Sadan

Introduction

As children, I'm convinced that each of us hears a Voice that guides us throughout our life. Call it our conscience, call it the Voice of the Universe, call it what you wish, but early in my life it was so clear that it was my constant companion. But somewhere between Bar Mitzvah and Boy Scouts, when values fall out of fashion, the Voice left me, and I, like many American youth, felt the material world, with all its temptations, corruption, and oppression, close in and I got buried. As I approached college, the need to find my purpose and define my integrity, again summoned forth my longing to reconnect to the Voice.

I left the U.S. in December 1970 in search of a Vision, the Voice that had been with me since childhood. The Voice had taken form and appeared to me in August of 1970 after I had just finished my studies and was waiting to see which path my future would take. I had studied what I had understood to be all the world's religions (at both the University of Rochester and Columbia, specializing in Japanese area studies and U.S. History). Yet there was a path of higher learning that was calling, and a methodology not found even in the world's best seats of learning. For what I sought and yearned for was Truth, and God the Authority behind Truth was not accessible through books. While I enjoyed the quest for knowledge during my college years it was the wisdom to use it wisely that was missing. So I followed the Voice and the Call and struck off on my own on a pilgrimage to points unknown, but totally confident that I would be led on the path that I needed to follow.

In telling these stories, I have tried to share only that which I have experienced myself or was personally told by the ones who had the experiences. I've tried to avoid any hearsay.

Charan chalo – Chalo marg Gobind
Let's travel together along the Path to God

Table of Contents

BOOK I – A PATH TO FOLLOW

Path I: *Looking for God behind the Ark*

Path II: *Constructing God's House without Walls:*
Building a New Community and a New Consciousness

Path VIII: *Reflections – Beyond the Notes*

BOOK I

A PATH TO FOLLOW

PATH I

Looking for God behind the Ark

The Calling

I was born, Ralph Neal Rakieten, an only child of loving parents in Syracuse, New York. My father was the youngest of eight and being the youngest grandson of my paternal grandfather brought an excess of adoration and attention. That was not to be matched by the love showered on me by my maternal grandmother. As my mother was also an only child, I was the sole focus of her attention. My Uncle and Aunt who lived a town away had no children of their own, so I also in essence had another very luxurious home. I wanted for nothing and actually, I never really wanted much materially. However, it was not the material world that called to me.

Voice of My Youth

I first began to 'hear' His voice when I was about six or seven years old. I had just mastered addition in school and was showing a younger boy how to add, drawing with a stick in the dirt near our driveway entrance on Vail Street, in what was then, the small South shore Long Island community of Islip. Suddenly a prayer ushered forth. I called out to the One whose presence I always felt, "No matter how much I learn always keep me like a child before you."

Then came the 'sound', the incessant ringing in my head. It was 1957. I must have just gotten my first transistor radio and Sputnik, the first Russian satellite was in orbit. One night as I lay down the noise appeared. It sounded like static at first. So much so that I opened my bookcase headboard to make sure I hadn't left my radio on. Then I remembered hearing stories of women whose rollers had 'picked-up' transmissions from Sputnik in space. This must be the explanation. I was receiving messages from space. But it never stopped, sometimes getting so loud I could barely think. Whether I was talking, sitting, sleeping, it was always there. So finally, I just accepted it as background noise.

Like many American youth, I had a paper route delivering newspapers on my bicycle in our neighborhood. That was year round summer and winter. One wintry day I loaded the papers in my basket, pulled my bike out of the garage at the rear of the house and set off. I had only rounded the corner and gotten in front of our house when my front wheel spun out on the ice. I fell into the road with the bike on top of me, blocking my way to the safety of the curb. I looked up and saw the grill of a black

Ford bearing down on me. "Run, run!" The Voice was deafening inside me. Jumping to its command I managed to crawl out from under the bike and rushed across the road just as the car swerved around my bike and ended up running up on the curb about twenty-five yards from where I sat – heart pounding, panting to catch my breath. The driver looked back at me and raised his fist in anger. Then he just backed off the curb and drove away.

Looking for God behind the Ark

My mother reminds me that I used to look for God behind the Ark in our Synagogue. It was an old house with the downstairs remodeled into a worship area and the upstairs into classrooms. I used to love to stand for prayer and try to read along with the old men whom I sat next to. I loved reading about the Prophets, and singing and calling out to One I couldn't see. The stories from the Bible were clear in my mind and served not simply as moral lessons but reinforcement that indeed God was a Power beyond the world we lived in.

Some time later, I was playing with a friend in the attic of our garage. One area was finished with wooden planks so we could store the screens and storm windows and other paraphernalia for the various seasons. Beyond the boards lay an area of unfinished paper-thin cement board. We were jumping on the wooden floorboards when I missed the boards and went straight through cement-board ceiling to the concrete floor some 10 feet below leaving a gaping hole behind me. I landed like a frog with my knees above my ears, and my tailbone hovering just above the floor. The wind was totally knocked out of me but with God's grace I had no other injuries. My friend, Jesse, peered down through the hole, "Are you all right?" I couldn't answer, couldn't find my voice for several minutes. Finally, I was able to stand up and catch my breath. As I walked slowly through the back gate that led to our house, Jesse following close behind making sure I was really okay, The Voice spoke again, "You will be a prophet to your people. But now, just as Joseph foresaw, you will have seven bad years. Then I will come for you."

Growing up in the America of the 60's was tumultuous in many ways. And just as the Voice had cautioned, somewhere between Bar Mitzvah and Boy Scouts, when values fall out of fashion, the Voice left me and I, like many youth felt the material world with all its temptations, corruption, and oppression close in and I got buried.

Camp, Boarding School, and the 'Lost Years'

At age 11, my parents sent me to what we called a 'sleep-away' camp, Winnebago, for the summer in a pristine part of Maine. And while I had a great time the first year, the second summer triggered the start of the worst years of my life. Prior to that moment, I had been absolutely fearless. I'd climb the tallest tree in an instant, jump into deep water without a care, grab anyone even twice my size and start wrestling, or ride big boys' bikes even if I had to stand up the whole way.

But standing in the woods one day at the beginning of camp I suddenly felt the Voice and all its power leave me. For the first time in my life, I experienced fear. Although I had been forewarned, nothing could prepare me for the force with which it hit. I remember leaning against a tree for support and when I opened my eyes it was like the whole world had literally turned upside down. I was alone in a strange world. The happiness had left. I felt totally abandoned and very afraid. I struggled to the dining hall and kept on struggling, groping my way through a strange new world. I had lost touch with my 'lifeline'. Left to swim alone in the ocean, I found myself calling out for help more often than I can remember.

Boarding school at The Gunnery was only slightly better. At least I could apply myself to studies and sports. Here my mind was continually challenged by teachers and coaches who wanted to squeeze the best out of me. And even if I resisted they still managed to get me to perform at levels which clearly showed my penchant for learning. This dedicated group taught me to think critically, and to express my usually unstructured thoughts in a mere 50, 100, or 350 words on a daily basis. Wally, my English teacher was also my Wrestling coach and kept me locked up until success was assured. What's more, by the time I graduated, I had been forced to read more classic literature than I would normally have read in a lifetime. Although I still have a few close friends I stay in touch with, living among a totally different class of people than I was used to, proved daunting indeed. Emotionally, I was still adrift.

Archetypes and Japanese Studies – turning the corner

In college, at the University of Rochester, intellectual history provided me with a framework to view the world. I chose to look at the United States as the culmination of Western Civilization and Japan as the culmination of the East and study everything from comparative mythology and religion to the political and economic theories that brought them into conflict in WW II. While college was no doubt a 'secular' experience in worldly knowledge, in reviewing my old papers, I found an old freshman college essay defending the existence of God, and from there on my quest for Truth was as central to my education as social concerns were to my life.

The Candle and the Light – Early meditative experiences

During the summer of 1969, I drove cross-country from New York to California with Mark, one of my childhood friends. It was a beautiful 3500-mile trip over the top of the Great Lakes, across Montana, onward through Idaho, then to Oregon and down the Pacific Coast to San Francisco. While there, we visited the beautiful Zen Monastery of Tassajara in Big Sur. It was there that I had my first disciplined experience with meditation. Sitting in line with the monks in a traditional Zen Do under the watchful eye of the Master, I was able to begin to glimpse the mind as separate from my being. And sense that there was another power within me which I could in fact use to control the mind. Moreover, for the first time I began to feel separated from my body. The floor beneath no longer solidly supported me.

Later that year, on yet another trip, this time to Montreal, I started using a candle to meditate. I don't know where I got the idea, but like a moth, I was drawn to the light. I fixed the candle to the floor, sat before it, and began to visualize that light within me. I would concentrate unwaveringly on the flame. Then closing my eyes, draw the flame towards me until it would appear in my mind. It was a wonderfully empowering experience. Once again, I would totally lose track of my body.

Then one day, I was sitting on the floor talking with a friend, when suddenly the floor just started to fall away in the middle of the conversation. It was a little startling but I was still there and in one piece. But from then on, I began falling through the floor more regularly.

Organizing Columbia during the 1970 student strike

I spent my senior year at Columbia, in New York City. It turned out to be the fateful year of the 'Kent State' killings. National Guardsmen shot and killed several student protestors on a university campus. A national student strike ensued, closing down classes across the country. The nation and campuses were polarized, and on our campus the students voiced their displeasure with institutional support of the 'establishment', the evil nexus that was responsible for injustice and war. I determined it was the people not the institution which made the difference and organized the graduate schools to focus on serving the community. We called it 'Work Action Group', those within the university community, both faculty and students alike, dedicated to serving the people not the 'establishment'. We held several dialogues, which drew the likes of Margaret Mead, and encouraged the medical and law students to start clinics, and the other students to seek community projects in which to volunteer. It was my first experiment in community building: to create a sense of community among diverse individuals and overcome the strident politics and alienation. I thought a university could be a community model but then came the GREs (graduate school admissions exams) and the university community's commitment to social change vanished before the practical call of the world. I myself graduated in June. With my Bachelors degree in hand from the Rochester, I could continue my studies at the University of Michigan or find some other line of work. Neither choice was terribly appealing. I wanted to find another path.

1970 – He Reveals Himself the Truth to Change Our Minds and Change the World

I had just finished college but wasn't satisfied with what I had learned. I had tried my best to understand how we humans had gotten ourselves into such a mess. We were constantly embroiled in wars, constantly heaping inhumanity after inhumanity on those who were different, and often in the name of religion or some other lofty ideal. I wanted to find a system – social, political, or economic that would lead us to a New World of peace and justice. We had seen the decimation of every basic social institution including the very values themselves: no family, no religion, and no moral leadership. I had searched the stacks of many libraries in the literature of the East and West and while I gained much knowledge about the history of our attempts, I found no answer. It seemed that no matter what 'system' we used, whatever formula we applied, that whenever human nature was injected into the equation it failed. The solution then must lie in changing human nature. There had to be a way to change the human consciousness to elevate our thoughts from our baser selfish instincts to search for the ideals of Truth. We had to be able to act out of love rather than self-preservation. The only allusion I found was in the sacred texts of religions. Yet the religions themselves or their practitioners were as much a part of the problem as their teachings were the solution. There must be someone, somewhere, who was following those teachings. If only I could find Him, I could learn and see how Truth could change our minds and change our world. The answer came sooner than I could have ever expected.

The Vision

When a student sincerely takes one step towards God, the True Guru will rush 1000 more to meet him.

Bhai Gurdas

It was a typical summer day in New York City. There was nothing unusual. The August humidity soaked my shirt with sweat as I trudged along the Upper West Side on my way to visit a friend. Reaching his 117th Street apartment beyond Columbia's back gates, I stopped in the lobby waiting for the rickety elevator to take me to 6L, caught my breath and reflected for a minute. Royall was moving on with his life. He almost had his doctorate and his path to academia was clear before him. And I, the young graduate was taking over his apartment. A step up for both of us. But my path was far less clear or was it?

We were sitting on the floor, Japanese style, across a low round table as we often did, chatting over a cup of tea. I don't remember what we were talking about or that there was anything remarkable about that point in the conversation, but then I blinked. And in that split-second, a tall, bearded figure stood before me.

I was face to face with the One who had been speaking to me all my life. A diamond-like light radiated from His head and His eyes literally held the universe. He held up his hand and said, "Don't be afraid." It is startling to say the least when someone invades your consciousness. I was in another dimension, with a Spiritual Being standing as clearly before me as my friend had been before I had been whisked away. Any initial surprise just melted away.

He drew me out through his eyes and toured me around the universe. The space within me expanded to regions previously totally unknown and unexplored. I felt like a baby wrapped in a blanket of light, held up to play with the heavens.

He made me feel like He possessed all the wisdom that I could possibly want to attain and as a role model was everything I could ever aspire to be. He brought me back, showed me something like an atom, and said, "Meditate on this", then left. I opened my eyes to be greeted by my friend in our familiar surroundings, having no concept of how long I had been gone or where indeed I had been.

I was totally at a loss for words. One second we were absorbed in conversation, the next I was somewhere else. I truly didn't know what to say, as I myself had no idea what had just happened. So I thanked Royall for the tea and left.

I made a rough sketch of the Being in my diary then spent the next month trying to find someone who could explain this vision to me, to see whether it fit some sort of archetype, but to no avail. While anyone I consulted marveled at the experience, they could only suggest that it was very much mine alone and pointed to my personal quest.

I began to see the world differently. I remember noting what became a favorite phrase, "there is no such thing as coincidence." Random events started to take shape and the puzzle that had been my life started fitting together.

All I knew was that my course had been set and each day was bringing me closer to leaving everything that I had known all my life for my journey into the unknown. Yet each day I felt more comfortable and confident that what lay ahead was more secure than the life I had been given so far. So the thought of giving up a life of relative comfort never even entered my thoughts. Besides, I figured that if I took the time and money allotted for graduate school and spent it in 'practical research', I perhaps could glean something of benefit for both myself and America. I badly needed and wanted a discipline, one that would bring me and keep me close to Truth and give me the power to maintain my integrity in the midst of this corrupt world. Further, I wanted to find models of how to rebuild a sense of community in a society that had broken down all the basic social institutions, and divided and politicized itself so no commonsense of social responsibility remained and no common standard was visible.

I loved children, and I had taught at summer camps. I knew I could teach. But before I returned I wanted to learn for myself and learn to be a teacher of men. I had to be able to face the responsibility that society demanded. And I was not ready at all. I also knew that unless I could find something I loved enough that I was willing to die for, life had little meaning.

Preparations

Having spent the last four years immersed in Japanese studies, I determined that the best way for me to structure my 'course' was to look at Buddhist societies, starting with the Tibetans and work my way through Sri Lanka, Burma, and finally to an extended stay in Japan. My target was to arrive in India in time to celebrate the Tibetan New Year in Dharmsala, the capital of the Tibetan Buddhist community in exile, learn what I could and then move on. I knew that in the figure of the Dalai Lama, the Tibetans had combined both spiritual and temporal power that I interpreted as a positive way to maintain a value-based society. I was curious to see if they had been able to resist the powers of acculturation and maintain their spirituality. I had collected many addresses and contacts for Japan, including the address of 'The Tribe', a Japanese commune, given to me by Gary Snyder who happened to one fine day stroll into the Kent Hall library, where I was studying, asking for a professor of mine. But except for the address of my friend's sitar master, the India section of my address book was blank.

I gave away all my prized earthly possessions to friends – a pottery bowl, a hand-hewn knife from Montana, and my various tea sets, then packed the remainder of my books and personal belongings into some trunks that I left in my parents' basement. My parka and backpack arrived in the mail. My boots and other paraphernalia I found on forays into the camping and outfitters shops.

The rest of the time, I spent scouring lower New York for the various consulates of the countries I expected to pass through. Some were only small second floor walk-up apartments. Leaving my passport with them, for the time it took to have the visa stamped, seemed like clear test of faith. I had never been out of the country, so the pages were completely clean, but by the time I was done, it looked more like a stamp-collector's mini-album.

14

My parents and grandmother were reconciled to the fact that they had lost me, for the time being at least. After much explaining and cajoling, it was obvious that my mind was made up. I had gathered a group of family friends to explain that the guideposts on our paths were different. There was no turning back.

Finally, I was ready. A few days before I left America on my quest, I was at a party, and someone asked me, "Aren't you afraid of finding the Truth." I was astounded. "What if you don't like it?" he continued. This was beyond my comprehension. To me Truth was the essence of Love, and to face Truth, while often difficult, is nothing to fear. When in fact I was brought face to face with Truth, I was indeed overwhelmed with love.

Six months after the vision, I was to come face to face again, but this time in person.

4

A Quest for Truth and
a Community of God

One of the greatest gifts my Mother ever gave me, was a complete
set of the letters I had written to both her and my grandmother from
the time I left home in December of 1970. Those in addition to my
diaries further document my experiences and help an aging man
reinforce his memories.

The notes from my sketch-pad diary clearly (though not so legibly)
outlined my quest. Leaving the U.S. in December 1970, I had written
my goal:

Plan
*Create a self-sufficient (learning environment) community centering around
spirituality.*
*A Center for Truth-studies, research to show truth in all religions,
and mythology in man's mind.*
*Bent on putting our technology of living in harmony with nature within us and
around us.*
*Architecture, technology, and environmental design (psychology) supporting their
research through patents or sale – we will live in the community.
In general we will be a model community; each member developing
himself, to the advancement of the community and society. In
turn, the environment created by the balance between individual
growth and community growth will provide the most conducive
environment for learning, for growth of consciousness and an
environment especially aimed at raising children (of God).*

My journey
I flew Icelandic airlines to Luxemburg, traveled by train to Basel,
Switzerland to stay with a friend for three weeks, then on to

Belgrade, Yugoslavia for another three week stop (till the New Year) and then boarded the fabled Orient Express to begin the journey to India. From the snowy platform I looked up to meet the smiling eyes of my 'guide', standing arms crossed shivering between cars. He was a Californian in a bean-bag parka and soft-soled moccasins caught in a European winter. He spoke no foreign languages, and had been crammed in with some laborers returning to Turkey. In my L.L.Bean parka and green backpack, he recognized a fellow American, and came to greet me. I was able to get him a seat in my couchette and as he thawed out he shared that he was to have flown from England to Bombay to be with his Guru, Swami Muktananda, but thought maybe a trip overland might prove more interesting.

There have been few statements that have proven to be more true. For we ended up traveling all the way to India together, and it was he, dear Ron, who had the address of 9 Teen Murti in his pocket, Satnam on his lips (with which I spent countless hours meditating on the long train rides) and the name of this Saint, and his ashram Gobind Sadan in Delhi. But this was not revealed to me until we actually arrived in Delhi, so for all intents and purposes I was still on my way to see the Tibetans.

The Voice Shows the Way
We stayed in Istanbul for a week, long enough to enjoy Turkish food and hospitality, wander through fascinating shops and bakeries, and to determine that the best way East was the train to Erzerum. Our hotel on the top layer of one of the hills provided a striking view of the Bosphorus. But given the modern nature of the city, it was hard for me to imagine that simply crossing that body of water into Asia meant stepping back in time. Paved roads gave way to dusty streets and by the time we arrived in Erzerum a day later, we were greeted by a frontier town with one unpaved main street bordered by raised wooden sidewalks and one hotel for tourists. On the way, I was forced to learn patience. Crammed into an upper birth of a three-tier couchette, I had about a foot between my face and the ceiling (or so it seemed). Anxiety attacks were not an option, so I just relaxed and went with the flow.

17

The bus to Iran left every other day so those of us traveling onward, determined to rent a mini-bus to take us to the Iranian border and then fend for ourselves from there. Among the fifteen or so, were a Danish couple and an Afghani businessman. It was again time to step off into the unknown.

As we were passing the Ararat region, I prayed for guidance and safe passage. The answer was very strange but perfectly clear.

In the vision, the van met with an accident. Everyone was killed but me. As I stood feeling sorry for Ron, he suddenly came alive and stepped out of the wreckage. As I surveyed the scene, my eyes fell on the Danish couple and they too stood up and joined us. The four of us started walking away when the Afghani businessman shook himself alive and ran after us.

While the vision was strange, it was even stranger to watch it play out. As we pulled up to the lodge at the Iranian border crossing, I noticed a VW minivan with British plates parked next to us. The nice looking young couple, Doug and Sandy, were in line just ahead of me. As we came through border security I asked them whether they had some room to take us to Tabriz. They replied they could accommodate four of us. So I went to the small restaurant where Ron was waiting and told him I'd found a ride. Then surveying the crowd of fellow travelers, I approached the Danish couple, Michael and Margrete, and asked if they'd like to accompany us. And just as we were making our way out the door, Arkum the Afghani came running after us to become our final companion.

Arkum, fluent in all the local languages, proved invaluable as he guided us through all the small towns finding us the best places to sleep and eat, from Government guest houses on the Caspian Sea, to small carpet town hotels. Driving on through the deserts of Iran with fresh dates and nuts on roadside stands for snacks, we were enjoying watching storks land in the trees when we looked across the sands to find a large city looming in the distance. It was Tehran but while we were bird watching, we had missed the one road into the city. We had to turn around and find our way back. After a few nights in a modern Tehran hotel we moved on through herds of goats and finally through the Shah's game preserve and across the border from Mashhad, into Herat, Afghanistan. A short walk from our multi-storey government operated hotel were the tourist shops, raised wood shacks with fold-down doors stocked full of embroidered leather jackets and jewelry. Having left everything behind and looking to travel further unburdened, I avoided the temptations of cheap ware. Besides, the leather was not fully tanned, and the smell in some shops was enough to keep even the boldest of us away.

Kandahar was almost summer-like and we were able to relax a few days before heading onward. As we strolled, comfortably through the open markets in short sleeves, we felt we were being watched but couldn't see anyone. Suddenly we realized that there was a small crowd of school girls staring at us from under the camouflage of their full black burkas. They scurried off as we returned their gaze.

My son, you'll be home in seven days

While the climate in Kandahar was most pleasant, the food apparently did not suit me. I had contracted dysentery, so by the time we reached Kabul I was not feeling well enough to tour the town with my companions. But, I was by-no means 'alone'. The Voice and the Visions had clearly become my main traveling companions. Lying on my cot in the attic room of our tourist hotel, I was shown an elaborate plan to set up a business in Afghani imports, lamb-skin coats and jewelry, that would make me very rich. I rejected the idea. I had not come on this journey for wealth.

Immediately a spiritual path lay before me and The Voice spoke loudly: "My son, you'll be home in seven days." As we moved to the Kabul Hotel, the Ritz of the city, with its large marble halls, the Voice seemed to echo off the walls, "You'll be home in six days." The Visions and teachings continued almost constantly so that I was very much overwhelmed. "Who do you miss? Your mother?" And she would speak. "Your father? And he would speak. Your friends?" It was as if they in turn were next to me. Nothing was separate. It became so clear that the Voice and the Force behind it were in control of every detail of my life, and I had no choice but to play the role given to me. Finally, on our last day in Kabul, the Voice instructed me to sit at the window. There displayed in the sunset, ushered in by a

19

huge flock of birds streaking across the pastel sky, was a pantheon of prophets and saints seated on the clouds. The message was clear. I was on the right path and they were all there as witnesses that it was in fact True. Moreover, they would be there to help and support me on my way.

The next morning we left Kabul, Arkum, and my illness behind us. Coming down out of the turquoise and pink mountains across the chocolate landscape, bordered by crystal clear rivers all rushing ahead, we nearly flew through the Khyber onto the plains of Pakistan with India stretching before me. I could barely wait to see where the seventh day would have me.

The Golden Temple

With stops outside Peshawar and a night in Lahore, by the evening of the seventh day after my call from Kabul, at dusk just before the border closed we crossed from Husainiwala into India. In a small tea stall near Ferozepur, I glanced up from the rough-hewn wooden table and had my first divine vision of Guru Nanak Dev ji, revered as the first Sikh Guru. He extended his hand from the wall calendar and drew me up above the clouds. It was truly serene. I knew I was close and that this figure who I had never seen before was central to my life, past and present.

Then following the only logical route, we arrived in Amritsar, the holy city of the Sikhs at 11p.m. Though I had been educated at some of the finest schools and studied what I had understood to be all the world's religions I had never seen a Sikh in my life, nor had I ever seen even a reference to the religious teachings known as Sikhism. But as I walked into the precincts of the Golden Temple, a stunningly beautiful two story edifice rising out of its shimmering reflection in the midst of the sacred pool that surrounds it, I looked for the Voice. For this was where I had been led. I was home.

We spent three relaxing days at the Golden Temple, but for me it was a difficult time. There was no doubt in my mind that this was where I had been led but there was no one physically to guide me outside of the now familiar and comforting image of Guru Nanak Dev ji who presided over the entrance to the Temple. All was familiar and comfortable and I was fascinated with these people, these Sikhs who walked barefoot on freezing marble and bathed in the sacred pool surrounding the temple while I was bundled in my parka. I often shared with them that it amazed me to think where their power came from to withstand the cold. These tall strapping men and strong stately women did not fit the image of starving India that I had been taught. Moreover, the fields in the surrounding areas were lush with crops. They were clearly a breed apart. This was a different India. But all my fascination only added to my confusion. Amritsar was the stopping off point for my trip to Dharmsala, and Ron was moving onto Delhi and Bombay.

The visions in Kabul had made the Tibetans a distant reality. There was definitely a different path, but how to find it? I succumbed to my exhaustion and followed Ron to Delhi. And it was there that Ron revealed Gobind Sadan.

5

I Find Him

Arriving in Delhi at the Lodhi Hotel, now a condemned skeleton next to the Oberoi, Ron found that Swami Muktananda had left Bombay and was on his way to Delhi. We would wait for him here. In the meantime, Ron would go meet a Saint he had heard about and ask if we could stay in his ashram 'Gobind Sadan'. After traveling for almost two months an ashram meant some welcome permanence to me. By evening, Ron and Michael came back glowing and said we were welcome there.

So the next day we parted ways. Michael, who had been an economic advisor to the King of Denmark, along with Margrete had paid $2000 each to become *sanyasis* and leave the world. Doug, Sandy, Ron and I followed directions to 9 Teen Murti Marg where Mata Rarewala and Baba Joginder Singh were waiting. After a nice lunch, moongi dal and my first taste of coriander, we piled into the VW bus and were guided to Gobind Sadan.

As we left the manicured streets of New Delhi, the road became less populated. The INA market, now a bustling landmark, was a short single strip of fruit and vegetable stands. Ron stopped to get a basket of fruit. "Never go to the Guru empty handed." By the time we reached Qutab the road was almost deserted. Anderia Morh was simply a bend in the road with some fruit stands. The land from the wireless station onward was barren and covered with scrub. Outside of a few poor villages, there were only a few kilns along the way where the land had been excavated several feet below road grade to provide the dirt for the bricks. Otherwise it seemed we were heading off into nowhere.

An ancient Pipal loomed ahead with the roof-lines of the small village Gadaipur behind it. As we turned off the road to the right passed Wadhalias (Qutab Stud Farm), the walls of a compound rose up across an open field. We drove through the gate to be greeted by a low line of buildings. It fit the vision of the night before. While praying to Swami Muktananda to relieve Ron's headache I had seen this same line of buildings and an empty train leaving the station. It was clear now. I was to stay here. My travels were over.

Standing in the corner against the retaining wall was Harvinder Singh (the tree and bougainvillea still mark the spot) in his classic trench coat, his broad smile spreading above his neatly groomed beard. He greeted us heartily in perfect English, eyes twinkling behind wire-rimmed glasses. Beyond in the field, people were picking chilies. As they stepped out they too greeted us in English. Randhawa Sahib (RK Puram) B.B. Singh, Gill Sahib, S.P Sahib, Mala Wala Bibi all government employees working in the field with the farmers. There were men, women, and children all working together. Well-dressed women carried baskets of dirt or manure on their heads. I couldn't believe that in a caste-ridden society like India that I would find the answer to social equality. Sitting on the irrigation wall, we waited patiently until Harvinder escorted us into the small room behind the *havan*.

Then Face to Face at Last
There beautifully framed by a small window sat the One who had appeared to me in New York. He was all in white, his black beard stood out strikingly against his immaculate clothes. His eyes just beamed love and I knew now that I was really home. Brig. Sahib translated as Maharaj ji looked at me and said: "You're a student, have you found God in your books yet?" We both laughed.

"Of course not," I managed to say.

"Why do you think it should be so easy to find God when it takes 30 years to become a doctor, lawyer or engineer. This is God's school and just as you need to learn to read, write and count

23

before you can really begin to learn, so in God's school, *Nam*, meditation is the *pahilu* (prerequisite)."

Maharaj ji said that He could tell me many things from his own experiences but until I felt them myself I wouldn't understand. Here was someone who knew God and who openly spoke of God's love and His relationship with us. Not only that, He was making this knowledge available free without asking anything from me. He simply said: "Take this prayer – *Ek Onkar Satnam Siri Waheguru* – Understand that tomorrow God is going to come to take your exam. You are way behind in your studies so recite this prayer like you are cramming for that test. Ask God's help. Ask that you want to meet Him."

Reciting the Lesson

Then He tapped me on the head and gave me some *patase* (white sugar puffs) that I learned to call 'candied *nam*' and sent me to my room to begin studying with instructions that tomorrow I should meet him and tell him of my progress. I wrote my first lesson '*Nam*' down on a piece of paper, in Romanized script with the translation: There is One God Whose Name is Truth, Praise to the Ever Greater Ever More Wondrous God.

Believe it or not, while the translation echoed true to my mind, it wasn't important to me. I had met the Guru and this was the lesson. So I would have recited it even without knowing the meaning. And I am sure the meaning in English never entered my mind while I was reciting it. I was too busy concentrating on the words themselves. So after a simple dinner of *roti* (coarse pan bread) and *gajjer sabji* (beet-red carrots), I took my lesson to the room provided with Gyani ji. I began reciting *Nam*, at first with great trepidation. I had heard of the power of 'mantras' and other incantations, and was worried that if I mispronounced a word something terrible would befall me. I vividly remembered Mickey Mouse, in 'The Sorcerer's Apprentice', being overrun and flooded out by an army of water-carrying brooms. But Gyani ji assured me that no such thing would happen. And to be sure, within a short period those 'foreign words' began to echo inside my head. Soon they gained such force that I could not

24

think let alone sleep. I slumped against the wall wrapped in the quilt I was given and let the visions play off my brain. They ran like 'Cinerama' with a wrap-around screen, a question springing up from one side, an answer from the other. All night I was literally consumed with *Nam*. When I finally realized it was morning and ventured out into the daylight I felt like I was five feet off the ground. Maharaj ji met me, put his arm around my shoulder and asked, "How goes the struggle?" It was amazing. He was guiding my lessons.

For the next several days, I literally didn't know which world, let alone which country, I was in. *Nam* was driving my every move, my every thought. I could barely sleep or barely eat. I didn't want to. I was being totally overcome.

On the third day we went into Delhi and outside the Imperial Hotel on Janpath a soothsayer confronted us. "What is the most beautiful flower in the garden?" he asked handing me a paper and pen to write with. "God," said the Voice. So I wrote 'G O D' with absolutely no further thought. He looked astonished. "God is not a flower," he almost shouted and then turned away.

Just accept it
We drove from the Tibetan shops along Janpath to the small brass market across from the Jain temple in Chandi Chowk, kitty corner to the Red Fort, to pick up some souvenirs. *Nam* was pounding in my head like huge waves on the beach with such force that I couldn't stand it and crawled into the back of the van to lie down. Again and again *Nam* would pound in my brain until my mind felt totally subdued. Finally the Voice said, "Just accept it." "OK," I submitted, "I accept it." Suddenly there was peace so deep that it was indescribable, as if the whole sea had calmed to glass and from its depth *Nam* was reverberating. But there was no tension – just peace – not a wave, not a ripple.

When we returned to Gobind Sadan someone was waiting for the van. As soon as I stepped out he said, "Maharaj ji is calling you." I practically ran all the way.

He was sitting with some army officers visiting from the Cant. in the small room where I had first met Him. I went in and purposefully bowed before Him. He looked at me and said with a smile, "Now do you accept that God exists or not?"

I just laughed. "Of course," I managed to say.

Maharaj ji continued, "Now what do you want to do?"

The questions of a lifetime had just been answered at age 22. He'd brought me 'Face to Face' with God. What else could I want but to stay at His feet and learn from Him. I could only say, "You tell me. You appeared to me in America, brought me here to Your Feet. You showed me this Power and made me understand that I have absolutely no control over my own life. God is so Powerful, what is His Order for me?"

Maharaj ji smiled, "All right, you may stay and we'll teach you. But, you have to think this through several times. This is a serious decision."

"Maharaj ji, I can't think any more. You tell me what I should do."

Pleased with the determination in my voice and in my soul, Maharaj ji consented: "From today onward don't cut your hair. We will teach you."

I bowed and returned to my room, my head still swimming with *Nam*. But at least now I was confident that I had found my Path, and keeping my hair, while it was a commitment, seemed so small a price for admission to this school of God, that I didn't give it a second thought.

Charged

I awoke from a deep sleep to a state of what I can only call 'limbo'. Unable to rise from the bed I just lay there waiting for the next command. Suddenly I was enveloped by an energy field so strong that I couldn't move. It felt like nothing I had ever experienced before. I just lay still, which was all I could do anyway, and let this current course through my being. When it finally released me, I was able to stand up immediately. I felt greatly refreshed. I stepped out into the sunshine to find Maharaj ji standing nearby. I explained the experience, and he responded simply, "You are blessed."

Early Letters home to my mother

Envelop labeled '8', postmarked 5-8-71 (8th May) from Janpath Post Office, New Delhi...

26

4ᵗʰ May, 1971 – I share the Vision in New York and the trip with my mother;

"I might as well begin the story which I've described to a few people and hinted at in the first letter to you from India. I was sitting in Royall (Tyler) and Pat's apartment shortly before they left (my 117ᵗʰ Street apartment) and briefly closed my eyes – and was put into 'Samadhi' for the first time as a tall bearded figure with stars in his eyes and a bright light shining from his head said, "Don't be afraid." I just stared in total rapture, looking into his eyes which seemed to contain the whole universe. I kept going deeper and deeper into them, then he showed me an object which was a vision of Brahm, the Creator of the Hindu Trinity, and then released me. I didn't really know what to make of it but it was the event that gave impetus to my trip – or from my present point of view – Maharaj sent for me."

3ʳᵈ October 1971

Most people consider Maharaj a saint, a pious man whose thoughts and life are devoted to God and who has thus been blessed with divine powers. But I know him to be the Guru – a Christ – who has no power in himself outside of God, has no thoughts of his own outside of God's – thus is God on earth, the son or servant of God. He himself said, "I am not a saint, but here to make saints." And because I bow before Him, my own conceptions become unclear and indefinite. The identity which we work so hard to form is firmly rooted in the self. God's way is a firm and constant denial of self-will in recognition of and devotion to what is the goodness in ourselves or any one else we love and what is the 'highest' force which not only orders our self but also all of creation – the Supreme Authority. God willed our self (into being) if you wish. So where is our will? So I know God orders all things – and I believe that when one is blessed by God with love and devotion to Him – God makes His orders known to him in thought or vision – so one can 'hear' God give the orders for the day, for a loved one's life, or for the world – as God chooses to speak them. So bowing to Maharaj I learn to listen to these orders – His will…

27

We are all One

As I sat in the *havan*, I was drawn deep into *samadhi*. There before me stood eight figures. As I was ushered into their presence, they introduced themselves and I was totally in awe.

Jesus, Moses, the Prophet Mohammed (PBUH), Lord Krishna, Lord Ram Chander ji, Lord Buddha, Guru Nanak and Guru Gobind Singh ji.

"We are all one," they began. "It is a shame that our followers have divided us and created conflict in the world. They are disgracing God and our good name. We have appeared to you so as you go forth, you will have no doubt that we are the same and our teachings are the same."

Then, as if that wasn't a powerful enough lesson, Jesus and Guru Gobind Singh ji rose into the air from their respective sides and merged into One figure. It was Maharaj ji. That image is forever fixed in my mind.

6

My Early Experiences

For the first several months, Maharaj ji kept me with Him just about all the time. He used to joke that if He hadn't secured the gate that led to His residence, He would probably wake up to find me waiting patiently, or impatiently, to start the lessons again.

I still remember the first time Maharaj ji left Gobind Sadan without me, almost 6 months later. I stood and cried like a baby whose parents had just gone off and left him with a babysitter.

But the rest of that first February, Maharaj ji took me on several trips in this world and beyond.

You are my firefly
For the first time since our arrival Maharaj ji took us with him on his travels.

Destination Bareilly, in U.P., a four hour drive from Delhi to visit the resident Muslim Pir who was a descendant of Pir Budhu Shah, Guru Gobind Singh ji's great devotee. It was this Pir who had preserved a *chola* (gown) of the Guru, and Pir Budhu Shah's walking stick. Maharaj ji had seen in a vision that these relics were in the Pir's possession and called for them. The astonished Pir, recognizing Maharaj ji's power, gladly offered them, and in a wonderful ceremony had brought them to Gobind Sadan with great reverence where they were received with great pomp and now lie in Maharaj ji's own prayer room.

We all packed into the van. Maharaj ji was sitting on the back deck and the rest of us on the floor before Him. He asked Ron to give me the Bible and told me to randomly open to a passage. It was John, 'a voice crying in the wilderness', preparing a way for the Lord. Maharaj ji turned to me, "You will be my firefly sending out the message to a darkened world. So people will know I am here." When I look at the state of the world, I often feel I have failed miserably in this duty.

Pir Sahib was not only thrilled to have Maharaj ji as his guest but liked the idea of entertaining us four foreigners. So he asked Maharaj ji if we could stay with him. It was our first time outside of the comfortable security of Gobind Sadan, but Maharaj ji assured us he would call us back soon, so we relaxed and enjoyed the Muslim hospitality and especially the Muslim *qawwal*, one of the most joyous musical expressions in the world, that thrilled us every evening. The Pir would sink into a trance of ecstasy for so long that his disciples worried that he, like his father, would leave the world if they did not at last disturb him and bring him back.

Though the hospitality was wonderful, my trance was still connected to Maharaj ji in Gobind Sadan and I longed to return. So we begged our leave and returned to Delhi.

Destination, Sarawan Bodla, Maharaj ji's childhood village and place of enlightenment in Punjab...

In Muktsar district, Punjab, the villages have long names like Manianwala, Giddhervaha, Sikhanwala. Their occupants are just as large, many of whom were well over 6 feet with big hearts to match. The people came pouring out to greet their Guru. *Langar* appeared in the middle of the street, no need to set the table, just roll out the mats and serve anyone and everyone who showed up. It was like an endless pot of God's grace in the form of warm hospitality and hot food. And I mean hot. While my heart drank in the love, my stomach couldn't handle the level of heat in the food and I often had to excuse myself or limit my diet to bananas and chapattis.

Maharaj ji's own family compound in the village of Sarawan Bodla was surrounded by a large enclosure. The now famous Beri tree under which Maharaj ji used to sit for hours, sometimes days in meditation, dominated the courtyard. Here the miracles of his youth took place: curing the incurable by simply offering a leaf from the tree or the dirt at his feet, and the leprosy or any other malady disappeared. Here the dead had risen, from a dead buffalo to a dead boy. Maharaj ji simply says, God told him that a perfectly healthy buffalo would fall dead and that he was to say that it would come alive. When he did, it stood up again.

It was here that you could hear the saints and angels come to bathe in the morning at the pump that still stands next to the tree.

Maharaj ji ushered me into the small room in the string of adobe buildings. Pictures of every saint and prophet imaginable still covered every square inch. The Guru Granth Sahib in which Maharaj ji had found a small piece of dirt was kept with the same respect and cleanliness. As the story goes, Maharaj ji was complaining that something was irritating his eye, yet no one could find anything. He directed them to check each page of Guru Granth Sahib and sure enough there was a piece of dirt. Once wiped clean, Maharaj ji's eye stopped watering. He wanted people to know that Guru Granth Sahib was indeed alive.

It was almost another world. To be taken to the place where Baba Siri Chand ji, Guru Nanak Dev ji and Guru Gobind Singh ji had appeared to him as a child, by Maharaj ji himself, and to walk the fields where he first felt the presence of life in the sap flowing from fresh cut fodder and begged to be excused. Each inch of the compound vibrated with the Holy presence as if the earth and all those above were there to welcome Him back. And I'm sure that is the truth.

Abohar – Brar Sahib's house
I had the privilege of staying with Maharaj ji in Abohar, at Brar Sahib's house, on the outskirts of Sarawan. M. S. Brar was in charge of the extensive canal system responsible for much of the lush crops in the region. He and his wife, Vicky Bhenji, serve Maharaj ji to this day.

Sometimes God comes to your house and you don't even get out of bed to greet Him
That night, after the long trip, I was lazy. Though I was awake, I lay in bed instead of getting up early to take my bath. In the morning as soon as I came to greet Maharaj ji he counseled, "You know sometimes God calls you and you don't even answer. He comes to your door and you don't get out of bed to welcome Him." That was a real wake up call.

Hold onto my feet and I'll never let you fall

Maharaj ji was sitting in a chair speaking to the gathering on Brar Sahib's front lawn. He was always so kind that while talking to people in Punjabi he would give me my lessons in English. All I had to do was close my eyes and tune in. It was like turning the dial on a United Nations' console to get different languages. That morning's lesson was one that I've never forgotten. And whenever there is change or stress in my life I return to it.

In the vision, I was sitting at Maharaj ji's feet. As I bowed to kiss them, He said, "Hold on tight." I clasped them and began to rise. Up and up through the clouds into the Heavens, He grew and grew carrying me along. "Don't ever be afraid," he said. "As long as you hold on to my feet, I will never let you fall." He has shown me again and again, that the Path is so wide you can't fall off, as long as you follow His Order. For *hukam* (God's order) is 'His Feet'. And by holding tight, you are always clinging to God's order. That does not mean that you don't fall down. I fall all the time, only to be picked up by His gracious hand, and set back on my feet.

Maharaj ji loves questions and answers

Walking along a canal near Sarawan with me tagging along, Brigadier Sahib turned to me and said, "Maharaj ji wants you to ask a question. Engage us in conversation." I think I remembered asking about life on other planets and whether we would ever reach there. Maharaj ji's response was that indeed there was life on other planets (as he subsequently showed me) but they had hidden themselves from us and that it was unlikely that we would find them. And that they were so far away that we couldn't reach them. With new computerized radio and bio-telescopes it may be time to put this question to Maharaj ji again.

Some time later friends were visiting from the U.S. After Maharaj ji had spoken to them he invited questions in a way I'll always remember. "Ask me any question," he said, "When you ask, the One inside me will answer and I will learn too." We need to look no further to understand what it means to be truly humble, knowing that the One within you possesses all the Power and Knowledge yet seeing yourself only as His servant.

My first experience with Maharaj ji guiding me in a strange place was when we were returning to Chandigarh from Abohar in a dense fog. Even though Bibi Nirlep Kaur, whose house we were staying at and others were in the car no one could see a thing. So Maharaj ji told them to ask me. I was totally bewildered. Why ask me? I've never even been here before. But without giving it any further thought, Maharaj ji told me to go ahead and give directions. I started telling the driver which way to turn. Sure enough, some 20 minutes later, we ended up in the driveway of Bibi ji's house in Sector 4.

Chandigarh adventures

As day dawned and the fog cleared, I could see that Nirlep's house, like Chandigarh itself, was an architectural masterpiece. Designed by the French master, Le Corbusier, out of cement and huge stone, the mansion had 5 bedrooms all with their own balconies and attached baths, a swimming pool, and a second story 4-tiered library with a beautiful skylight. The living room had a vaulted ceiling, and the largest elephant tusks I'd ever seen dominated the central wall. The dining room could seat 20 easily, and the expansive grounds provided an unobstructed view of the foothills of the Himalayas. All in all, it had the feel of royalty as indeed it should, for Nirlep Kaur and her family were as close to royalty as one can get in Punjab (outside of the Raja's own family).

The balcony behind my bedroom, which overlooked the front of the house, had a carpeted area where we sat whenever Maharaj ji and Nirlep Kaur came to visit me. On one memorable occasion, Maharaj ji had me read from the Old Testament and at the mention of Moses, He would stop me and begin to describe Moses, standing in his brown cloak, staff in hand, very tall and powerful. Maharaj ji liked him very much. For me it was like taking a walk through history.

Maharaj ji takes me on a tour of the Cosmos – Planets with life

I was aware of Dr. Timothy Leary's work with LSD, (the psychedelic 'trip-inducing' drug) at Harvard and the new 'religion' he had started. But I was more concerned that 'turn on, tune in and drop out', was seriously injuring not just the individuals involved but also taking kids who were sensitive and socially conscious and removing them from their active participation in any social movement. So I had never read his book, *'The Politics of Ecstasy'* in America. But when suddenly it showed up in a friend's library in India, I skimmed through it and was amused that someone thought that drugs were the pathway to God. So I took the book to Maharaj ji and asked him to comment. He smiled, "Do you want to see something?" As if to say, 'So this person thinks that drugs will give you enhanced vision!'

He was sitting cross-legged on his bed and Bibi ji (Nirlep Kaur), Baba Joginder Singh, and I were on the floor. "Come here," he beckoned me to come closer. He reached out and tapped me on the head. Immediately I was almost engulfed in the flames of a blazing inferno and could feel the heat so intensely that I literally pulled back just as a child jerks his finger away from a hot stove, and sat in total darkness, waiting. I was floating comfortably in space when Maharaj ji asked, "What do you see?"

"Nothing," I replied. "Don't you see fire?" Bibi ji was translating. While I was millions of miles away, I could hear them clearly. "I did but now I'm in darkness". "Go back to the fire and go beyond it," Maharaj ji directed.

And so the tour began. "Do you see water?" "Yes." "Go to the source." A stream of water led to a giant fall. I could hear the deafening sound of the plunging water. "Go beyond it." As I rose above the falls, a portal opened. "Go through it." I was ushered into a corridor and swept out into an endless stream of lights barreling by at blinding speed. The cosmos unfolded before me in a dazzling display that not even the most spectacular Hubble images can rival. I was inside the very heart of Creation with the One the Creator had entrusted the worlds to as my personal guide. On and on further than the term light years can encompass at speeds no instrument could measure, He led me through countless orbs, pausing only long enough to observe planets with

34

life. On and on I was propelled along until I saw a planet with people. There was absolutely no doubt that they were human beings! Then Maharaj ji took me to another planet. This one had two suns. Then on to another with red soil. I could almost feel its sandy texture. The next stop was again inhabited with a civilization incredibly more advanced. Their faces radiated with a beautiful calm, their simple tunics and pants were made of iridescent thread. It was like entering a science fiction dream world. But this one was undoubtedly real. One planet had two steel-like orbs connected with a corridor and many other remarkable sights.

Totally awed by the breathtaking beauty, I was returned to my quiet state on the floor. I felt the carpet and solid marble rise up to meet me. While not dazed I still couldn't open my eyes. I was totally aware of the experience yet strangely unaffected physically. I'm someone who becomes breathless after a marathon or even a good sprint around the block, but this was soul travel and while I could 'sense', see, and sometimes even feel, I was not tired. I had been cradled in the Hand of my Guide. Maharaj ji asked, "Who showed you this?" Baba Siri Chand ji spoke, "Guru Nanak." But as soon as His name was mentioned Guru Nanak retorted, "Baba Siri Chand." It went back and forth several times neither wanting the credit. And certainly Maharaj ji would never take credit though He did everything. He often says "at that level they are all One. There is no competition among them. If someone praises Guru Gobind Singh, they all praise Him. Or Guru Gobind Singh will reply by praising Baba Siri Chand."

Regardless of the duration or sensation, this experience was forever imprinted on my consciousness. Time and space had collapsed into a singular expression of the infinite Power of God, and the extent of the Presence of the Cosmos, not just a pool of knowledge, that lies within us.

It was clear that everything is visible from within. From that moment on, the visible heavens had forever shrunk to a tent-like canopy from which I could reach up and pluck a shining star at night or ride the clouds across the morning sky. Often when asked to describe the experience I become lost in the enormity of the moment. The more I try to say the less adequate the words seem and I begin to lose sense of the Power. Sometimes it is best not to speak.

When we finally settled back into the reality of the room Maharaj ji looked at me and said as if to reinforce the validity of the experience. "Bring me a scientist someday and I'll show them. Then they can draw maps of these places." I've met many top scientists and shared the vision, but as of this writing Maharaj ji's offer is still open.

Back to Earth

With the warm weather starting I was not properly prepared. I still had blue jeans and flannel shirts. So Maharaj ji called Mr. Kalha, the former Chief Engineer, Canals, Punjab, and asked him to take me to get properly outfitted. Kalha Sahib was a tall hulking man who exuded enormous warmth. His kind eyes beckoned to me to follow him to his car. Outside stood a beautifully preserved DeSoto convertible. "Climb in." He didn't have to make a second ovation. I was soon enjoying his company riding through the streets on the antique leather seats. He took me to a *khadi* (handloom) emporium, and was kind enough to purchase sets of *kurta pyjamas* which lasted long enough to figure prominently in my early photos and finally end up as a present to my Mother that she wore and enjoyed for many years.

Just as Kalha Sahib looked after my clothing needs, Bedi Sahib, another of Maharaj ji's oldest devotees, who had hosted Maharaj ji at his home early in His visits was kind enough to make sure I had enough to eat. Standing on the back lawn beside Maharaj ji, he explained my tender stomach and saw that I had digestible food. Many years later at his home in Ambala, where he was confined by a stroke, he asked me to return the favor and pray for him to Maharaj ji to bless him. When I hesitated, he said, "It's just like my asking Maharaj ji to take care of your food. Think that Maharaj ji is standing right in front of us and plead my case." Alas I waited to return to Delhi, and put the case personally before Maharaj ji.

Chand's prayer room

One of Maharaj ji's earliest and certainly most colorful disciples is Ms. Promilla Chand. Oxford educated Professor of

Philosophy, Cukoo as she is known to those who love her, is so intense in her devotion and so headstrong in her will that just being around her one can be assured of an amazing adventure. The first time she met me in Nirlep's living room, she came right up and said, "So you are the new sant." I was shocked. I certainly didn't see myself as a saint. Fellow student yes, saint, not by a long shot. Anyway, Maharaj ji knew Chand and I had many lessons to share with each other so He sent me to her home for a few nights. Her house in Sector 5 is a virtual museum of Maharaj ji's early history. It was Cukoo who with her camera documented the early days of Maharaj ji's rise. In fact Maharaj ji stayed in her home in a room which still lies untouched from the time He was there. Gobind Sadan's logo of Maharaj ji plowing behind the bullocks was taken from her famous photo. Mata Chand, Cukoo's mother, was as doting as possible on me. And I was given the run of the house.

Now Chand had turned her library into one of the most remarkable prayer rooms I've ever seen. Ever corner of every shelf had pictures, sacred items or scriptures, not just of Maharaj ji but of many of the great saints and Prophets. Along side the Guru Granth Sahib, in one corner she had made an elaborate *Gaddi* for Baba Siri Chand ji. I had a penchant for finding comfortable spots for meditation; quiet, out of the way nooks, where I wouldn't be disturbed. So without thinking about the sanctity of the spot, I quickly settled myself into the recesses of the pillows and lapsed into a beautiful deep Samadhi. Meanwhile, Cukoo and her mother were frantic. They couldn't find me anywhere. Apparently, Maharaj ji was coming and they wanted to clean up and get me ready. Finally, their calls broke through the 'mist' and I responded. The looks on their faces were worth framing. To this day, Cukoo reminds me and laughs about how disrespectful I was to sit in Baba Siri Chand ji's *Gaddi*.

Maharaj ji's birthday

That year we celebrated Maharaj ji's birthday in Chandigarh and some of the first pictures I have of me at Maharaj ji's feet were at that wonderful event. I was allowed to sit near Maharaj ji and just feel and see some of the power that flowed through His Holy Being to those around him. This was a true exchange of love from the Guru to His disciples. And something which Maharaj ji showers on His devotees in the form of song, *Nam*, *parshad*, or just plain Light. It is said that being in the presence of the Guru is akin to one sandalwood tree spreading its perfume to all the neighboring trees. So just being in His Divine Presence is enough to give us a fragrance for life.

But what we do with that scent is the real story. Do we hoard it or share it, covet it or spread it across the world? For if we in our pride keep this gift to ourselves, perhaps it will not grow within us at the rate it would if we understood it is not ours but His, and continue to share it with all we meet. Then we can understand the concept of the endless bounty, of the gift that is inexhaustible. As Guru Nanak has described it,

"The Giver continues to give for His capacity is endless. It is the recipients who get tired for their ability to receive is limited."

Off with your head

Back in Gobind Sadan, I had just started to settle into a routine again after all the traveling and new experiences, when I was summoned by Maharaj ji. He was sitting in the small room silhouetted against the window. Gurcharan was there to translate for me. A sword lay in front of Him. "Today I'm going to take your head. Are you ready?" I wasn't sure, but from the look on Maharaj ji's face He was ready. He began to draw the sword. With more than a little trepidation, I put my head down on the mat before Him. "Let me show you what you'll get," was all I heard. Then I didn't know whether He actually cut my head off or just tapped me but it seemed like my head rolled off spewing the universe. I had no sensation of pain, just a sudden visionary whoosh and once again, I was streaming past orb after orb of lights. On and on into endless space, I was propelled at an ever dizzying pace. Once again, Maharaj ji showed me the planets with different civilizations as He had in Chandigarh. It is hard to say that these had become familiar sites, but while the experience was breathtakingly beautiful, it was somewhat less overwhelming. The descent came quickly. From the outer reaches of the cosmos, Maharaj ji brought me to a vantage point where Jesus stood on a hill overlooking a beautiful green valley. "This is what the Kingdom of Heaven will look like," He said. It seemed that all at Jesus's feet was in place and at peace. Just as deep space echoed with the silence of God's power, so the 'Kingdom on Earth' held that dynamic tension reverberating with God's Holy Name. The experience was over. I slowly sat up to find my head in tact on my shoulders and Maharaj ji smiling back at me. I had passed the test. Gurcharan still laughs about the look on my face when I first came into the room. Now I was completely serene. Maharaj ji excused me. I slowly got up and proceeded back to my room, to make a note on my diary. Words once again failed me. I lapsed into a reverie remembering where I had been, and that I had actually been shown the coming of God's Kingdom.

What makes it more special is that Maharaj ji has allowed me the privilege of witnessing and playing a small part in its development.

7

Adjusting to Campus Life

As with any new student, there was a period of adjustment. Having been to 'sleep-away' camp from the age of 10, followed by boarding school and university, I've had to make my share of adjustments. But, India, and Gobind Sadan presented many new challenges – climatic, dietary, and physical. No matter. I had been accepted in the toughest school in the world, by the Headmaster Himself, and the rest was just a formality. He knew He was going to help me over the hurdles, and frankly regardless of the early difficulties, most of them resulted in humorous lessons. I'll share a few.

Are you still hungry?

Maharaj ji would serve *langar* every day himself. One day I returned from Delhi where I'd stopped at Randhawa's house at IIT. He had insisted that I eat before I left so I was quite comfortably stuffed by the time I returned. But seeing Maharaj ji himself serving, I could not resist sitting with the others for His blessings. When He reached me with the bucket of vegetables, He started to laugh. "Are you still hungry?" and then proceeded much to my embarrassment but also to my delight to tell everyone exactly what I had eaten at Randhawas.

I wash my food thoroughly

After months of dysentery my stomach just couldn't handle the *langar* food, but every once in a while I'd be tempted by a special dish, and *kaley chhole* (small black chick peas) were one of them. Served in a brown curry they were simply delicious. Except the curry was laced with red chilies. As a matter of fact you could see the pieces floating in the soup. So I had a simple solution, I took my bowl to the tap and washed them, and came back with a bowl of the chick peas without the sauce. When word went around that I had washed the curry away, the *sangat* couldn't stop laughing. To this day, there are those who still tell the story.

My introduction to a local delicacy

Every culture has its own delicacies and undoubtedly one of the most famous and sought after dishes in Punjab is s*aron-ka-saag* and *makki ki roti* (mustard greens on fresh corn bread). Before you pass judgment, or let your stomach turn you away, this dark green mound served on a bright yellow circle of coarse pan bread with butter dripping off the edges is one of the most succulent tastes you could ever encounter.

Standing at the gate that separated the *langar* from the inner courtyard, Maharaj ji stood with a bucket of greens, scooping dollops of the saag onto the bread. This was a double blessing – a delicious meal served with blessed hands.

Candied *Nam*

Sweets are a part of India's daily life. There is little subtlety in Indian sweets. They leave no doubt on your taste buds. As a matter of fact, most people divide their food, and plates, by sweet and salty. Once you've enjoyed your sweet you don't want to spoil your taste, or vice versa. I would divide Indian sweets into two categories – milk/cheese based, and vegetable or lentil based. The milk-based sweets are called *burfi* and the dal or vegetable one's are called *laddoo*.

You cannot go through a day without a sweet being offered, either as a simple dessert or in celebration and thanks for some auspicious occasion. Gobind Sadan was always filled with sweets, and whenever Maharaj ji Himself would serve them He'd ask which one I wanted, I'd always reply, 'NAM.' Then lovingly he'd say, "All are filled with *Nam*, have anyone you want", and proceed to place several in my outstretched hands.

My teachers

While Maharaj ji oversaw my spiritual progress, he assigned wonderful people to teach me Punjabi, Music, and History. Gurcharan was my Punjabi tutor and Bibi Jaswant Kaur taught me kirtan (classical music

41

with harmonium and tabla). Major Sahib would teach me Sikh history and Gurbani.

Sometimes, after we had shifted to the hill, Maharaj ji would call Manjeet Singh who has, until recently, served as a senior Sikh religious official. While Maharaj ji sat on the sofa overseeing and clarifying the lessons, Manjeet, Gurcharan, and myself would review Sikh history, often referring to MacAuliffe's popular 'History of the Sikhs'.

T not Tea

Punjabi is a wonderfully lyrical language and relatively easy to learn, gender not withstanding. But for an American who is used to consonants only having one pronunciation (excluding dipthongs) making oneself understood is a virtual quagmire. Punjabi has four varieties of T's and D's, two Ch's and Jh's, and an Rh which gives the Danes no problem but I still can't pronounce without really straining.

Gurcharan would patiently start my lessons, sitting on a small marble block near Baba Siri Chand ji's shrine.

"Say Th." "T," I'd reply. "No Th." Still T was all that I could manage. "Th – T", by this time she was laughing. "Like the Th in Tea." Well for me there was no 'Th' in Tea, so that made her laugh so hard that she nearly fell off the stoop.

Good man the laltern

All the villagers who went to school learned to read at least some English. And they would all come up to me and say, "Good man the laltern." I would smile and nod my head and they would laugh. I figured this must have been some affectionate greeting they had learned for a new friend. I was "Good man the laltern." Some years later I was touring Punjab and picked up an English school book in my host's home. There on the first page, was the story 'Good man the lantern'. I couldn't stop laughing. It was about someone who had to shine a lantern at night to help people find their way (to the best of my recollection).

Kirtan – Singing God's praises

Having taken piano lessons, the concept of ragas was very similar to scales in different keys, and the harmonium at a basic level was relatively easy to pump with one hand and play with the other. Chords and stops were another thing (which our son Chetan excels at but that frankly I never mastered). Learning to control my voice to follow the tune was a different matter, as I had never been known to sing. If I did it was always from the rear of a chorus line so my voice wouldn't destroy the beauty of the song.

But this was a new experience. Perhaps *Nam* tuned not only my mind but my voice as well. For as I began to sing, a better, not beautiful by any means, but somewhat melodic sound actually came out. I am convinced that one sings out of joy (or pain). But joy automatically *began* to tune the voice.

The basic scale – SA RE GA MA PA could be played in any raag. Adding sharps and flats.

Within Guru Granth Sahib there are some 30 *raags* and Bibi Jaswant Kaur was and is one of the only people in the world who can sing all of them. Even today at age 87 she wins any competition she enters and is the envy of young ragi (or singer).

Although she was trained in classical music in Amritsar at the feet of some of the greatest masters, and was an accomplished professional singer on All India Radio she left public life to become the 'hazuri ragi' (musical artist in residence) at Gobind Sadan. One can still hear her melodious voice float across the compound every evening.

Tabla was another challenge. Each drum had its own notes which were to ring forth when struck in just the right way. The larger 'bass' drum with the metal shell was to be coaxed with the left hand cupped on top. As the heel dug in to the rawhide, the 3 fingers were to 'scratch' down and back to produce the resonance of the 'back-beat'. The smaller drum was made of wood and could be tuned by banging the wooden 'dowels' strung between the rawhide thongs (which held the head in place) and the wooden base. The harder you forced the dowels down, the tighter the head became and the higher pitched sound it produced. Professionals, or even those amateurs who know what they're doing, tune the drum to the 'raag' or key of the harmonium before singing. For me, I was happy if I could tap away with my index finger and get anything more than a thud!

Rhythm was less of a problem for I could always keep the 'beat'. But in classical Indian music the melody alone doesn't define the *shabad* or hymn. Each selection has its own rhythm with which it must be played, and each rhythm (or *Thal*) has its own name and song associated with it. I learned only three.

Tin Thal or 3 beats – Ta Din Din Da, Ta Din Din Da

Dadra or 2 beats – Ta Din Da, Da Tin Da

and Kehrva – a bouncing Ta Din, tuck a Din; Ta Din, tuck a Din

Of course, these were the very basic beat sounds, like the A,B,C's, and when heard rolling off the fingers of the Masters, the tabla produces more sounds and rolls than one could possibly ever imagine.

Cleaning up – digging up a fresh plowed field

As an educated American, I felt I had to find ways to help improve my new community. And I thought a garbage or compost pit would be a wonderful addition to improve the area. So early one morning, after I finished my role at the *havan*, I grabbed a spade and began to dig a pit in, what I thought was, a strategically ideal location. It was close enough to the *langar* for access, but far enough that it would not leave any smell. The area I had chosen was relatively soft ground and being the strong young man that I was, by daybreak I had managed to dig a shoulder deep pit about 5 feet across. As the community awoke the men started running towards me shouting for me to stop. As they took my spade I thought they were going to help. But instead they started to fill in the pit. Without my knowing I had just dug up a freshly plowed field and while they were laughing they were pretty annoyed that I had destroyed their work. So much for American ingenuity.

Washing machine or butter churn

The ingenuity of these villagers never failed to amaze me. They had just begun to manufacture washing machines in India. They were simple affairs, steel cylinders with a small plastic gyrator in the center, and a hose to drain the water out. I walked into the *Langar* one day to find a new washing machine standing near the sink.

44

"Oh, a new washing machine," I remarked to Bibi Surjit Kaur. "Washing machine! Are you crazy? That's our butter churn," she retorted briskly.

I laughed. I thought she was pulling my leg. "Come on, everyone knows it's a washing machine."

She grabbed me by the arm and pulled me over to the machine, lifted the lid and revealed a tub full of yoghurt ready to be churned into butter.

"Now tell me, does this look like laundry to you?" she said triumphantly.

It was an amazing adaptation of technology. Instead of washing clothes, with a flip of a switch, the machine would churn the yoghurt, the whey would drain out the hose, leaving a beautiful hunk of pure white butter in the bottom. The traditional clay *matka* with its wooden churn attachment had left the premises, banished back to the villages.

My Prayers

Sikh prayers are divided into three sections. The morning or daily prayers – *nitnem*, the evening prayer – *rehras*, and the prayer before going to sleep – *kirtan sohila*. I would for sit for hours and memorize the prayers myself. I heard that a 'proper' Sikh was not supposed to eat before they finished their morning prayers.

As long as I couldn't read Gurmukhi (the phonetic script), I was naturally exempt. But once I crossed that magic line where I honestly felt I was proficient enough to read, I felt obligated to follow this discipline.

Early on it was torture. I would be starving, but kept plodding along through the prayers. Finally, I was able to get them down to a reasonable time and from then on it became a simple routine.

Jaap Sahib is the most difficult

Once I was sitting on a charpoy (cot) at the back of the *langar* by the low wall trying to memorize Jaap Sahib, one of the daily prayers, when Maharaj ji strolled by. He asked what I was doing. I told him

45

I was memorizing Jaap Sahib. He replied, "Jaap Sahib is very difficult." I smiled and said nonchalantly, "Not at all." WRONG answer. From that point on, I have had difficulty reciting Jaap Sahib without a mistake, even though I do it seven times a day (or try to). The correct answer would have been, "Yes it is hard, please bless me."

But despite my early mistakes, bless me He did.

Mata Rihana

Prem Swaranjit would often take me out to shop when I needed something. But today was different.

"Today we're going to see Mata Rihana," she said after we had picked up some much needed groceries. We drove through Delhi to Raj Ghat along the Yamuna. As we pulled in, the parking lot was totally empty. The large landscaped lawns were equally bare. At the far end was a small thatch hut which Prem was heading for with me in tow. We bent our heads to enter, not really being able to see clearly. The entry way opened up to a small room where a thin old lady sat balanced on the edge of her bed. She was as small as a sparrow but the love in her eyes filled the room with light and warmth. She was happy to see Prem and accept this waif she had brought in tow.

This was the famed Mata Rihana, one of Gandhi ji's original disciples who had developed spiritual powers through her years of prayer.

"So you've brought me a visitor." She said in perfect English, smiling at me.

"Yes, this is Baba Virsa Singh's American disciple."

"I know. He will serve him all his life and be a worthy disciple." There was a warm rush coursing through me. It was not a simple affirmation, but a blessing that was being bestowed by another Saint. She put her hand on my head and the love flowed through to my toes. I thanked her profusely.

Prem told me that it was Mata Rihana who had told her that Swaranjit needed a Guru and described Maharaj ji to her. These connections were truly marvelous. Those who never see each other, know each other better than we do. They know who has come to serve whom and where to direct each one who enters their presence. Just as Maharaj ji had said that Swami Muktananda was standing before me as I had invoked him in my prayer for Ron's health.

Clockwise: Author at age 11

Press photo 1973

Diaries, sketch pad and letters home – 1970 and 71

Author with Maharaj ji and Baba Inder Singh, 1971

Baba Inder Singh Family Collection

top: Chetan with Maharaj ji in dairy on hill (below current auditorium) 1978

middle: Our house under construction, Maharaj ji's current Kothi in 1973. (the view of pahari from the tank)

bottom: Maharaj ji in the rose garden – with Langar wall in the background

Our marriage – leading Joginder around Guru Granth Sahib in GS Darbar Sahib room, and Sukhwant Singh seated behind Guru Granth Sahib, 27 January, 1973.

Sikhs or Sikhi – Author speaking at the All India Akali Conference, Ludhiana, in 1978 – seated (l to r) Jarnail Singh Bhindralwala, Tohra Sahib, Talwandi Sahib, Sardarni Nirlep Kaur, Badal Sahib

Longman Studio

Maharaj ji with us following marriage

PATH II

PATH II

Constructing God's House without Walls: Building
a New Community and a New Consciousness

Transforming land – Transforming Souls

The process of building Gobind Sadan to some may seem strange, especially in this day-and-age, when organizations that do considerable good simply approach wealthy donors, governments, or foundations for funding, hire top-rate professionals and build their name and infrastructure.

Not Gobind Sadan. To say that Maharaj ji built Gobind Sadan one brick at a time would be an understatement. He literally built it one soul at a time. The process of building the physical structure to house the community of 'God's House without Walls,' was paralleled by the process of building each individual's consciousness and ability to carry their share of the weight and to carry their share of the message to the world. It was not just barren land that was being transformed but barren souls. Just as the land thirsted for nutrients and brought forth beautiful crops, so we who worked it were hungry for spiritual nourishment.

Far from all being professionals in any of our work, we were a 'rag-tag' bunch of individuals with different skills, some more obvious than others.

Maharaj ji insisted on building it from the bottom up and was driven by the goal of self-sufficiency no matter what the price to his person. He has literally given himself to the cause from the time in the fields, to the time counseling and blessing millions, to construct a new paradigm: a world without borders, a world in which people understand we are all God's children.

8

Gobind Sadan: The Early History

From a Small Family to the World

In the late 60's and even through the 70's the area beyond Qutab Minar, the Monolith at the South End of Delhi, was pretty desolate. There wasn't even a single house on either side of Gobind Sadan Marg, the road that runs from Andheria Mohr past Sultanpur to Mandi Village. Beyond the wireless station, the only change in scenery was the kiln half way to the Village Gadaipur. The dirt, from the roadside back to the kiln was dug out four feet deep for bricks. The monsoons used to turn it into a giant pond. Sometimes it rained so hard that the water would wash over the road.

Only two buses ran from Mehrauli-Qutab to Gadaipur. One at 8:30 in the morning to take people to work and one in the evening to bring them home. If you missed the night bus, as Joginder often did, you'd have to pray for a ride or walk.

The bus stop hasn't changed since then. People still board and are dropped off at the little bridge where the main road turns off to Gobind Sadan. If Babaji had wanted to attract a lot of attention or draw a huge following to his center this was definitely not the best location. But Baba Virsa Singh has never been and never will be motivated by what the world sees or hears. And to him 'location' is totally dependent on spiritual direction and the 'presence' of God. So while few at that time could understand why he would leave the comforts of a large tract in Amritsar, he was called away and shown this 7 acres of barren land. And when in 1968 Sardarni Nirlep Kaur, daughter of Gyan Singh Rarewala, the first Chief Minister of what was post-partition Punjab, who herself was a Member of Parliament, offered the plot, though Babaji sent Baba Amritsaria and Baba

Joginder Singh to inspect it, he had already known what was waiting, a place where God dwelt.

The Blessed Place

To hear Maharaj ji or Major Sahib (our resident historian and 92-year-old Chief Research Scholar) tell the story, the area around Qutab was originally called Mehar Wali, the Blessed Place. Old maps actually show the notation. At one point, legend has it that the four great Muslim Saints Hazrat Moinuddin Chishti (who had brought Islam to North India), Khwaja Qutubuddin Bakhtiar Kaki, Baba Sheikh Farid and Hazrat Nizamuddin Aulia had gathered and recited their *namaz* together there. That sacred spot still stands. But over the years the name morphed into Mehrauli.

In Gadaipur where Gobind Sadan is located, Sufi saints came to meditate. Thus the name Gada - pur literally means, 'the place of saints'. Maharaj ji himself used to enjoy sitting in meditation. on the large rocks that stand overlooking Qutab.

Digging further, records show that this was also the place of the *Pandavas*, Arjun's family from the famous epic the Mahabharat, that is best known in the West for its jewel, the great sacred scripture, the Bhagvad Gita. Exiled from their kingdom, the *Pandavas* were given a desolate stretch of land from which they, with Lord Krishna's help, erected a beautiful new capital. At that time it was called Indraprastha.

So the farm also needed a name, one which would revive the spirit of the land and reconnect it to its heritage. It lay waiting, until June 11th, 1968 when Maharaj ji called Major Kirpal Singh and told everyone that he would name the place. Throughout the day, Maharaj ji spoke to Major Sahib about Guru Gobind Singh ji. Finally, as the sun was setting, Maharaj ji asked him what name he thought best fit the place. Major Sahib replied, *"Eh Gobind de Ghar hai"* (This is Gobind's house) and suggested Gobind Sadan. Maharaj ji was very pleased, and it has been Gobind Sadan ever since.

When Maharaj ji was still in his remote childhood village of Sarawan Bodla he had already seen and told his disciples that they would one day find land that was so blessed that it would be known throughout the world.

But, as my wife Joginder who was one of the first people to set foot on this sacred soil, tells it, "When we arrived in 1968, the only things prominent about the property were the weeds and wild bushes. There wasn't even any water. We had to carry buckets from the farm next door. There was no electricity and no place to sleep so we could only work during the day and then go home when it got dark."

And this is where I came in.

When I first walked through the gates on February 5, 1971, the fields to the immediate right were planted in chilies and teeming

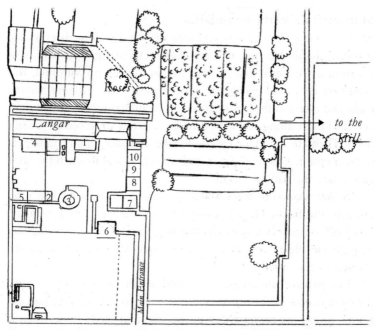

Map of the Early Gobind Sadan Compound 1971 – 1976

1. Darbar Sahib room	7. Gurcharan's room
2. Havan Sahib	8. Col. Baweja's room
3. Baba Siri Chand ji's room	9. Bibi Jaswant Kaur's room
4. Maharaj ji's first room (kothi no. 1)	10. Bibi Shanti's room
5. Maharaj ji's second room (kothi no. 2)	11. Ralph Singh's room
6. Bathrooms	

with activity. Men, women and children were working, either picking chilies or carrying baskets of dirt and manure for various projects. To the left were vegetables for the *langar*. Irrigation lines ran from the well in the far corner and the running water sang along with the *sangat* as it flowed into the fields. Everything was humming with *Nam*. You'd have to be deaf not to hear it.

There was a special kind of symmetry about the place. Not that it had any remarkable architectural features. As a matter of fact, it was rather simply and sparsely designed. But the buildings clung together to form the compound which provided us food and shelter and supported the prayer life which was our lifeblood.

Maharaj ji walks the boundaries

Every evening Maharaj ji would take off on a walk with everyone trooping behind trying to keep pace. His stride and pace was enormous. We would almost have to run to keep up with him. But even here he would engage us in questions. From Gobind Sadan's main gate down to the bus stop at the Mandi Road corner, then right and again left along what used to be another of Gobind Sadan's fields. Then He would turn around and come back, often coming via the rear entrance along the now walled-in field and through the back gate where the flats now stand.

If you wanted to meet Maharaj ji it was very simple. Just walk out into the fields. He was easily identified even from a distance. Just look for the black umbrella that he carried. He often would talk with people while overseeing our work, standing on a path while we planted or harvested.

For private meetings, he would sit in Gurcharan's room, the chair is now in the office. Sometimes he would use Bibi Jaswant Kaur's room, the center room in the line, and rarely mine when it was clean enough.

Gobind Sadan was a small family at that time. Maharaj ji used to distribute *langar* with his own hands to the thirty or so of us, sitting on the veranda where Bhagat ji's room is now.

Most evenings after *langar*, He would stand in the dera, sometimes on the veranda in front of the Darbar Sahib room and sing. This was heaven. The whole atmosphere reverberated with his Voice. It was as if the entire Heavenly Hosts were dancing and singing along, and I'm sure they were.

Only once do I remember him pulling up a chair and gathering us at His feet near the *pipal* in the courtyard outside the screened-in rooms: "I am not a Saint. I have come to make saints. To turn people back towards God."

This was a time when Maharaj ji was not only accessible, He was visibly active in every part of our daily life. As the compound and the work grew, His ability to be physically present every places diminished. So slowly, He had to replace His personal presence with Spiritual guidance either directly or through those He empowered. This took some of the burden off of Him. But, if He could, He would still be out in the fields every day, meeting people and supervising the work.

Every road or pathway in Gobind Sadan was built by hand. The main path from the dera to the hill is approximately two hundred yards long and elevated three feet above the fields. That meant that the *sangat* had to dig, lift, carry, pile and pack a three-foot high mound of gravel and dirt over the entire two hundred yards. Sound hard. It was. But there was never a more joyous crew. There were several stations, the diggers with the spades, the lifters, the carriers, the dumpers and packers. I usually traded off between digging, lifting, or carrying. The dirt or gravel would literally fly off the diggers spades into the waiting *tuslas*. These were large steel pans about three feet in diameter and about six inches deep. The dirt would be heaped on top until it peaked without falling off, then the entire pan would be lifted onto the waiting carrier's head. Now the carriers usually wound a cloth to shield their head's from the weight, but once firmly settled, they would take off almost running with one hand balancing the pan, and the other keeping pace with their stride. Once they reached the site, sometimes a good five minutes away depending on where we gathered the dirt, they would dump their buckets and return just as fast as they went for a refill. Meanwhile the packers would compress the dirt with a thick bamboo pole with a flat weight attached to the bottom. The whole process reminded me of a giant relay race. But with Maharaj ji standing and encouraging us, and blessing every movement, the medals came directly from heaven.

Irrigating the fields in itself was a special duty and Geeta, day and night with or without waders, would stand sometimes knee deep in water or the mud it produced. Men were stationed at strategic locations to scoop out enough dirt from the dyke of earth to allow an area to fill and then replace it with a soggy clod once the water had reached its optimal level. The fields were laid out like patchwork, in symmetrical squares, into which water could be metered out. Once one square was filled, the opening was blocked and the water proceeded to flood the next.

Four foot kale

Maharaj ji had me bring some seed from America so I gathered up some Burpees vegetables without really paying attention. Once in Gobind Sadan I passed them on to Lalu Ram, the gardener, who planted them in the field in front of the *havan*. The field was rich in organic matter and within a month these giant green plants had sprung up. No one including myself knew what they were and the seed packs had long since been discarded. The leaves were a good 3 foot long and looked like a giant mustard. The ribs on the leaves were more like sinew than vegetable matter. The women in the *langar* hadn't the slightest idea how to deal with it and so our giant kale, enough to feed and nourish a small army, went to seed and vanished from Gobind Sadan.

Bathrooms with a view

The dysentery from my travels was still with me and I often found myself in the embarrassing position (literally) of streaking out the front gate in broad daylight to crouch in the field to relieve myself. There were no bathrooms at that time. Night or day we would go out to squat in the field. The back boundary beyond the small tubewell in the corner was only strung with wire.

I remember Brig. Sahib leading me out early each morning before our bath and then sitting together in Baba Siri Chand ji's shrine. I enjoy recalling him singing *rogan te aur sogan te*, Guru Gobind Singh ji's beautiful invocation,

God please keep me close to you in sickness and in happiness,
Though I am surrounded by enemies You don't let them touch me,
as he bathed. Once he asked me, "Do you realize how much this means especially to a soldier?"

The showers were the two small rooms on the front of the water tower (the electrical workshop), the first rooms you see on entering Gobind Sadan. We used to get ten of us in there at once, two or three ducked under the *nalkas* (taps) while the rest of us were in various stages of dress or undress. The routine went, get wet, get out from under the tap and soap while the next person gets wet. As he steps out to soap, you duck back under to rinse and so forth. Quite the cooperative effort.

The new bathrooms in the corner were constructed in 1973 and afforded the luxury of five 'private' baths, still with *nalkas*, and five private toilets opposite them. An identical block was built for the women a short distance away. Bathing at 1:30 in the winter was a real advantage. While there was no hot water, the trick was to get someone to run the motor and draw fresh water from the well, where the ground kept it naturally warm. Once it sat for a while in the tank it was cooled by the outside air so we'd switch on the pump, get warm water, and bathe. Usually halfway through our baths we could hear the water starting to hit the overflow and cascade off the tower.

Today's central courtyard *was* Gobind Sadan in the early days. The rest of the land was under fodder for the buffalo on the hill, vegetables for the *langar*, and the roses that were an integral part of my life and of my early training. The inner ring of rooms, the Darbar Sahib room, Baba Siri Chand ji's shrine, and the *havan* except for some minor renovations, stand just as they did when I arrived. Little has changed. Except for the residents and perhaps the store-rooms which doubled as extra accommodation to handle any overflow, have been turned into the office.

Havan

The *havan* was a wonderful place, with barely room enough to squeeze a single row of people around the sacred fire. I used to sit back in

57

the far left corner and drift off into reverie for hours, often loving the picture of Guru Nanak, black background with golden appliqué, which hung over the near corner where the bananas and parshad are now placed. The sacred fire has burned continuously in that spot since 1968, with the prayers of Jaap Sahib and *Nam* continuing 24 hours a day. The power there is palpable and it was the 'lab,' the classroom where we practiced the teachings of Guru Granth Sahib. Here we learned to apply the Eternal Truths to ourselves and search for their meaning within our own consciousness.

It was the place to burn away our weaknesses, to kindle the sacred fire within our minds, purify the atmosphere within to welcome God, and to bring out the Image of the holy light, the sacred fire within us all.

When Maharaj ji ordered an all day *havan*, several of us would squeeze ourselves along the back wall between the *havan*. I being the smallest would often be sandwiched between Baba Joginder Singh and others. Holy smoke took on a new meaning as the fire blazed with every ladle of ghee and spoon of *smagari*, filled the small room with more and more fragrant (if not pungent smoke). While people often associate smoked-filled rooms with corrupt practices, here the smoked-filled room was a source of healing and peace.

The *smagari* was specially prepared from flowers, seeds and spices. I often had to go to the small 'factory' and had the pleasure of watching the dried petals and scents added to the mixer and then bagged in the 100 kg burlap sacks.

The Guru Granth Sahib room or Darbar Sahib hasn't changed except for the ceiling and the wallpaper. It is the same Piri sahib that Joginder and I walked around during our marriage ceremony in 1973, to the beautiful voice of Bibi Jaswant Kaur's kirtan and Sukhwant reading the lavan. Maharaj ji himself presided over our wedding which He had lovingly arranged, sponsoring this American with no credentials other than his love for His Guru, to marry a Princess.

Maharaj ji often sat in the room against the almirah holding the rumals which stood along the right wall as he listened to the *path*. Evenings he would stand on the veranda and sing or sit inside with those doing kirtan, while we sang and danced. Today, as part of my morning ritual I wave chauri sahib over these areas.

I was asked to bring a tape recorder back from my trip home to see my parents in December 1971. So we began taping Maharaj ji's kirtan on an old Ampex. Many of the tapes disappeared in a trunk with our wedding possessions en route to the U.S. Maybe one day they'll be found. It also contained the first movies of Maharaj ji in the rose garden and of the early Gobind Sadan from 1972 and '73. Fortunately, some other tapes remain and have been distributed.

Baba Siri Chand ji's Shrine – my early sewa

It was my esteemed privilege to maintain Baba Siri Chand ji's shrine. Maharaj ji had taken Ron and me into the shrine when we first arrived. It was almost like being introduced, but I was so in awe, that introduction is hardly the proper word. 'Ushered into His presence' is perhaps better. After Ron left (when we returned from our visit to Pir Sahib in Bareilly) I was given the duty.

The interior of the original shrine had plain cement walls painted in bright red (Baba Siri Chand ji's color). The square fire grate sat in the center of the marble-chip floor. As it was rather shallow, it had to be emptied quite often. A black metal hood descended to about 3 feet from the floor. A 2 foot plexiglass window had been inserted into a section of the pipe about eye level so we could see Baba Siri Chand as we entered the room or stood for ardas. Otherwise he was hidden from public view.

The picture and wooden *gaddi* still sit in Maharaj ji's own prayer room. I remember the day that Bibi Nirlep Kaur shifted the picture from the shrine into the prayer room in Maharaj ji's kothi number 2 behind the *havan* wall. Maharaj ji was in his old bedroom (kothi number 1) and feeling very dizzy. He asked me to ask why He's not well. We couldn't solve the mystery until it was discovered that the picture had been moved without asking. It was promptly reinstalled in the shrine and Maharaj ji's headache disappeared.

It's hard to describe how great the love Maharaj ji has for Baba Siri Chand ji. I've had slight glimpses. When Maharaj ji took me into Baba Siri Chand ji's shrine, Maharaj ji explained the significance of all the objects, the *carmandal* (water jug) hollowed out of a knot from a tree (I don't know where it is now) which sat on one of the small glass shelves. Under which there were wooden boxes for smagari. The *karavan*, Baba Siri Chand ji's wooden sandals, sat at his feet. The *chimpta* (metal tongs) stood next to him and could be clapped or used for tending the fire, but were used by Baba ji to bless people, either by dipping in water or by touching them. His visible form to me, was a beautifully framed picture which used to sit ensconced on a wooden throne. After bowing low to Him, Maharaj ji would spray Baba Siri Chand ji with perfume and wave the chauri sahib over Him.

It was part of Maharaj ji's daily routine to come out, visit the *darbar sahib* room while bowing at the entry and before Guru Granth Sahib. He would stand doing chauri sahib, sit and listen to Gurbani, then offer a prayer. Maharaj ji would then pray at the *havan*, offering ghee and smagari. He would often have me stand behind Him to show me what He saw. Agni Devta in beautiful shining gold would rise from the *havan* and greet Maharaj ji. As Maharaj ji stood with hands folded, the flames would embrace him, dancing all over his body, cleansing away all the difficulties he had taken on himself.

Finally, He would enter Baba Siri Chand ji's shrine.

I would have to arrive at the Shrine before the 2 a.m. ardas, dust and mop the floor, change the water in the *carmandal*, clean Baba Siri Chand ji's picture, light the fire and sit there in meditation. It was wonderful. At times, I felt like I was sitting at the feet of this gigantic mountain towering over me but totally consuming me with love.

During the rainy season, the courtyard would fill with water instantly and threaten to flood the shrine. At the first sound of rain, I would literally leap out of my room grabbing every cloth I could find and try to dam the front door to keep the water away. If that failed then my fall back was to actually open the door and just keep the water out of the *havan*, which was at that time recessed in the floor, and keep it from creeping up the frame of the throne. When the water finally receded, I was left with quite a cleaning job each day.

One morning as I sat there feeling how lucky I was, and, I must admit, how proud I was that I had reached this point (whatever that meant to a young student) I began to get a little too full of myself. At that very moment, the door opened and Maharaj ji entered. He appeared in Cosmic Form, so huge that all I could see was His feet, to which I quickly bowed and through which I quickly and quietly 'crawled' out of the Masters way, only turning briefly to again pay my humblest obeisance.

Audiences in Maharaj ji's court

Maharaj ji used to meet people in a small room behind the *havan* on the footprint of *kothi* (house) number 2. It was large enough to cram 10 people in. A curtain divided a small area with a cot where he could rest during the day. There was a bathroom off the veranda. The entry way is now closed off by the new *havan*. But if you go into kothi number 2 and turn around facing the *havan* you can see where the path exited around the original *havan*. There was a small metal gate where the white wooden arch stands today. Maharaj ji could enter his inner compound through a door where the car port now stands. Those green gates are still in their original position.

Maharaj ji's Kothi number 1 consisted of a large bedroom, bathroom (with the famous tub where he slipped and was knocked unconscious only to be revived by Guru Gobind Singh ji reaching out from the photo at his bedside) and the kitchen was off the large veranda which ringed the house on three sides. One of my other early duties was to cook for Maharaj ji, and that kitchen was the site of my introduction to a *papita* with Baba Joginder Singh and Baba Gurbaksh Singh.

The Case of the Delectable Papaya

Maharaj ji knew and knows everything. As children, we may try to put something over on our parents. But that can't happen with the Guru. People would offer fruit or other eatables to Maharaj ji and often His kitchen filled to overflowing. Baba Joginder Singh had his eye on a particularly large papaya that had been sitting there for a few days. When he felt it was safe, he told Baba Gurbaksh Singh and me that today was the day to enjoy this papaya as it had certainly passed the point where Maharaj ji would want it. So, we all consented and took the papaya out on the lawn, cut it and devoured it and cleaned up leaving no trace of our escapade. No sooner had we washed our hands, than Maharaj ji returned. As He stepped onto the veranda, He called out loudly, "Bring me that papaya." You have never seen such 'sheepish' looks on Sikhs' faces before.

There were double doors near the fig tree that was planted in the corner behind the *havan* over a small pool. I used to cut the grass with a lawn mower with a roller drum behind to level the ground. That entrance has long since been closed but the picture of Krishan Maharaj ji remains on the original wall.

Our rooms

The dera rooms are the same but their usage has changed as has their occupants. Bibi Kirtan wali occupied the center room from our time until she moved to her apartment in Noor Nagri. The veranda was originally open and the screens were placed about 1973. Mataji's room, the end room, which was the first room I stayed in with Gyani ji, became Col. and Mrs Baweja's room. Bibi Shanti's room was next to Bibi Kirtan Wali's. An elder of Gobind Sadan, who devoted herself to prayer and seva, she was always most kind to me. She often inviting me to her house in Delhi for a home cooked meal and making me feel part of her family.

I was shifted to the far corner and was able to build a brick tile wall and put my stove and refrigerator there as Maharaj ji had allowed me to make my own food to save my stomach.

Gyani ji's room was at that time the *dana* room, and the back store room (where I kept all the rose supplies) now is home to Sant Singh. The outer corridor rooms didn't exist. The original *langar* godown for wheat and *gur* and other supplies was converted into the 'guest rooms' along the Green Room that run behind the Darbar Sahib room.

Gurcharan's room hasn't changed at all. It was here that Maharaj ji would often sit and hold private audience. The large chair set in the middle practically filled the small room as His blessed presence filled the whole area.

The office was alternatively a store room and a place for more Singh's (the men) to sleep when needed. It was in this room that the sparrow hit the fan extending the life of a sewak. Now that may sound strange, but a person was seriously ill, and waiting for death to come. But Maharaj ji has shown us countless times that one being (human or otherwise) can take the karma from another. And so just as the family was pleading with Maharaj ji to give them more time, the bird came out of nowhere, flew into the room and without stopping hit the fan and died.

Langar

The original *langar* (when I first came) consisted of two *katcha chulas*, (mud and brick hearths). One held large pots and the other the smaller ones, and a very large *tava* about four feet across for the *rotis*. They stood in the area where the veranda of the Green Room is now. There was a special art in crafting these 'village ranges.' They were extremely efficient with wide mouths to stoke and hold the fire, fed mainly with dung cake that not only produced an extremely hot coat but also a pungent odor which unmistakenly flavored the milk. The horseshoe shaped opening was crafted to comfortably hold the largest pot or cauldron without any fear of its falling to the fire below. Later a *tandoor* was added to the configuration.

Bibi Surjit Kaur who now runs Shahi Data Darbar was the manager of the kitchen along with Mata Harnam Kaur who was soft-hearted as Surjit Kaur was tough. When we were truly blessed Maharaj ji's mother would also cook for us.

Regardless of the dish, a brass cauldron was placed on the hearth, often stoked with dung cake. Once the pan bottom began to turn red with the heat, Bibi Surjit Kaur and Bibi Harnam Kaur used to take 2 handfuls of red chilies and drop them into searing hot mustard oil. If anyone was within 15 yards their sinuses were instantly cleared.

While *langar* was prepared behind the walls, it was served on the veranda. Another wall extended from the gate and made a right angle around the Neem/Kicker tree that stands over the green room, giving those in the kitchen some privacy.

Maharaj ji and the crow

Every book of famous stories regardless of the culture seems to include the ubiquitous crow. Indian crows are grey with a black head and very pronounced beak which is open more times than it is shut. When the crows are not tearing into something, they are calling out with a raucous '*cawn*' from which it derives its Indian name. And a chorus of crows in India is only eclipsed by the grey babblers who will drown out even the most vocal crows.

Maharaj ji was sitting on the lower side of the hill beneath the dairy, on a site near where the current check point is. We were cleaning out the old manure pile at the base of the hill, (where Vakil Sahib's and Baba Kirpal Singh's quarters now stand) and he was overseeing the work. I had taken a break and settled near his feet when suddenly I heard a baby crying. I wasn't the only one. As the cries became more persistent others started looking around to see where they were coming from. There was no baby in sight.

But perched high in the tree, which still stands near the rear entrance to the 'Russian Kothi' was a crow. Every time it opened its mouth, instead of the '*cawn*' there came the distinct human cry of a baby. Finally Maharaj ji looked up and blessed the crow. Its cry returned to normal and it flew away. While Maharaj ji didn't share the full details, the person who had taken birth as that crow had just been freed of his karma and allowed to return as a human in his next birth.

Picking *loofas* from the back boundary

When I left America in the 70's, *loofas* were in vogue as a bath sponge and sold at quite the premium.

Imagine my surprise when I found them growing freely on the barbed wire fence which formed the rear boundary. I was even more surprised to find they were edible. In reality, they were a 'black' cousin of zucchini of an even deeper green, and were much more delicate in flavor. But left to their own devices, they would go to seed and dry on the vine, producing the tan fibrous filaments of perfect size for bathing.

Gobind Sadan's rear stone wall behind our flat has now replaced the barbed wire and where once the vines and yellow flowers of *kali tori* stretched, multi-colored bougainvillea arches gracefully across the landscape.

Kirtan on the veranda

Tuesday evenings Gurbachan Randhawa, head of horticulture at IIT (Indian Institute of Technology), used to bring his *malis* to Gobind Sadan for kirtan. And they would sing Nam Dev's tribute to God and Lord Krishna:

aisi mere lal tudh bin kaun kare

My beloved, You are the One who can (make a beggar a king), Protector of the weak, without You we are nothing.

Then Maharaj ji would join in, and everyone would sing and dance and celebrate.

Though I didn't understand the words the joy that came from everyone singing was tremendous. It just rolled across the compound and embraced you. Each evening the *sangat* would gather at the *havan* and sing *Chaupai Sahib*, and the unmistakable rhythm would send vibrations all through my body.

Those vibrations spread to every corner of the area, pulsing through our work and our prayers. Not only did Gobind Sadan emerge as a spiritual oasis from the desolate surroundings, but once Maharaj ji stepped foot on this land and began to develop it, people started to buy property around the area and began to build. Today, this remote area has become home to large country estates (farm houses) and the once barren land has become some of the most valuable real estate in Delhi. Many of the villagers who used to deliver milk to Delhi by bicycle now drive Mercedes.

Studio Pammi, Chandigarh

Maharaj ji in Gobind Sadan's fields circa 1971

9

Lessons from Work –
Stories from the Fields

"Work with your hands and feet, keep your mind attuned to God."
Guru Gobind Singh

Starting at the bottom

For most of us in modern societies, the opportunity to start at the bottom is lost. Many might say 'and thankfully so'. We expect comfort from the day we are born and are so dependent on maintaining that comfort that we not only mortgage our houses, it seems that we mortgage our souls.

Maharaj ji's way is different. It is based on old-fashioned hard work, and a farm is the perfect setting. Standing knee deep in manure and loving it, dripping with sweat as you turn the chopping wheel, having mud dripping down your neck from the bundle of greens cut in the rainy season, gives you a significantly different perspective on life.

No air conditioners, no beds, no fancy food, just hard work. Work until you're so tired that all you can think of is sleep, then rise to pray and back to work again. Boring, perhaps, but the result is incredible development for both the individual, the community, and ultimately society at large.

We've grown soft, out of shape physically and the habits which keep our mind and character aligned have not only slipped, they've atrophied.

Gobind Sadan, provided and still provides people the opportunity to experience what it means to work your way up from the bottom, no matter how rich you are.

These are some of my most memorable lessons.

Into the fields – You must work

Maharaj ji would often work in the fields himself, either plowing behind the oxen (the picture on Gobind Sadan's logo is real not posed) or come up at four a.m. to the dairy when we were short-handed, tying up his *chola* (gown), to sit and milk.

One day, Maharaj ji saw me in the *havan* in broad daylight and called me out. "You can't just sit and meditate. You must work. The world won't remember you for your visions they'll remember you for your work." He took me into the field behind the *langar*, grabbed two spades, and explained, "We need to irrigate our fields so we build *'vuts'* to hold the water in each area. Follow me." Then he proceeded to walk effortlessly down the row raising dirt from the left with the inside of his spade and letting it slide off on the right to form a neat small hill. In His path, the mound rose straight and true. I labored to follow him, my efforts looking more like the undulations of a snake. While He smiled in approval, it took me many attempts to even approximate a straight line.

Next, He handed me a sickle. "We have to feed our buffalo fresh greens, so here's how we cut it." He crouched in front of a row of uncut *'berseem,'* Egyptian clover (an alfalfa like fodder), held the soft green stalks from the top with his left hand and raked the sickle across the bottom stems with his right. I followed suit but in those first weeks, I must have cut my fingers more than I cut the fodder.

Then on to the *toka,* the chopping machine. Fodder is fed in one end, the gears grab it and pull it into the path of the rotating cutting blades bolted in opposite directions along the diameter of a large steel wheel. It's usually a two person job. One feeds the fodder, the other rotates the wheel applying pressure to the wooden handle so the wheel spins effortlessly chopping the greens. While the wheel may spin effortlessly, there is tremendous effort required of the spinner. And more so when on many summer mornings following my 2 to 4 a.m. 'role' at the *havan* I had to work alone to beat the hot morning sun. I would stand at one end loading the fodder and then run to the other to keep the wheel spinning. This area is now occupied by the rooms at the base of the Russian *kothi* wall.

The last lesson was tying and carrying the cut fodder on my head. Usually an empty cloth, burlap, or nylon *borie* (sack) cut open at the seams to form a large rectangle was laid beneath the *toka* to receive the chopped fodder. Once full, two ends were crossed and tied followed by the crossing and tying the other two ends to secure the bundle. Then it was hoisted onto a fellow worker's head to be carried up to the buffalo. One smooth procedure, except when I had to carry it. Though I was assured that the most efficient way to carry heavy loads was on my head taking full advantage of our spinal system and supporting muscles, my body somehow found that somewhere between the head, neck and shoulders was the natural resting place for heavy bundles. Until of course, I finally got the knack of it.

The most difficult and comical experience was carrying a large pot of *'dana'* (the grain mixture) we mixed with the green fodder and fed to milking buffalo, from the *langar* to the hill. With my head and shoulders draped with burlap, the heavy pot was hoisted up and placed squarely on my head. It was a good 40 pounds worth of boiling hot grain. At that time the original path from the *dera* to the hill (now a beautiful tree lined shady walkway) had just recently been completed and was completely open. I was about halfway up the path, when the first globs of burning mixture began finding their way onto my neck. By the time I got within shouting range, I had already been well-coated. Fortunately for me and the buffalo, my fellow workers heard my cries for help and rushed down the hill to save what was left of the mixture.

Our code

Though our team was few in number, the work that Maharaj ji generated through us was enormous.

We had a few simple rules. Swaran went down the list: No one 'called in' sick. You didn't have a fever unless it was over 102. Everyone worked hurt. And 4 ½ hours sleep was plenty.

I'm reminded of Maharaj ji's childhood story that once when he was lying sick with fever on a cot, his father came in and told him that work was the best cure for a fever. "Get out in the fields and the fever will run away."

On seeing me cutting fodder in the fields some time hence, Maharaj ji remarked smiling, "After this nothing in the world will seem difficult by comparison." Nothing could be more true.

Each part of work was your spiritual lesson. If I allowed my mind to focus and not get frustrated Maharaj ji would constantly instruct me, as much perhaps even more while working than in the *havan*. Each action had a spiritual corollary. If we cut fodder, we were cutting through the jungle of our minds. If we lifted heavy loads, we were relieving the suffering of the world. If we walked long distances in the heat, this was our pilgrimage. *Nam* linked every action and held our movements in balance. Indeed it seemed that 'we' were not working, rather there was a power flowing through us.

Maharaj ji had no fixed time for discourses and at that time if you wanted to see Him you would have to catch Him in the fields overseeing the work, when He wasn't working himself. He would often stand on the hill and look out over the fields at the forms of his devotees bringing dead land to life again.

One day He showed me a wonderful vision. Maharaj ji had me stand beside Him and shared His view of the world. Suddenly I saw that none of us were working. Rather everything and everyone, down to the minute actions of the beating wings of birds to the movements of the oxen and the hands of the men and women at work, was being directed by an enormous all pervasive force which kept everything in balance just as it does the stars and planets of the universe. And at the center of it stood the One who could see it, the One who could hear the Orders, and in fact the One who is empowered to Give them.

Everything was playing out as He saw it or foresaw it. No one was working through their own effort. Everyone was in harmony with the Divine. Some have even gone so far as to say that when we are attuned to God, then He sends His angels to work through us. However, it happens, it's clear that in Gobind Sadan the Divine Power is always present and it takes only stepping out of our ego for even a second to perceive it.

So often Maharaj ji will allow His power work through someone else

This serves two purposes. First and foremost, Maharaj ji never wants to show people His power. He never wants to be given credit for all the wondrous things He does. So, He deflects it by telling others to pray for someone sick, or make *jal* (holy water) or have someone else give directions.

The second purpose is to show that God can in fact work through anyone. It not only proves the point, but increases the faith of the ones who are fortunate enough to be chosen for this grand experiment. But, it is critical that we never feel that 'we' had anything to do with it. Rather it is always Maharaj ji's gift, a small glimpse of what His power is like. Almost like a parent giving a toy to a child, or a Master tossing a bone to his dog. Out of love all is given.

We are all part of that Divine Order

While we become aware of the presence of God through meditation and learn to hear His voice and orders, it is through work that we learn to follow them and in so doing, help bring His order to a chaotic world. For the lesson is the same as Maharaj ji puts it, "What use is it to the world if those who say they love God sit idle, or retreat to the seclusion of the mountains and forest to 'perfect' themselves, when the world is burning?" It is only when those who love God work in the world, tackling the problems head on, and allowing God to work through them to overcome the problems, that God's order in the world will begin to emerge. It is we humans who have destroyed the harmony of nature. And only when we finally find that harmony within ourselves, will we learn to serve our Creator again, and the order on earth will be restored.

Sadan Roses and Ralph the Roseman

Early on, I would help around in odd jobs, washing cars or doing whatever chores needed doing. But people kept asking me, "What is your duty?" I was probably getting more in their way than helping them.

71

Then came the roses, my true learning ground, both beautiful and thorny. Maharaj ji put me in charge of cultivating and marketing the four acres of roses that Gobind Sadan grew as a cash crop. Other than being entrusted by my mother to weeding her beloved rose bed, and using FTD billed to my parents' account to send them to relatives on important holidays, I knew nothing about roses. But such is Maharaj ji's way of teaching responsibility. I had two expert *malis* (gardeners) Brij Lal and Lalu Ram under me, though it should have been the other way around. Brij Lal was a tremendous worker but he and I nearly got into fights at times. I'm sure it was over my stupidity. While Lalu was as kind hearted and patient a soul as one could ever find. Together and with the help of the whole volunteer crew of the *dera* at weeding and fertilizing time, we ran 'Sadan Roses', which boasted up to 250 dozen a day during the main winter and fall flushes.

And it was the challenge of getting rid of that many roses that forced me into my first 'sales' position, marketing roses at $1 a dozen to the diplomatic community of Delhi. I started taking samples by bus to a strategic point in the well-frequented Greater Kailash market. I found a few willing and sympathetic customers. I asked one, the husband of the head of The Library of Congress in Delhi, whether he thought his friends would be interested in roses delivered to them for Christmas. He referred me to some friends and I knocked on any door that had a foreign (especially American sounding) name plate. I'll never forget the Sammels, whose daughter Becky went running back saying, "Mom there's an American at the door with a turban." To the Guptas, Sammels, the Bennetts, the Eytons, the MacPhersons, Campbells, the Fishers, the Belkinds, the Hustons, the Andereggs, and Phelps, Titus, Drummonds, Geithners, and the many more who were not only loyal customers but remained our friends, I can only send my eternal thanks and gratitude. I was able to deliver almost 10 dozen roses on foot for Christmas to those who had placed orders. From Greater Kailash the word spread across Delhi to Friends Colony on one end to Vasant Vihar and Chanakyapuri on the other; from Americans to Mexicans, to the French and Russians, Ford Foundation, World Bank and Embassy parties and all the foreign journalists. Many people just wanted 'a dozen a week'. The business growth required me to move up to a Lambretta motor scooter with custom wooden boxes each side lined with plastic containers for the roses, fitted like saddle-bags over the rear skirting. Finally, the business expanded so much that I needed a 'three-wheeler'. This was a *Vespa* scooter covered with a cab with an extended two-wheel rear axel covered by a flat bed which could carry enough buckets to hold any and all quantities. Just substituting a covered passenger seat for the flatbed, this same body became the famous 'auto-rickshaw'. By this time I had become 'Ralph the Roseman,' an epithet emblazoned in an L.A. Times article for all my friends and family to read at home.

Onward my warriors

Whether it was planting new stock or weeding, through rain or heat, Maharaj ji would stand on the path and literally shout encouragement while we squatted in the carries racing to finish before sunset. He would literally inject us with his energy. Like a general urging his men on in battle, Maharaj ji would call out, *"Chalo Bhai Surmai"* (Onward my warriors). And no matter how tired we were or how fast we were already going the pace inevitably doubled.

Langar and tea were served right there in the fields and the work continued. Someone would always be on water duty, or better yet bring *lassi* (buttermilk) to cool you off.

Many a mistake did I make, but despite it all Maharaj ji forgave me again and again. I'm sure I would have been fired a dozen times if I were in a 'real' business situation. It is typical of Maharaj ji to entrust a valuable commodity or project to someone whom He has faith in just to show that God will give that person the ability that will someday 'pay off'. It was truly a long-term investment in human capital.

Mommy, the Milkman's here!

The roses were finally plowed under when it was determined that despite their beauty they were not as economically viable as milk. Not to mention that strong Punjabi farmers didn't like sitting on their haunches all day with *rhumbis* (little trowels), weeding around

73

the thorny bushes. So Maharaj ji made me a milkman of Delhi. Delivering Gobind Sadan's milk to housewives and hotels through out town. Each morning I would have to help in the milking, then load the milk into old fashion metal milk cans, place them in my three-wheeler and head out to Delhi. The days were exhausting, for often I was required to shop for supplies or service the scooter before returning home. At each stop the customers would surround the scooter, I would ladle the milk into whatever containers they presented, and take the cash in return. The hotels and sweet shops usually just took a whole milk can (or two).

On my first runs, I never realized that the movement of the scooter caused the cream to rise to the top of the cans. In total ignorance, I would give my first customers the milk at the top and proceed to reach further down in the can as the day wore on. Within a few days, I was getting rave reviews from the first customers and complaints of selling 'separated' (skimmed milk) from the latter ones. Confused, I was gently counseled to mix the milk on arrival and then ladle it out. Despite my mistakes, to this day people still remember me as their milkman, as the kids would run upstairs shouting, "Mommy, the milk man is here."

Working with the animals

While I always loved animals, besides the horses I rode occasionally, the largest animal I was personally responsible for was a cocker spaniel. So to be given major responsibility for a herd of buffalo and cows was a big step up. I started at the bottom literally, under Maharaj ji's watchful eye, learning how to identify calves and their mothers. I then had to bring the calf to the mother prior to milking, let it suck and then quickly pull it off so the mother could be milked. This was the ingenious way they started the milk flowing in each animal.

Maharaj ji loved the animals and would oversee the morning and evening milkings and often just tour randomly. On days when we were short-handed, Maharaj ji would tie up his *chola* and sit and milk himself.

I had to learn which mineral mixtures each animal would be given depending on where they were in the milking cycle and check

74

for mastitis or the presence of any other disease. The calves were prone to worms and if left untreated they would kill the animal in a matter of weeks. I lost a valuable calf in the learning process.

If animals were seriously ill or when they would come in heat, I had to drive my two-wheeler Lambretta scooter for 15 miles to the Gurgaon experimental station where our good friend Dr. Abhi presided. Even through heavy storms, he would come at all hours riding on the back of my scooter, help the animals and then accept my ride back.

There are many stories from the dairy that taught me that Maharaj ji was always watching over me while I worked, but none as vivid as this:

It was a bright sunny day and I was working with the buffalo moving some straw with a pitchfork that had accumulated around the troughs. Suddenly Maharaj ji said (from within), "Watch out, there's a snake under there!" I froze for a minute and looked down at the seemingly harmless pile of straw, then replied, "Please don't joke with me." Maharaj ji's retort was simple, "Would your Guru ever kid you?" and with that, I turned over the next batch of straw revealing a huge pit viper, one of the most venomous snakes around. I quickly called the men and they dealt with it.

Surajpur and the foundations for Shiv Sadan

With the work in Delhi well under control, Maharaj ji's vision drew him to a plot of land across the Yamuna in a small village called Surajpur.

Maharaj ji set up base camp next to the large 5 inch bore well, that not only provided plenty of irrigation water, but served as an instant shower to wash the mud off our bodies and our clothes.

Two thatches were constructed, one small private thatch for Maharaj ji and a larger one for the *sangat*. Summer was holiday time and the student contingent, sons and daughters of Delhi families could join us for their vacation.

No Joke

On clear days, one of my early duties was helping the carpenter, *Mistri Sahib,* cut some trees and haul them back to camp to construct the huts. While the flood plains were not totally barren, trees were few and far between. The most common was the date palm, so one of the benefits of the work was having fresh hearts of palm as the dates were not yet in season. The wood was relatively soft and the semi-sharp axe heads thudded through them easily. Once felled, we would cut off the tops, harvest the clean white hearts for immediate consumption or wrap them for later, and look to the shortest route back to camp. Sometimes it was an hour's walk. Having trudged back and forth several times, I was constantly on the lookout for an easier route. A small *nala* (rivulet) flowed through the area and I kept it in sight whenever we went looking for trees. I mentioned it to *Mistri Sahib,* but he kept telling me it was just too far away. Finally, I was tired of hauling trees and took a firm stand. It was far simpler to float the logs down the stream than carry them. We could even do several at a time. This time the older man relented.

As we got to the waters edge, we rolled the logs down the banks, rolled up our trousers, and proceeded to wade chest deep into the water. Suddenly the old man let out a scream: "Joke!" At least that's what it sounded like to me. He was squirming and heading for shore. As he came out of the water, I noticed several very large brown shapes on his back – leeches. I flashed back to the 'African Queen' and quickly exited still unscathed. I helped him remove the creatures and then humbly apologized for forcing him into such an uncomfortable situation. From then on, the trek across land didn't seem so bad.

Mired in Mud

It was towards the end of monsoons and the mud was thick. Our only tractor was mired in mud about 2 miles away from camp. I was posted out in a tent with Amarjit and Bachittar watching over the tractor and waiting for the rains to break so we could get it moving again. But in the weeks I was there, the tractor could only be started to keep the engine in tune. Any thought of moving it would have to wait.

Every morning, I would take the horse, a brown mare, and ride the two miles to base camp to get our rations for the day. Usually I was able to time the rain so I could at least make it one way without getting drenched. The clouds move quickly across the flood plains sky. You could see them coming and whenever the grey closed quickly over the light blue patches, I knew that I'd never make it to camp in time. But the horse didn't mind a bit more mud and I was careful to let her find the driest path rather than force her on what I perceived to be the best way.

A can of milk for tea, *parantha* and mango *achar* and some *gur* (raw sugar) served as breakfast and lunch. For dinner we all would go to camp for a hot meal.

We had to trench around the tent to keep it from flooding. Often in the middle of the night I'd be awakened by water creeping up my toes, grab the spade and torch and proceed to rebuild the dyke where it had been breached. Watching the monsoon from a room in Gobind Sadan or running in from the fields soaking wet to a dry space was a much different experience than actually living in the monsoon. The tent was the only shelter and when it rained (which was 75% of the time), the sheets of water were so thick, they spread across the entrance. All one could do was settle down inside and wait. Or watch to make sure that the dykes were holding. When it did clear a bit we could see our closest neighbors a few hundred yards away: Balwant Singh's family farmhouse and Dara Singh's lean-to. Both were equidistant yet worlds apart.

Dara Singh

On rainy days we had little choice but to visit our neighbors. On one side the fields were planted with sunflowers, seemingly hundreds of acres of them. When the sun did shine the yellow from the flowers just arched up to greet it. It was the duty of Dara Singh to keep the sparrows from eating the seeds and see that the crop was watered when necessary. He was tall and scrawny like a scarecrow with rather tattered clothes to match. It was a wonder how he could ever fit into the shelter he had made by draping an old tarp reinforced by plastic fertilizer bags over the tubewell spout. Like us, he would go to his masters house each morning for rations and then spend the rest of his time in the fields, weather permitting. But given the downpour it was a good bet we'd find him home.

He could hear us sloshing through the water and came out to greet us. He welcomed us warmly and immediately stoked the small fire that set the tent aglow reflecting the shadows of the animated tales of his travels. He grabbed a jug of milk and proceeded to make tea for the four of us. I was amazed by this hospitality. The man literally had nothing but the clothes on his back. He must have understood what I was thinking and so he said, "I live here alone, but I know some weary travelers lost in a storm or guests such as yourselves will happen to come by. So when I take my rations I always put some aside so I can serve them."

I was completely bowled over and tears welled up in my eyes. Here I was, a relatively wealthy American being hosted by someone who had nothing. We consider ourselves generous. Surveys show US to be one of the most philanthropic of nations. But we give out of surplus. We give away what we don't need or don't want. Here was a man literally taking food from his own mouth just in case he needed to serve a total stranger. This was true generosity. Years later, I was at the Marriott Marquee in New York for the United Nations Association Annual Dinner when Ted Turner pledged his billion dollars to help the United Nations. What was so genuine about his act was that he looked down at Gerry Levine, then Chair of Time Warner and said, "I really didn't do anything to earn this. My stock just went up in value." I was able to memorialize Dara Singh in an op-ed on Turner's generosity, "We give out of surplus, remember the poor who give."

Balwant Singh and Biji's absolutely wonderful *aloo parantha*
On the opposite side of our tent from Dara Singh's lean-to stood a sturdy farmhouse that would make anyone stop and take notice even if constructed in the farms in America. A fence stretched around its perimeter as far as we could see. On a day when the rain was so bad that I couldn't get to camp for morning rations, we set out to meet our neighbors and 'beg' a little milk for our tea.

As we passed through the steel gate, a strongly-built hulking man stepped out onto the porch to receive us.

We were ushered inside into the warmth of a family who were to become some of Maharaj ji's closest devotees, and Balwant Singh, the man at the door, one of my dearest friends and Maharaj ji's constant companion until his death.

"Milk, you want milk for tea?" they laughed. "You are just in time for breakfast. Sit down." They quickly made a place for us and smells of Indian spices filled the air. Soon after *aloo parantha,* as big as our plates began to appear. This was Biji, the family Matriarch's specialty. After we finished eating, the family enjoyed hearing stories of Maharaj ji in my broken Punjabi and they pledged to come see him. We thanked them and left knowing we would see more of each other later.

As roads improved, the trek from Delhi to Surajpur became easier. So easy, in fact that this once deserted spot came under the eyes of developers, and today what was once a remote farm in the middle of nowhere now sits in the middle of Greater Noida, one of the higher-rent small cities that have sprung up around the Capital region. Maharaj ji was able to sell the land at a handsome profit and put the proceeds into developing Shiv Sadan.

Shiv Sadan itself

By the time Maharaj ji called me back from America in the 90's, Shiv Sadan was a fully functioning model mega farm. And Dara Singh and Balwant Singh had now become main characters in its story. From keeping sparrows off sunflowers, Dara had been assigned to be the key person to protect the land against the locals who would often steal every pump handle or any moveable part that was installed in the area. He laughed when sharing how Maharaj ji had cautioned him not to take strict action against anyone but simply pray. Sure enough in a few days the missing parts would reappear. Maharaj ji always said that it would take time for the people to realize that we were developing the area for their benefit. Once Shiv Sadan was settled, Dara Singh became the host at the guest house.

Balwant Singh was now not only in charge of the farm, but Maharaj ji's driver and constant companion.

Many times I had the privilege of riding in the back of the Jeep while Bant, as he was affectionately known, drove Maharaj ji on his rounds of the farm. At first, I thought that Maharaj ji was going to inspect or supervise the work, but one day I realized that he was actually going to inspect the crops. And when I say inspect, I mean he would not only look at the crops but engage them in conversation, much as he did the workers.

Maharaj ji's soil lab

As we made our rounds, Balwant Singh always shared his favorite stories.

"As I was taking Maharaj ji around the farm, he specially told me he wanted to inspect the rice. It was standing in water and we were worried to see it waterlogged. Water is great for rice in the early stages but then too much water could damage it. As we approached the fields, Maharaj ji ordered me to stop and He just closed his eyes and sat still. Suddenly he said, 'Zinc, the rice wants zinc.' Now I had farmed this area for many years and no one had ever mentioned zinc in regard to rice. 'Let the water stay, they like it,' he continued, 'but be sure to give them plenty of zinc.'

"Now as with any good farmer, we have our soil tested regularly to see what nutrients the soil has lost so we can replenish them. We had sent the samples to the lab the week before and were awaiting results. When the results came the next day, we were shocked. There was a noticeable deficiency of zinc in the soil. We laughed and told the technician that we had already received the report. He was obviously confused. 'But Sir, I have just come directly from the lab.' Then I explained, that Maharaj ji had told us from his vision what the rice wanted. The man was totally amazed."

Havan *ash*

Those of us who are associated with Gobind Sadan know of the power of the *havan,* and the curative powers of the ash that is produced from its sacred fire. But, as Bant told it, the power of ash went far beyond human applications.

As I came to understand, red rot was like a plague for sugarcane. Once infected, its core pulp developed a red streak and there was no cure. The crop had to be sacrificed. Bant made sure that the cane agents came regularly to inspect the crop and was surprised when one day the report came that indeed red rot had infested a particular stand of cane.

Bant reported immediately to Maharaj ji who told him without a second thought, "Don't worry, sprinkle ash from the *havan* on the cane and there will be no damage." Bant followed the instructions and by the next week when the agent made his rounds, the rot had disappeared.

On another occasion, when red rot had infested a different stand, Maharaj ji told them to take holy water from Pir Sahib's *dargah* (tomb) and spray the seed before planting. When the agent came back six months later, he was shocked to see a perfectly healthy stand of cane that had grown out of the infected seed.

Keeping the wheat dry after harvest

The one thing wheat doesn't need once harvested is rain. If you know how quickly moong beans sprout when dampened, you can imagine what freshly harvested and threshed wheat will look like if dampened before it can be bagged and stored. The loss from mould can be enormous. Wheat is harvested in the month of April, the beginning of the hot and dry months. But rain does come.

As Bant shared, they had just finished the harvest and the wheat was waiting to be bagged when rain clouds began to threaten. "At that time Maharaj ji was in Delhi. I called and asked what we should do so the rain would not damage the crop. Again he said, 'Don't worry, sprinkle ash around the perimeter of the area and no rain will touch the wheat.' We followed his instructions and though it did rain, not even a drop touched the wheat."

Maharaj ji himself would spend the whole day in the fields. Morning was spent touring, like a General inspecting his forces, then He would set up his chair wherever the work was going on, planting cane, plowing fields, and stay til the sun went down. His lunch and

81

tea was served there with his *fauj* and if anyone wanted to see Him they would have to find a way out to the site.

Mukhtiar Singh and his teams

Mukhtiar (Mukha) whom we can recall was the young man who had burned the engine on Gobind Sadan's first Ford tractor in 1972 because he forgot to change the air filter, now kept over 20 tractors going around the farm. He literally lived on his motorcycle, (reminiscent of the stories of the Sikhs of old, who lived on their horses) riding the farm's roads overseeing the work.

When the disheartened youth of Punjab would come to Maharaj ji, he would challenge them, "If you want to do something for your country, here's a tractor, see how much food you can grow." Then he would divide them into teams and let them plough for the record.

It was Mukha's job to see that their work went smoothly and the farms kept moving. And move they did. The record still stands at over 24 hours at a stretch. Fertile fields just sprung out of the barren land, and in no time record crops followed. The boys' pride swelled to see the wheat heads and oats waving in the breeze. It was as if a magic wand had been passed across this desolate area and they somehow had been made a part of the play.

Development short – there should be no poverty

Older now and quite a bit out of shape, I spent my time documenting the work with an old beat up video camera. Even with a broken view finder, a casualty of a rough ride, Maharaj ji kept delivering beautiful scene after scene, that ultimately became the footage for our first introductory short: "There should be no poverty," that was produced for the Parliament of the World's Religions in Chicago.

Meanwhile, a more professional team were filming the scenes for Swaranjit's movie, 'Spreading the Light of Truth', catching the most beautiful light coming through windows and trees on Maharaj ji as he moved effortlessly around his 'kingdom'.

When I didn't have a camera in hand to record the visible progress, my pen was busy filling diaries with the amazing visions of things that Maharaj ji would show me while I sat at the *havan*. One day I

82

saw people from every nation and every religion coming with banners and laying them at Maharaj ji's feet.

Then the Voice spoke: "Today is the day that the door between heaven and earth is open."

I was so excited I ran down the road telling everyone I could see. I embraced Mary Pat and told her the good news and it found its way into Mary Pat's wonderful book about her experiences during this period in Shiv Sadan.

The Charged Tree

Maharaj ji was standing under the large tree near the *langar* in the Tejpuri courtyard, a fresh cup of tea in hand, taking questions from Mary Pat who was standing a few feet in front of him with tape recorder in her hand. It is common in villages to build a small terrace around the base of the larger trees out of *paucha*, the mud and dung mixture that serves as plaster on everything from brick walls of houses to new surfaces on top of brick flooring in courtyards. (It's easily maintained by applying another coat whenever the previous one begins to show signs of wear.) While it beautifies the area, it's also a practical solution for keeping people from tripping over the extensive above ground root system.

Preferring the shade of the tree, I stepped back on the raised portion while translating Maharaj ji's talk for Mary Pat. By this time Maharaj ji himself was standing on the skirting of the tree. Now this has never happened before or since, though I am constantly translating for Maharaj ji in different settings, but as my foot touched the skirting, I felt an instant and incredibly strong current literally lift me off the raised spot and place me back on ground level. I had somehow entered sacred space when the 'shield' was still up. I say that only as a metaphor because Maharaj ji has always made himself accessible to the general public, let alone to those who are fortunate enough to serve him. But perhaps today as a reminder to me and a demonstration to Mary Pat that wherever he stands (or is) the energy field around him is so enormous that no one can enter his presence without his permission.

Tea with Mata Ganga

We knew something special was afoot when early one morning Maharaj ji summoned us to quickly get ready. Maharaj ji had been 'invited to tea' with Mata Ganga.

It was still pre-dawn as we drove out from the compound leaving the neatly plowed fields, to make our way through the elephant grass and across the sandy stretch to the river banks. For those who have not seen Mata Ganga I can only make a feeble attempt. At her widest point, even on a good day it was hard to make out the opposite shore. And depending on which vantage point you had, you could try your best to follow her course as she caressed the entire border of Maharaj ji's land. In the end, you would lose site of her around some distant bend. Her smaller tributaries stretched out like strands of hair across the face of the earth, as if she still filled the locks of her beloved Lord Shiv ji. So wherever you went, there were signs of her presence.

She presents herself with different faces at different seasons and constantly changes shape like the beauty that she is, as a woman changes clothes. At some points, she would meander lazily along a low lying bed where one could enter for one's traditional cleansing bath from a gentle slope while at others she would literally chop away huge chunks of the bordering fields and deposit them in other areas, constantly rearranging her 'home', redecorating the surroundings. It was best not to stand to close to the edge, for at any moment the ground you were standing on would literally fall away and descend into the water as if neatly carved by an invisible Chef.

Maharaj ji directed us to a point on the cliffs a good twenty feet above the water. Balwant Singh laid some *daris* on the ground and set up Maharaj ji's folding chair. We gathered around him and waited. Sitting close to his feet, I could see Maharaj ji deep in *samadhi*. His face was literally aglow as he communed. If we closed our eyes we could sense the Being present and feel her gentle touch, but we waited for Maharaj ji to share the details of what had transpired.

Soon Maharaj ji's eyes opened and his focus once more descended to this world: "Mata wants to 'donate' all the surrounding land to us.

She said she likes what we're doing to grow food and feed those in need. In return we must build a temple to Lord Shiv ji."

By this time the sun had begun to shed some light on the surroundings. Balwant Singh poured tea for everyone and opened a box of special *khoya* brought in from a surrounding village. It was a wonderful start to the morning and whenever I visited Shiv Sadan thereafter I could see the promises fulfilled. The acreage grew each year, as Mata deposited more and more land on Maharaj ji's side. And the temple to Lord Shiv ji stands as promised.

Pir Sahib

No story about Shiv Sadan would be complete without including Pir Sahib, the powerful Muslim Fakir, who had left the world several 100 years ago but was still very much present. As a matter of fact, when Maharaj ji was purchasing the land around his *dargah*, people cautioned against it. Everything in the area was 'bad luck'. Nothing grew properly and the families who lived nearby were always suffering some sort of calamity: an untimely death, severe disease, an unexplained fire, and continual financial loss.

Maharaj ji prayed and the Pir came to pay his respects. Pir Sahib said, "The people around here have shown me utter disrespect. They've left my grave unattended and the place has gone to ruin. Construct a new place and ask people to show me a little respect and I will reward these small acts many times over."

From that day, the order was given to construct a simple structure to enclose the grave. Keep it clean, put new *chadars* (green sheets) regularly and keep the *jots* (oil lamps) and incense burning. Within the year, the field that had been useless, produced a record crop, and peace descended on the residents of the area.

Today, a new Mosque stands on the site, visible from all around and Pir Sahib continues to shower blessings on all who visit.

Maharaj ji's singing lights up the night

There's a special stone marking in the yard of the Shiv Sadan guest house, between the large central tree and the pump near where the cane fence used to stand. It was a warm evening, and we'd just finished weeding the cane in the field that ran along the guest house boundary road. Maharaj ji was waiting for everyone to come in and as the darkness descended he gathered us around and started to sing:

Zimin asaman vikhai chandna hi chandna

Heaven and earth are dancing with Your Light.

And we sang and danced along. The whole area was charged with the most amazing streams of energy that the fatigue from the hard day's work was literally drawn out of our bodies and the more we sang and the more we danced the stronger and stronger we became.

Koi Kisai da Kisai da Koi
Mera Eko Bajanwalia
Everyone has someone they love and for me it is only Bajanwalia

Horaihi hai teri Jai Jai Kar
Oh God, Your victory and glory is at hand
Tenu bhakshanhar saray akhday Sahiba manu bhaksh laiyo
They call you the forgiver of all our sins, My Lord please forgive me

Sahiba tera mera pyar kadi na badal ai
Oh Lord don't ever let the love between us change
Ek tu na badalay ek mai na badala
Don't you ever change and don't let me ever change
Zimin badalay asaman badalay,
The earth may change and the sky may change,
but don't let our love ever change

Ek Onkar Satnam Siri Waheguru
There is One God, Whose Name is Truth, Praise the Ever Greater,
Ever more wondrous God
Siri Waheguru, Siri Waheguru
Praise the Ever Wondrous, Ever Greater God

Tera jiya na Dayal Bajanwalia – mera jiya papi koi na
There is no one as kind as you, Bajanwalia,
There is no greater a sinner than me

Sahiba sanu bhaksh lao
Please Lord forgive us

86

Meharvan sahib mera meharvan
You are the forgiver of all our sins

Chau kuntan vichkar, Bajanwalia
Bajanwalia, you are glorified to the four corners of the world
Sahiba pher kadon avangai, zaroor dasda
Oh my Lord, please tell me when will you come again

Ki lehna dar dar ton, ek dar ha hoja
Ki lehna dar dar ton, Bajanwala da hoja
What can I gain (begging) looking from door to door
I just look to the One door, to the door of Bajanwala

On and on into the night, rejoicing in all God's gifts, Maharaj ji taught us what it meant to truly thank and praise God. That He cares for us, more than a parent can ever care for their child, is almost inconceivable. With the millions of creatures He is responsible for, it is amazing and most humbling that He even knows our names.

But, His greatest gift is meditation and the more He allows us to meditate, the more that God has hidden from our normal view becomes clear.

PATH III

Lessons from Meditation

If Maharaj ji's days were focused on sowing crops in fallow land, the evening was spent sowing the seed of *Nam* in our souls. He would stand and sing:

Nam bij lo karma walio – ayee rut bij laindi

Come lucky ones and sow the seed of *Nam*, the season has come, let's sow God's Holy Name

10

Meditation According to Maharaj ji

During my first audience, Maharaj ji had told me that meditation was the prerequisite for entering God's school. We in the West are taught (incorrectly) that meditation is an 'Eastern' practice and many from the East who have brought meditation to Western countries often integrate it with other physical practices, stressing posture and breathing. I feel this confuses the issue. Further, today it is being popularized medically as a way to reduce stress. But in essence while meditation does affect our body, it is first and foremost meant to affect our mind, to change our consciousness. The state of our mind then impacts our bodies and our actions. As Maharaj ji says, "The body is simply an instrument of our mind."

I had then asked Maharaj ji directly:

"There are many forms of meditation and prayer, what do you mean by meditation?"

He replied, "Meditation is thinking of God 24 hours a day, thanking Him every moment."

I interpret that to also mean, being mindful, aware of God's presence in our life at all times. A very simple concept, but how do we achieve it?

Maharaj ji simply says, "Recite *Nam*".

Later, I was asked by some foreign guests why one should meditate? The only answer I could give was, "Just do it and you'll understand." What did I know? I was a student deep in my studies with little experience of practical applications to our worldly lives. I was so caught up in the practice that I had taken little time to look at it from an outsider's point of view, much like a scientist who is constantly playing with his formulas and theories. If someone asks, "Why are you doing this research?" he has almost forgotten what to say.

So what is *Nam*?

"Like a mute trying to describe a delectable sweet"

Guru Granth Sahib

Nam, God's Holy Name, has been described in many ways. All are inadequate. For me *Ek Onkar SatNam Siri Waheguru*, was enough. It didn't matter what the philosophy behind *Nam* was or even what it meant. I was just happy reciting it. But if pressed I would answer that *Nam* is both the 'Word' of God from which all creation springs, and the name or form of the Holy Spirit within us.

We might say that *Nam* operates on three levels. On a cosmic level, *Nam* is the sound of creation. While it is expressed slightly differently, scriptures teach that God spoke and from that Voice all creation took form. Some traditions speak only of the visible taking form from the unseen. Regardless of how it is expressed, that voice or force of creation remains imprinted on all things animate and inanimate. That primordial sound continues to reverberate throughout the cosmos. It will never stop. It is the unceasingly melody.

We might call the second level, creation. In our created universe, according to the scriptures of India, from the Vedas to Guru Granth Sahib, there are 840 thousand life forms. These include everything from single cell organisms to human beings and, if I might say, beyond to spirit forms which some feel haunt their lives. That is not to mention the inanimate, from the rocks and mountains and the minerals that lie below them, to the distant stars and planets. *Nam* ties all forms together. It is the very thread of existence upon which everything is strung. It is also the part of all creation which never dies.

However, what differentiates human beings from other life forms is not our ability to reason, it is our ability to experience God. (I had this conversation with Jane Goodall when I asked her how life was among the 'lower species', meaning human beings). *Nam* exists in all things, animate and inanimate. We note in the New Testament that as Jesus was entering Jerusalem, "If the rocks could speak, they too would shout Hosanna." But it is only human beings who are so blessed that they can recite it.

Other beings may hear it and act according to its orders. In this way they may be far better than us. But God has given humans the ability to raise their consciousness, to become one with God. That does not mean we can ever become God, but we can become more Godlike in our behavior.

In *Nam*, time collapses and we are drawn into the Center of Creation, closer to God. While there is no time, space actually expands so we are able to experience the infinite, that which has no time or space limitation. And in that space, all knowledge and wisdom is contained. Everything is within us.

So on a personal or internal level, when we do meditate, we find that *Nam* is the very essence of our being. If we are to rise above our ego, the 'I' within us, how else do we exist outside of God? What other name can we take? What else is there besides God?

Instead of thinking of ourselves all the time, calling out to God by reciting His Holy Name, keeps our minds filled with God's love at all times. This is the essence of what some term unceasing prayer.

Meditation is listening to *Nam* echo throughout our consciousness. Maharaj ji quotes Guru Nanak in Japji Sahib:

sunia sidh pir sur nath
sunia dharat dhaval akaas

All creation is attuned to, or more accurately, is held transfixed by, the Word of God.

God's Holy Name reverberates throughout the universe. It is the primordial sound from which everything emanates. From this sound both the orders and visions of God come forth. *Nam* is the sound that emanates from the Light of God, and perhaps by following the sound we are able to find the Light within us.

Enough of philosophy. Maharaj ji always stresses the practical experiential from which any philosophy can be deduced or corroborated. The rest He likes to say 'is just in the air'. "After all,"

He'll quip, "spirituality is not complicated philosophy, it's very simple." In fact it is reality.

Nam prepares your mind for the Light

One of the earliest lessons Maharaj ji taught me was that without Nam our minds could never withstand the power of the Light. If we are grounded in the world, lightning will destroy us. Conversely, if we somehow are not attached to anything then it will pass through us. So while reciting Nam we are somehow detached from our ego and become attuned to God.

The Guru tunes your mind

Whenever I enter Maharaj ji's presence, I suddenly feel the sound and strength of Nam increase in my mind. This is no coincidence. It radiates from Him like sunshine. But there is something more going on. Sometimes in the middle of a talk, He will even interject a comment, "The most important thing you can do is meditate." Or, "Now it's so important to meditate." Suddenly I look up at Him and He is literally listening to my mind. Like a music teacher checking his students' tuning or scales, Maharaj ji is actually tuning my mind. And once He's satisfied that Nam is 'humming' along, then He will even nod and then turn His attention to the rest of the gathering. Such is the greatness of His love and the greatness of the Guru.

Maharaj ji has us repeat after Him

Maharaj ji may have us begin by reciting the words out loud. He Himself will have us repeat after Him several times and then tell us to go on reciting the lesson. For those who ask him how long to meditate, he may tell them to spend a minimum of twenty minutes in the morning, to set our alarms twenty minutes or ½ hour earlier and then again before we go to sleep at night. Then let the love increase naturally from there, so that you yourself are drawn into God's love and want to spend more time yourself. For those more serious about their practice He will assign more rigorous lessons of 2 hours at a time. Sometimes he will say 1 and ¼ hours.

For those who ask, "Why can't I control my mind immediately? Why don't visions appear? Why don't I see light?"

94

Maharaj ji tells us not to worry if our mind is wandering. Just sit and meditate. I suppose it's a little like piano lessons for those so 'inflicted' as to have to struggle with a metronome and learning scales only to be able to achieve after hours of practice the most feeble rendition of the beautiful piece the teacher had played the week before. So too Maharaj ji may give us glimpses of God's Glory and then expect that we through our 'own' practice reach that stage. Of course, it may be lifetime before it happens, but we only need to know that God or that state exists and allow our love to pull us along the path.

There may be some who are impatient, who expect instant enlightenment and do not like the idea of arduous hours of practice. To them Maharaj ji has a simple message, this is the game of life. These are the rules that God has given us to play with. And as with anything it must be a labor of love. As He told me in our first meeting, "Why should you think it should be so easy to find God when it takes 30 years to become a doctor, lawyer or engineer?" But of course, the 'work' we put in during our past lives not only counts, everything we have today is because of what we placed in 'our account' from previous lives.

So enlightenment never comes easily. However if in this life we are quick to grasp a lesson, it simply means that we were good students in the past. More likely, the Guru has taken pity on us. Maharaj ji often says, this period, while it may seem the darkest in civilization, is actually the easiest to find God. As there are so few pursuing God, His door opens quickly to those who knock.

Hearing Him sing

Maharaj ji may give *Nam* by song as a way to train our minds. We all have experienced going to sleep after listening to music or after hearing an especially beautiful song in a play or movie. In the morning, we wake up to that song still playing in our minds. Sometimes throughout the day and for days on end it keeps playing and we are continually touched by it.

Hearing Maharaj ji sing is like hearing the Heavens burst with celestial song. His voice creates waves that echo endlessly, reverberating through our every cell and to all corners of the cosmos.

To be in His presence when He sings is perhaps the single most powerful spiritual experience anyone could have. He Himself is drawing all the power of love from God and transmitting it to those around, not just to the people, but to the entire environment, the trees and flowers. For days (perhaps forever) after there is a glow that remains. I suppose one could argue that His talks or His very Being have the same impact, for God is always present in Him. But, when He sings, there is nothing like it. He may stand for hours teaching those gathered around Him what it really means to 'sing God's praises'. And sing we do and dance for the power is irresistible.

Unceasing prayer with every breath

Sahas sahas simro Gobind, man   anter ki utre chint
With every breath let us recite God's Holy Name
All the worries of our mind will be dispelled

Guru Granth Sahib

One morning after I'd finished cleaning Maharaj ji's room in kothi number 2, He was in a beneficent mood and beckoned me to sit next to Him on the floor. He sat near the doorway cross-legged with his arms stretched over his knees, and proceeded with a lesson I'll never forget.

"It says in Gurbani to recite *Nam* with every breath. Watch."
He began to inhale and exhale. With each breath he began:
Bhakhs lo —
(Lord) Forgive Me
After several minutes, Maharaj ji switched to *Nam*:
Then inhale
Ek
Exhale
Onkar
Inhale
Satnam
Exhale
Siri Waheguru

96

Nam is also the sustenance for our minds

Maharaj ji often quotes Gurbani:

man ka tosa har nam hai hirde rakho sambhal.
The true nourishment for our minds is *Nam*, keep it close to your
heart.

Just as we are concerned with the diet for our bodies, we should
pay attention to what we feed our minds. The only thing that will
quiet a troubled mind is *Nam*, like a crying child calmed by its bottle.

It is the medicine for our 'disease' of human weakness and if
we go without taking our medicine we will certainly never get better.
Perhaps our condition may even worsen.

In the early days, the force of *Nam* within me was so
overpowering that concentration was never a problem. I would be
awakened at 1:30 a.m. with four to four ½ hours of sleep, which
were considered standard for Gobind Sadan, have my bath and
report to the *havan* promptly at 2 a.m. for my two hour shift.
I would offer a brief prayer, sit in my favorite corner, simply
close my eyes, and *Nam* would take over. When people said
they had trouble focusing, I literally didn't know what they
were talking about. I couldn't even understand how someone
could get sleepy during meditation.

However, with the many changes in life, my routine was affected
and I've had to struggle with the same problems of wandering mind,
dozing off, dealing with worries, that I shrugged off when others
had shared them with me. Maharaj ji used to console me by saying
these were stages that I was passing through and not to worry. Because
at first I thought I had lost the blessing. My sense is rather that early
in your studies God appears with such force and grandeur that you
are literally dazzled and lifted to untold heights. Then He brings you
down to earth again and expects you to learn how to find your way
back.

Over the years, Maharaj ji has taught me some wonderful
and often amusing ways to control my mind and focus it on the
task of cleaning house. For Maharaj ji has always said that meditation
is an active process. Often quoting Guru Nanak:

vakhat te upar larh marai – amrit vele shabad alaape.
Seize the moment and strike at the right time – take *Nam* at the
ambrosial hour.

The most important guest

While *Gurbani* is an ocean of peace, its instructions often refer to the
struggle between good and evil in our minds, and how to control
our errant thoughts and bring light within. Often I think of how
pure I have to make my mind if I am to invite the Lord to come
and dwell there. If we invite guests to visit, we clean our house. The
more important the guest, the more we clean and may even go out
of way to buy new furniture. For really important people we might
even make renovations. So, if we are inviting God to visit us, our
meditation should produce as thorough a cleaning as possible.

Maharaj ji's lessons can be broken down into 3 parts:

First - focusing our mind on the task.

We have to recognize that our house needs cleaning and that
now is the time we've set aside to do it. Half the battle is being
able to recognize the dirt and not being afraid to face it.

Second – controlling our thoughts.

Once we've determined that we will clean our minds, how do we
keep all those thoughts from interrupting the process?

Third – the actual cleansing process.

When we recite *Nam* and Jaap Sahib what images can we maintain
to see that our mind is in fact cleaned and we are not just
mouthing the words and missing a lot of the dirt or sweeping it
under the carpet?

Some of my Favorite Lessons

While Maharaj ji, as all Masters lecture his students, these are
lessons 'dictated' from within while I was practicing meditation,
what I refer to as doing my homework.

Disturbing the Peace

In the United States, people can be arrested for disturbing the peace.
If someone is especially noisy, rude, or unruly, neighbors or an owner
of an establishment can call the police and have the person taken off
to jail. I often think that we should ticket our thoughts for

disturbing our peace of mind and have them carted off to a cell until they can learn to behave themselves and act in a more orderly fashion. Of course, it is we ourselves who must learn to 'police' our thoughts and hold them accountable to the Law of Peace. The only way this can be done is by inviting the Guru, actually entreating the Guru, to keep your mind clear of such thugs and ruffians. And it is only through calling out His Holy Name that we can properly invite Him into our minds.

The classroom

Once as I sat in Baba Siri Chand ji's *havan* my mind was roaming. Maharaj ji became a teacher in the classroom of my mind. He went to the 'door' and told my thoughts, "Ralph is busy in class now. When he is done with his school work he'll come out and play with you again." And with that He shut the door. And if that wasn't enough, if ever my thoughts began to wander, or I'd 'look out the window,' He'd quickly pull down the shade.

The children

Then Maharaj ji taught me to treat my worries or thoughts as my children and discipline them. Tell them, "I'm busy, this is my private time for prayer, and I'll deal with you later. In the meantime don't bother me. Go amuse yourself someplace else." What was amazing was that thoughts can be trained just like our children to amuse themselves. And often by the time I finished meditating the problem that was worrying me so had already defused itself, or at least diminished in its demands and no longer bothered me. For often it isn't that the problem itself, it's how we react to it that makes it difficult to control.

Just like we burn *smagari* and ghee in the *havan* Maharaj ji has shown me to use *Nam* to light the *havan* in my mind. Then whenever an especially troubling thought manages to sneak into the classroom I simply throw it in the *havan* and let it burn away.

There is another much deeper aspect to kindling the sacred fire within. While we can be on guard for our conscious thoughts, Maharaj ji quotes Guru Teg Bahadur ji when he says,

nar achet pap ton dar rahe

Be vigilant, for your subconscious thoughts also create sin.

99

Many times I thought, how when it was hard enough to control the bad thoughts that beset our minds, could we possibly control our subconscious. The answer came one day in Baba Siri Chand ji's *havan*. In the *Ramayana*, one of India's first Spiritual Epics, Lord Ram created an invisible ring around Sita Mata (his wife and queen) to protect her from evil. At the end He made her walk through the fire to allow her true self to emerge unharmed. If we create a *havan* in our minds, and pray that 'Lord please make each thought first pass through Your Sacred Fire before it enters our mind,' then we would have a chance where only pure thoughts would dwell in our consciousness. I had understood the theory. However keeping that fire burning at all times is another matter.

The broom or mop

Make *Nam* a broom and with every recitation watch the dirt from your mind being swept away. Then mop up neatly afterwards to catch any flecks remaining and leave everything smelling fresh.

Garbage bags

Just as we bag our garbage and discard it, so too we can take our troublesome thoughts and seal them in a garbage bag and dispose of them.

The sword

Make *Nam* a sword and let it cut a path through the jungle of your mind until you can see the Light clearly. It will vanquish all the negativity and evil and leave your mind clear.

Bathing old wounds

Much of what troubles us is our memories of painful events. There may even be sores that have festered. Too painful to be touched, we avoid them completely. But with *Nam* we can bathe our minds with such a soothing solution that these old wounds heal. Then we are able to lance the sores allowing the darkness we've held within to escape, even if it is literally nauseating. Then *Nam* once again cleans these wounds deeply, cauterizing them if necessary to keep the infection from recurring.

Change the tape or the channel

Often if my mind is chattering, playing a particular annoying refrain, or showing a troubling scene, Maharaj ji would simply say, "I don't like that ... change the channel," or "play another tape." Almost like a parent monitoring the music, TV/movie, or Internet viewing of their children to protect them from damaging messages. And we should change it to – Nam, Path, and Praises of Him. Of course, it is a constant struggle to keep our minds from flipping stations, or pushing the remote or surfing. But it can be done.

Don't let your thoughts run away with you

When our child starts to misbehave, we often say, "Don't get carried away." Likewise we can clamp down on the variant actions of our minds. Don't let our thoughts run away with us.

In some ways whatsoever we think may on one level or another come to pass. And we want to make sure it is good for us and those around us, and good for the world. Our negative thoughts not only pollute our minds and affect our bodies, but pollute the world around us.

The washing machine

Mary Pat once asked me why her mind seemed to dredge up all these thoughts while reciting Jaap Sahib, while when she recited Nam she was able to be absorbed in God's love. Suddenly Maharaj ji showed me the image of a washing machine. First, the clothes are churned. As the soap sinks in the dirt loosens its grip and rises to the surface. Then the dirt is rinsed away. Finally, the clothes are rinsed again with clean water until they are clean. While it is usually enough to run clothes through one cycle, extremely dirty clothes may need to be pre-washed or soaked for a long time in stronger solutions to get the stubborn stains out. Similarly, our minds are covered with dirt and though we wash and wash, they never seem to come clean.

Video Games

Someone once asked why it seems that just when we feel we have achieved some level of peace through meditation that suddenly we are beset by problems that disturb us. Maharaj ji immediately showed me a video game. With each level we clear, the next levels become progressively harder. The problems, while they may look familiar, actually come at us at an ever-quickening pace to test our concentration. Meditation is no different and God is constantly testing us.

The Horse

Maharaj ji has often likened our minds to a horse that is allowed to run wild all day. "You are not going to turn him for home easily." In meditation we learn to 'reign in' that horse and keep him on track.

Form the habit

Maharaj ji always stressed that we must develop the habit of *Nam*, of turning our minds to *Nam*, and being conscious of it at all times. We must also cultivate the habit of rising early in the morning, to sit in 'God's office or God's classroom,' as Maharaj ji puts it, before we start our day in the world. We shouldn't worry whether we can concentrate or not. Maharaj ji said, "Just do it, and let God take over."

Dozing off

For those who lament the fact that they may tend to doze off in "class" or fall asleep while meditating, Maharaj ji has these kind words: "If you do fall asleep while reciting *Nam* you are actually sleeping in the lap of God." But of course we can't use that as an excuse. We should try to stay awake. If we have ever dozed off in class, the teacher may wrap on our desk. In Zen Buddhist meditation, the Master walks the hall with a stick to whack on the shoulder of those who doze off. However, in Gobind Sadan we are left to our own devices, which means we have to visualize that teacher or Master standing before us, and maintain that alertness so we don't want to fall asleep in the Presence of the One who would shower us with love. This is no idle exercise, for He is definitely right there before us whether we can see Him or not.

Moving to the rhythm

Laughing, smiling, sitting or standing,
Nam will merge you with God

Maharaj ji once said, "When I think of *Nam*, I see everything moving with *Nam*. *Nam* is even the driving force behind the fan." From that day on, every time a fan is turned on, *Nam* is blown across the room. When I jog or walk, my feet beat out *Nam*. The birds' wings, their songs, the insects at night all are humming *Nam*. Listen, it's unmistakable.

The cup in the gutter

Maharaj ji once said to me, "You are like a cup that I put out in the gutter (of the world) and every so often you become so dirty that I have to bring you in (to Gobind Sadan) to polish you before placing you out again."

Jesus in the boat

One of the most beautiful stories of the power of *Nam* and meditation is one that Maharaj ji often tells. Jesus is in the boat with his disciples when the storm comes up. Jesus is lost in meditation, one with His Father and doesn't even notice anything wrong. As the waves begin to break over the sides and the boat begins to fill with water the disciples try to rouse him. "Master, Master," they shout, "the boat is sinking." But Jesus doesn't respond. Again they shout, "Master, Master, the boat is filling with water." Finally, Jesus hears their calls and stands up. "What's the matter," he shouts, "don't you know that the wind is under my Father's command." And the wind stops. "And the sea as well." And suddenly the sea calms, and He steps from the boat and walks to shore on the water.

"Master, what are you?" they ask. "Oh ye of little faith, if you had the faith of a mustard seed you could move mountains."

Away from the power of the story itself and the praise it engenders for Lord Jesus there is an important lesson: how to maintain our faith in the midst of turmoil.

Gurbani says:

Nanak nam jahaj hai, charhe so utre par
Nam is our boat that carries us across the sea of life.

Let us see our consciousness as the boat being powered by God's Holy Name. As long as we focus on God through *Nam* then the boat sails smoothly even through difficult storms. But the minute we take our mind off *Nam*, our connection with God is lost and we lose our faith in Him. Then the boat begins to take water. We begin to pay attention to our problems thus giving them more importance than we do to God, thereby giving them more power over us. So we slowly begin to sink with our problems. All that is necessary is for us to return to *Nam*, to once again acknowledge the presence of God, and the boat will begin to cut through the waves again and our problems will recede.

This in fact is how our life progresses. Our faith is strong until faced with new difficulties and then we panic. Shouting out "Master, Master help us," without even realizing that He is sitting within us waiting to help us if we would only ask.

Settling Disputes – Forgive us our trespasses
Much of what deeply troubles us is our dealings with others. All of us have either been hurt by someone or hurt someone else. And, when Maharaj ji has said that it is a 'sin' to even hurt someone's feelings, then it is indeed a difficult hurdle for us to overcome. Maharaj ji often quotes the Lord Jesus, saying that: We must forgive others if we expect God to forgive us.

I remember standing with Maharaj ji at Princeton when a young man approached Maharaj ji for His blessings. The man told of how his parents had been killed by 'enemies,' and how could there ever be peace in the world as long as hatred existed between such groups. Maharaj ji looked at the man and asked: "Have you forgiven them for killing your parents?" The man was stunned. "No, he replied, it's very hard." Maharaj ji continued, "Hard or not, this is Jesus' order. If you are not able to follow it in your own life, how can there be peace in the world?"

One meditation that Maharaj ji has shown is that if you bring the other person before you in the center of your mind, and if you've hurt them, beg their forgiveness. If they have hurt you, tell them that you forgive them. Then go with them into the presence of God, however you see God, Maharaj ji, Jesus, the Light, and ask that you both be forgiven. Once you have forgiven them internally in the presence of God then it is much easier to overcome your pain, when and if you finally meet again. Moreover they will no longer have control on that part of your mind because in forgiveness you have let it go or risen above it.

Bless don't curse

In Punjabi culture there is a very interesting, even enlightened way to react to someone (often a child) who misbehaves. Instead of cursing them, you shout, "Oh, may you improve." Maharaj ji teaches us to pray for your enemies. Don't curse them. God will change their minds and also raise us up. This is a very practical, positive and direct way to offer forgiveness.

The Comic in our Textbook, or imprinting our thoughts on our prayers

Prayers are supposed to leave their imprint on our minds. However, the way we typically pray usually ends up in quite the opposite process. We open our prayer books and begin to look at or mouth the words. Meanwhile our minds are running rampant. Our thoughts are literally dancing across the pages. Sometimes it's so bad that I venture to say that we can get through an entire prayer book without paying the least attention to a single word, having been totally consumed by our thoughts.

Maharaj ji in a humorous mood showed me the image of children who bring their favorite comic books to school and cleverly place them inside the textbook they are supposed to be reading. They appear quite studious while all the while they are actually reading their comics. Of course this all breaks down when the teacher calls on them to answer a question on the material they are reading. Or, when they are ill prepared for the test.

Like those children, we will not receive the benefit of the prayers when our tests come. Our fears and foibles will continually block our progress until we can learn to allow the prayers to imprint their power on our minds and learn to control our thoughts.

Are we good students or daydreamers? We can all think back to our school days when the teacher stood at the blackboard and lectured us. Sometimes our mind would drift off – floating right out the window following the sounds outside – the kids on the playground or just thinking of what we would do after school. But every once in a while something the teacher said would click and we were so tuned in that it wouldn't matter what was going on around us, whether others were talking or fidgeting or what the weather was like outside, we totally tuned out the distractions and focused on the teacher's every word. Meditation is the same. God and the Guru is standing right before us talking to us but most of the time we're somewhere else not paying attention, worrying about what will happen to us or our loved ones, thinking about what we'd like to do to that nasty person who just offended us or remembering something or someone from our past. But then suddenly even for an ever so brief moment that glimpse of God or the Voice within us rises above the din of our worries and the clouds of our anger and we see a little Light. The Light is so powerful, so enchanting that we are drawn to it like moths to a flame. For those so blessed we too like the moth would be consumed by the flame – merging our souls into it. Oh to bathe in Your Ocean of Light – Your Holy Name resounding in our minds. That is meditation and unlike a daydream, it takes us into the reality that surrounds us, envelops us and seals off the negativity of this world that we call home. If only we would learn to be good students. Your peace would fill us and spill out into a thirsty world. And the greatest lesson of all – Peace on earth – could be achieved.

Mommy look at me – the ultimate ego trap

When I was little and learned to ride my bike, I was so excited that I turned while still riding and shouted, "Mommy look at me". That was my downfall, the bike started to wobble and I couldn't control it. Down I went. The exhilaration was gone, soon replaced by the hurt. The scratches were nothing compared to my embarrassment and damaged ego.

Damaged ego – that was the problem to begin with. It was not enough to enjoy the moment, I had to show someone else. In that moment whatever gift we are given is dropped. Not that we haven't experienced it whatever it may be – but it may take us time to climb back on the bike and in the back of our minds a little fear has been placed to dampen our enthusiasm. Falling by ourselves might just increase our determination but falling while showing off is a shame – damaging to our young self esteem. And so it goes.

Each time You give us a gift let not our ego blind us. As we enjoy we need only thank you first.

As we grow, the tendency is to forget that it is You who are doing everything and thanking You is the easy remedy for ego, sublimating all other loves in the fire of Your Divine light.

Surely, there is no more wonderful way to live than in sight of your love and divine grace. Hence the commandment – "Thou shalt have no other god's before me," is in one sense a covenant of love and not a mandate of a jealous God. But if we are true to our worship there would be no other that we seek and no other that we see – no other form that we long for – as You ARE all and within all. As with Guru Gobind Singh ji's watchword *'tav parshad'* (Oh Lord it is all with thy grace). Even in the midst of great victories it was *tav parshad*. Not look at me.

Maharaj ji counsels – Even when sitting in a car, or when dressing, whenever and wherever we should thank the Giver.

With a good cleaning, we might expose a real wisdom tooth
As Guru Nanak said it is only *Nam* that can clean our minds.

Let's look at it front the dentist's perspective.

We brush our teeth daily, at least twice, but still the plaque build up is heavy.

Our minds are caked with plaque. We may even need a chisel to pry it loose and yes, the surface will be sore for a while. But *Nam* will heal it.

We must take the protective coating of *Nam*, lest we allow the filth to build back up again.

As Guru Tegh Bahadur says, "After his bath the elephant just goes and rolls in the dust again."

Dare to enter the jungle and tame the wild beast

Maharaj ji often compares our mind to a jungle full of wild thoughts. With *Nam* we can brave the darkest recesses, rout out and tame the wild beast of our ego. But it is not easy. It is a constant struggle. But with Maharaj ji's blessings we must continue to try until we have succeeded.

11

The Power of Jaap Sahib
Guru Gobind Singh's Empowering Cosmic hymn in praise of God

Anyone who has ever had the privilege of sitting in Maharaj ji's 'court' has seen the scores of people come to him for blessings. They may be rich or poor and from any place or any religion in the world. Maharaj ji takes a small yellow booklet from the boxes next to him and says: "You are blessed, here take Jaap Sahib." Sometimes he will ask which language they would prefer and then accordingly, the Punjabi, Hindi, English, or Russian text is presented to them. "Recite this and leave the rest to God." I can't even begin to think how many Jaap Sahib's have been distributed in this way, but millions is the proper denomination. So what is special about these 199 verses?

Empowering prayer
Many traditions talk about centering prayer, a return to the meditative quiet of our inner self. But Jaap Sahib works quite differently, while it may ultimately quiet our minds, it does so by vanquishing our internal enemies and the impediments to our progress in the world. It is what I'd call 'empowering prayer'.

We have seen the power of Jaap Sahib to grant positions to those who would never have risen out of poverty, to open doors that were always shut, to calm even the most disturbed souls.

Athletes have won medals, cripples have walked, businesses have flourished, politicians have won elections, all because they put their faith in these 199 verses of endless praise for the Infinite One.

Medaling in Sports
For those interested in sports, there are some wonderful stories shared by the coach of one of India's top track and field teams. Actually,

they weren't always at the top, but according to their coach, as soon as they began reciting Jaap Sahib each one of their members improved so much that not only did they win individual medals but the team rose to the top in national and international competition.

One runner was so far behind he could barely stay on the team let alone think of a medal. But with Jaap Sahib, his times kept increasing until he to was able to medal in his event.

This team consisted of players from all over India, of all religions and cultures. But Jaap Sahib is so universal a prayer that it was accepted by all. Besides when they saw the results they all felt they should receive some of its blessings too. If ever there is a doubt in someone's mind, Jaap Sahib itself clears it away, as happened in this case.

Jesus appears in Jaap Sahib

There was a girl from Kerala, a silver medalist in track, who wondered whether it was all right for her as a Christian to recite Jaap Sahib. As she opened the prayer book for the first time, Jesus appeared to her from the pages in answer to her question.

Jaap Sahib in translation

Jaap Sahib has since been translated into English and Russian so those who don't know Punjabi can recite it and benefit from its power. What is quite amazing about Jaap Sahib is that it even works in translation. Usually people say that a translation is not, and should not be considered, scripture. While I usually agree, Jaap Sahib is something special.

A Case in point

Friends of ours had wanted to learn Jaap Sahib in its original, and had gathered at our home for the recitation. That night we called Maharaj ji for His blessings and told Him that people were learning Jaap Sahib. His response was quite shocking, "Why are you forcing them to learn Punjabi, let them do it in English or whatever language they want."

We begged forgiveness saying that this was their idea and we were of course not forcing the issue. But, the point was made and the order stood. Jaap Sahib in English it was. So from that point on, each month we sat in a circle and recited Jaap Sahib, each one taking a line we revolved around the room. By the second round, we could feel the whole atmosphere change. Our consciousness kept spiraling higher and higher with each verse, and by the end of the reading there was so much peace in the room you could literally cut it. We would just sit and drink it in.

It even calms spirits

Once while I was visiting friends in Toronto, a call came that one of their friends had committed suicide and the family was totally distraught, as we can well understand.

When we arrived in the small apartment, the room was so filled with negativity that it affected everyone. Everyone was in hysterics with no guidance at all. It was as if the spirit was bouncing off the walls. Maharaj ji immediately said read Jaap Sahib. We only had one prayer book to share. But the 2 of us started, line by line, she reciting one and I the next. As we read, we could feel the calm begin to spread. And even though I missed a couple of words, by the time we finished the hysterics had been replaced by peace and the soul had settled down.

Jaap Sahib – Praise Therapy

Harold Koenig is a world famous psychiatrist at Duke University Medical School, and has published a landmark compendium on the impact of Faith on healing in many different cultural settings.

I shared with him the forty year 'study' in Gobind Sadan on how praise changes thought patterns, he suddenly exclaimed with light in his eyes, "Praise Therapy!"

Healing is in fact a change of thought pattern, a raising of our consciousness, which in turn impacts our actions, both internal/physiological and external, how we deal with those around us and our environment.

We know that thought impacts, if not determines (predisposes us to) our actions; both in how we 'act' internally, how we treat our selves, as well as how we interact with our community and environment. Our negativity affects us at a physiological level often manifesting itself in different types of

111

'illnesses', as well as it affects our relationships with others around us. So in order to heal we must in essence change the way we think.

If healing is truly a change of our thought pattern, then praise may very well be the pivotal point of intersection between the human mind/consciousness and God through which we are 'healed'.

Through praise, the qualities of God we are praising become imprinted on our consciousness. It is that process which elevates us and overcomes the negative stimuli present within us or imposed by our environment. For it is not the power of reason and thought which separates us from the 'lower species' rather it is our reasoning and thought which more often separate us from God – leaving us alone in the world.

Praise and devotion counter the imprinting of the external stimuli of the 'material world.' It is said in most traditions that the human being is the pathway to God, that God created us a little lower than the angels. It is only in human form that one can realize, reach, or merge with God.

Babaji who has been demonstrating the power of praise to change and heal minds/ bodies, racial and religious wounds, the scourge of poverty, and the environment says beautifully in his introduction to 'Jaap Sahib: The Divine Hymns of Praise,'

"When we praise God, that quality manifests within us. If we praise God as the fearless one – fearlessness comes within us – when we praise God as all merciful – mercy flows from us."

At Gobind Sadan, a 30 year 'study' is in progress which shows emphatically the impact of Praise on behavior – of individual bitterness softened to love – of strident relations, both family and societal, overcome by peace. Physical and mental illnesses are also healed.

When we try to reconstruct an ego damaged through physical or psychological trauma – we are still limited by the building blocks of the ego, which we may try to shore up with external support or praise from others. This is not necessarily internalized. We are also limiting the 'self' to grow within the 'box' of its constructs. We need constant praise, constant approval to reinforce ourselves. When the support is not then forthcoming –

112

With Maharaj ji and Nirlep Kaur in Elbridge living room 1986

Maharaj ji at doorway of our Elbridge home, winter of 1999

Maharaj ji with family in our Elbridge living room: author, Maharaj ji, Chetan, Tegbir, Joginder 1986

Maharaj ji blesses the boundaries of our Elbridge home, summer of 1988

Maharaj ji in the foyer of 475 Riverside Drive, The National Council of Churches, summer of 1990

The 2 sided cross – "I am the Light" and the gift of a child

top: Portrait of Maharaj ji from his birthday celebration 25 Feb, 2007

below: author translating for delegates to GSI's Forum on Development and Civil Society – 'Enlightened Development' 23-24 Feb, 2007

Studio Pammi, Chandigarh

or doesn't answer our cry – we once again lose our sense of security. The thumb, the blanket, something to cling to.

In Praise we are providing the ego with 'tools' to reach beyond itself – to expand with the support of the Power of the Universe, which resides within – and allows the 'soul' to tap into its infinite support, which is always with us.

We begin to attune our minds to the 'Voice of the Infinite' instead of the finite voice of fear and anxiety which is constantly present, haunting our every action, questioning our ability to move forward.

Praise takes us outside and beyond the self and in the process forms a bridge to the limitless. It forms a link to the Limitless Ocean which lies within, a ladder on which our thoughts and our minds can ascend to Divine heights leaving our frailty behind.

Like daily medications, prayer and meditation soothe our wounded self, soften the physical and mental pain by allowing us to transcend or reroute the response: Thank God instead of pitying yourselves.

Hence the synaptic process is reversed. The triggers only work while we are focused on our physical body and our needs. When we refocus on God's strength we too are "made whole". In some cases, the illness may disappear, but in most cases our psyche is healed and we progress beyond our physical limitations.

Maharaj ji on Jaap Sahib

Jaap Sahib is not particular to any one religion. It has come from the Source of all religions, the Source of all Creation. Guru Gobind Singh ji has not created any separate religion, and as you recite Jaap Sahib, you will feel that there is only one God, one Love, one Truth, and one service to all Creation. There are no divisive boundaries.

When we recite Jaap Sahib, we are talking to the Creator. We are saying, "Oh God, nothing exists outside of Your command. Even darkness is under Your command; conflict is under Your command. Light and peace are also within Your command. Nothing happens without Your ordering it, and You exist within everything. Your Power is in everything, and thus there is life in everything."

When there is chaos in society, people think God has lost control. However, we should know that everything is under God's control. We may only perceive the outcome of actions long after they occur. Be assured, something good will grow out of our present difficulties.

God's nature is the subject of a university that only a chosen few have attended. How can we understand or explain a subject when we have not taken the course? Those whose words are enshrined in scripture, graduated from the University of the One who is both Creator and Destroyer. Jesus referred to this University as 'my Father's kingdom.' Guru Nanak called it the 'Realm of Truth,' and the Prophet Muhammad spoke of 'Bahisht' (paradise). They know, because they studied there. Though we cannot see it, it does exist.

We do not understand God. The Guru has said that God is like a farmer. If you see a farmer harvesting his rice crop you might ask him, "What are you doing?" "Why are you destroying the rice?" The farmer would explain, "I'm cutting the rice so that I can plant wheat." In God's order, there is no issue of virtue or sin. We do not understand why someone dies at a young age. So the Guru explains, "God is like a farmer who cuts his crop whenever he chooses, be it young, half-ripe, or fully mature." Humans are like His crop. And not only humans, the whole of Creation is His crop.

From a personal perspective, all that happens in life is the outcome of our karma (past deeds) whether in this life or earlier. Karma leaves its imprints on our psyche, and accordingly we pass through life's sunshine or shadow, happiness or misery. There is One Power that transcends karma and that is God Almighty. Therefore, when we pray seeking forgiveness and compassion, then God out of compassion may break the shackles of karma and set us free. At that moment, we undergo a wonderful transformation. Fear and anxiety give way to courage and tranquility. Falsehood and pride are transformed into truth and humility. Greed and attachment turn into renunciation and detachment. This indeed is the miraculous power of prayer enshrined in the divine words of Jaap Sahib.

When you praise someone's virtues, those virtues begin to arise within you. So when we pray to God as the most Fearless, we become fearless. When we invoke Him as the mightiest in Battle, He grants us strength and success in battle. When we bow to God as the Provider of sustenance for all existence, He grants us our sustenance and livelihood. When we hail God as the Fountainhead of all enlightenment, our minds are set on the path of enlightenment.

Jaap Sahib is a universal prayer hailing God's varied attributes, and in the process seeking God's grace. I earnestly invite you to plunge into it and enjoy its bliss. You will emerge transformed and rejuvenated, and you will find worldly challenges, problems, and trials so puny that you will sail through them successfully and seemingly effortlessly because God's grace and power will be operating through you. What is more, your spirit will be constantly soaring upwards to its ultimate goal of union with the Supreme Spirit.

It's God's order

After all the explanations are said and done, Maharaj ji will sum things up the way he began. "It was God's order for me to share Jaap Sahib with the world."

The fact that it is written in the *Janamsakhi* of Bhai Ram Koer, a 300 year old authentic document of one of the key Sikhs of Guru Gobind Singh ji's court, that the Guru himself said:

"As long as there is breath left in our bodies,
Recite Ek Onkar Satnam Siri Waheguru and Jaap Sahib",

which only affirms what Maharaj ji has already told us.

Japji Sahib and Jaap Sahib

There are three points that link Japji Sahib with Jaap Sahib in our spiritual practice.

Maharaj ji covers these beautifully in his 'Blessings' section of Surendra Nath's translation of Jaap Sahib. I had the privilege of exploring them further with Maharaj ji while Gyani ji and I were riding with Him around Shiv Sadan in His Bronco.

Guru Nanak says:

gavai ko tan hovai kisai tan

People can only praise that part of God that they themselves can perceive.

An author will see God as His inspiration or muse. The warrior will see God as his Champion, the Doctor will praise God as the Healer.

Then Guru Nanak continues:

jisno bakhse sifit sala, Nanak patshahi patshah

Those who are blessed to ever sing God's praises are the King of kings.

Now in Jaap Sahib there is nothing but praise. So by reciting Jaap Sahib we are following Guru Nanak Dev ji's course. But how does praising God raise us above others.

115

Maharaj ji answers this question very beautifully in His 'Blessings'. By praising God in Jaap Sahib, those qualities that we are praising actually come within us. When we praise God as the fearless One, we become fearless; as the Giver of all, we become charitable. So, in praising God we begin to imbibe those virtues associated with God. And, it is those virtues that distinguish us among humanity, and raise us to a new level of consciousness.

Prayers at the *havan* or at Jesus's place

In addition, Maharaj ji may tell you to go to Jesus's place and light candles and have Mary pray for you, or go to the *havan* and have Hardeep pray for you there.

It may be that God wants you to perform a *havan*, or mop the floor (on your hands and knees), do chaur sahib, offer *rot* (sweet bread) to Hanumanji, a *degh* (cauldron) of sweet rice for the Prophet Mohammed, *Jalebis* or any other type of offering for the poor. You may say, if Maharaj ji has so much power why would He tell someone else to pray?

There are several reasons. First as we have seen He wants to work through others. Secondly, like any good administrator, delegating your power is more efficient. And while there may be saints who can heal or bless, it is only Maharaj ji who can give another the gift to heal, or to hear Jesus speak, or hear God's orders in prayer. And He gives these gifts generously.

Chardi Kala – the upward spiral

The Sikh concept of *Chardi kala* is an expression of eternal optimism. Translated literally it means "always rising," and combines both a personal and social consciousness that allows us to ever rise above difficulties, or rise above it, as we often hear today. After all God's blessings are with us no matter what is happening to us in this material world.

ketia dukh bukh sad mar eh bhe dat teri datar
Whatever happens, be it sorrow or hunger, is a gift from God.

So as long as we feel God's blessings, our answer to 'how are you,' is, *Chardi kala*. Moreover, so often we bemoan the fate of the world that we are in an endless downward spiral. *Chardi*

116

kala says the opposite. That God's Name and glory is ever rising and we are in the most wonderful and marvelous upward spiral that the world has ever seen.

And at the center is Sarawan wale Maharaj ji ever propelling us to new heights, overcoming all our difficulties, inspiring great thoughts out of our small and petty minds, and always giving us the credit. He is the Lord of All, the Lord of All Lords, the King of All Kings, The Greatest of the Great, The Wonder of the Wonderful, the Marvel of the Marvelous, the Beauty of the Beautiful, the Glory of the Glorious, Majesty of the Majestic, Awe of the Awesome, Power of the Powerful, The Greatest of ALL.

Why do you seek Him here, He is with you on earth
On several occasions God has affirmed to me Sarawan wale as Guru, as His Chosen One.

Once in meditation I was raised up to the Heavens and brought before the throne of the Lord. It was empty. I was amazed. Then the Voice rang out: "Why do you search for Him here when He is there with you on earth." When I checked my old diaries, I found an arrow pointing outside next to this passage. Apparently just as I had been writing, Maharaj ji had walked by.

As I entered the Darbar Sahib room sometime thereafter Maharaj ji was sitting listening to the reading:

Gur Gur Gur kar man mor Gur bin nahi koi hor
Oh my mind always focus on the Guru, Nothing exists outside of the Guru.

Again and again, wherever I looked there was the Guru, whatever I thought, there was the Guru. He was standing in front of me. And I have been so poor a student that up until now while He had taught me so much and given me so much love that I have not been able to properly represent Him and repay all He has given. It is my prayer that He will forgive my weaknesses and always keep me at His Holy Feet. Without Him I am truly nothing. He is the only special One.

Two More Lifelong Lessons

While meditation, work, and seva were the basic courses, Maharaj ji added two more to my syllabus: marriage and preaching, and both became life long practices.

12

Marriage and the Path of the Householder

"Your marriage was arranged? That's impossible." Even after 34 years of marriage, new friends on both sides of the ocean, Sikh youth who were looking to express their freedom, and reporters interviewing me, all find it hard to believe that an American would accept a traditional arranged marriage.

There are several different ways I explain the subject.

First, as an American coming out of a period when the divorce rate was rivaling that of marriage and many were questioning the institution of marriage, I actually liked the idea of a lifelong commitment based on values as opposed to simply physical attraction. Further, I liked the idea of not having to be burdened with 'attracting' my mate. The mating dance of the western male took place in offices, bars, nightclubs, on the beach or practically anywhere the two sexes could get each other's attention. By that time, I'd had my fill of dating and was ready for a different approach. Most traditional societies had arranged marriages. We should remember Yenta the matchmaker in 'Fiddler on the Roof'. It was a way of safeguarding tradition. And one should never think that parents don't want to admire 'the beautiful couple'.

Secondly, there are arranged marriages and arranged marriages. There are matches really made in heaven. Even Shakespeare referred to Romeo and Juliet as 'star-crossed lovers'. I never really stopped to consider the term for more than its poetic power. But after being exposed to the concept of karma, my sense changed. In terms of relationships, the word used is '*sanjog*' (the link), one's connection with another soul. And it is used most frequently if not exclusively to describe whether you have really found your soul mate or not. Parents often come to Maharaj ji asking whether a proposed match (partner) for their son or daughter is suitable. Maharaj ji will close his eyes and see whether there is a link or not. It's very simple. We in the west have taken to matching 'signs'. We look at the Chinese calendar and the Indian shastras. The lesson is quite clear: never get a mouse married to a cat, or a rat to a tiger.

So much for theory:

During my first visit to Chandigarh in '71, Maharaj ji was speaking to the *sangat* from the top of the library in Sector 4. I sat on the lower level engrossed in my private lessons. At one point in the vision, he showed me my bride. A double staircase descended from heaven and a Princess slowly walked down. She was absolutely beautiful. It was a vision I'll never forget. But marriage was far from my mind at that time.

However the longer I stayed in Gobind Sadan, the question of my future arose. Was I to stay at Maharaj ji's feet and simply develop spiritually here, going out to preach from time to time? Or, was I to return to America, as I had originally envisioned to share some of my new-found wisdom in hopes of helping reshape the future course of our society and turn it towards God? If I was to go back, I felt I had to be married. I didn't feel I could live in the midst of a western world as a single person without constantly being tempted and moreover I felt it behooved me to live 'like everyone else' and show that one could maintain one's love for God even amidst the challenges of everyday married life. Besides, part of Maharaj ji's mission was to uphold traditional values and the sanctity of marriage was a cornerstone of society.

In December of 1972, Maharaj ji came to my room and began the discussion. According to Prem Swaranjit, the eye-witness to the proposal, Maharaj ji looked at me and said, "So you think you still have room to love someone else." My response was, "Guru Nanak was married."

So, Maharaj ji sent a message for Joginder to join us. Now this was the Joginder whom I had known and worked beside since coming to Gobind Sadan. But never and I mean never had I ever considered that we would marry. We were not particularly close and only spoke when necessary. I can't remember having any real conversation with her. My teachers were Gurcharan and Bibi Kirtan Wali. Besides Joginder held an outside job and only came in the evening to assume her duty of staying up to make tea for people. She stayed up all night then left for work in the morning. When she slept was a real mystery.

So when Maharaj ji called her into the room and began asking her who she wanted to marry, I didn't know what to think. When she replied, "I'll marry anyone who you say, Maharaj ji." "Marry Ralph!" His response caught me totally off guard. That was it.

We still needed her family's approval, so one day her father and her older brother-in-law came to Gobind Sadan to interview me. My father-in-law's questions were very straight-forward. Here I was living in a religious community, how was I going to support his daughter? More importantly, they had heard many 'horror' stories about life in America. What was the guarantee that I wasn't going to drag her off to the U.S. and divorce her? I must have answered satisfactorily, since he consented. We were given some time to get to know each other, but the engagement was held soon after.

It was a simple ceremony called *shwara*. We gathered before Guru Granth Sahib. Joginder's family had brought a tray of sweets, saffron and oil for the *tilak*, and the *shwara* (a large dried date). Maharaj ji acting as my "father" took the *shwara* and placed it in my mouth. Rings were exchanged and we were engaged.

The wedding was set at a time when my father could attend in January 1973. Unfortunately, my mother was too sick to travel. Having no family in India to help, I designed and printed a simple invitation card, and delivered it to my rose customers along with their flowers and circulated the rest among other close friends in the *sangat*.

Joginder's father took me shopping for suits as was customary, and I went to get my wedding suit stitched. Vaish Brothers was the tailor of choice in Connaught Place and I picked a charcoal pinstripe and had it done up double breasted with high-pointed lapels. Unless the moths finally got it, it still hangs in our coat

123

closet. More than a memory, it's a piece of life's art. I added a yellow silk tie with black floral print. The day of the wedding, Bibi Nirlep tied a bright yellow turban tighter and more stylishly than I ever had been able to master.

My father arrived and was greeted by a chauffer-driven Jaguar convertible, a loan from my close friend, Chilu. I don't know what he expected but everything including his meeting with Maharaj ji was way beyond his imagination. He kept remarking how nice everyone was.

He stood face to face with Maharaj ji, the one, in the words of his family (my aunts and uncles), who had all but seduced their favorite nephew to a dark life, and said with a smile:

"You are the figure of God."

To which Maharaj ji replied, "I am simply a servant."

"But you speak God's words." I was astounded.

Later he would defend Maharaj ji and his work to the family. From then on, any misdeed was all my fault. Maharaj ji, Gobind Sadan, and my wife (whom he defended like his own daughter) were now beyond reproach.

The day of the wedding was typically cool, but the warmth of the occasion filled Gobind Sadan. The roses were in full bloom and I found an orange 'Superstar' (Tropicana in the U.S.) bud over two inches long. It was so heavy that it was hard for my father's lapel to bear the weight.

As the guests from the Embassy community began to file in, Joginder made her appearance coming up the driveway on the field side. Now my father had not seen her before so he quickly made his way through her family and kissed her right before her shocked parents. Such cultural slips are quickly forgiven, but long remembered.

The pre-marriage greeting ceremonies speak of the marriage of the families. My father stood facing Joginder's father and garlands and hugs were exchanged. Small in stature as he was and several years older, S. Krishan Singh, Joginder's father, was so enthusiastic, that he managed to lift my father off the ground (at least his feet cleared the ground). My father laughed good naturedly but didn't return the favor.

As we had no other family members, close elders from the Gobind Sadan community, Baba Inder Singh and Col. Baweja had to stand in for the exchanges with Joginder's other family members. Under normal circumstances where the full contingent of both families are present, it is not uncommon for the gifts, garlands, and hugs to extend down to the uncles, both maternal and paternal. Little doubt is left that the family bond is forged and is to be called upon whenever the couple is in need.

Anand Karaj – the Path of Bliss

The Sikh marriage ceremony is as simple as it is elegant. Four passes around the Guru Granth Sahib, groom leading his bride, connected by a silk cloth handed to him by the girls' family. It is actually three marriages: The one between the couple, between the families, and between God and the community.

The couple and parents stand to pray for the success of their marriage. Then the lines from Guru Granth Sahib are recited. As the music starts and the same lines are sung, the couple bows then walks slowly, circumambulating the scripture, imbibing the words in recognition that this is the path of their future that they are embarking on. The sacred words of God remain the center of their life, their mooring. They are bound inextricably by the sacred ties, and the family and friends present will always be there to support them.

Lavans – sacred rounds

Actually composed as hymns to the 'courtship' between the seeker and God, the *lavans*, have been adapted for the marriage ceremony.

In the first round, the Lord instructs you to take an active part in worldly affairs

Commit to the righteous path of Dharma taught by Brahma in the Vedas, and renounce your sins.

Meditate on God's Holy Name, and enshrine it in your mind as is mentioned in the Smitris.

Contemplating the Perfect True Guru, your sins will be destroyed.

By great good fortune, celestial bliss is attained, and the Lord seems sweet to the mind.

125

Nanak proclaims in the first round, the process has begun.

In the second round, the Master leads you to meet the True Guru, the Cosmic Being.

The mind has become fearless and the filth of ego has been dispelled.

In the pure love, singing the praises of God, you will see God's presence before you.

The soul is illumined with the love of the all pervasive God.

Within you and outside as well, there is only the One Eternal God. Meeting together with the devotees and singing songs of joy

Nanak proclaims in the second round, the internal melody of God's Holy Name resounds.

In the third round, the devotees mind is filled with a desire for God's love.

Meeting the Saints of the Lord, it is our great fortune to be joined with God.

Singing the Glorious Praises of the Lord, I Uttered his Holy Words, and met the Immaculate Lord,

By good fortune, the Saints are able to recite the Unspoken Story of the Lord.

Reciting God's Holy name, it resounds in my mind, by my good fortune

Nanak says in the third round the mind is filled with Divine detachment from the world.

In the fourth round, my mind is at natural peace; I have found the Lord.

The Holy Saint has met God with spontaneous ease; the Lord seems so sweet to my mind and body.

The Lord seems so sweet; and I am pleasing to my God. Night and day, I remain continuously attuned to my Lord.

I have obtained my Lord and Master, the fruit of my mind's desires. The Glory of the Lord's Name resounds in my mind .

Merging with the Lord God, the bride feels the elation of God's Holy Name in her heart.

Nanak proclaims in the fourth round we have found the Eternal God.

I was seated before Guru Granth Sahib. The newly stitched trousers strained a bit as I crossed my legs. But I was far too excited to focus on any physical restraints. Joginder was led in by her mother and sisters and seated to my left. She kept her face down as was traditional, and though the gold fringe on her crimson *chunni* hid her face I could sense the tears. We had both come to serve and love our Guru, and didn't want anything to come in our way.

The goal of the ceremony is to complete each round in time with the music, and in time to bow, sit, and listen to the reading of the next verse, before bowing, standing, and walking around again. All this must be done in a dignified manner, no rushing, when you are normally nervous, and your bride is weighed down by several pounds of jewelry, hanging from her hands and neck.

The prayers said and the opening lines read, the singing began, signaling the start. We bowed, rose and started our life together. I led with sword in one hand and holding the silk cloth that bound us in the other.

Bibi Jaswant Kaur was in especially good voice and her melodies almost lifted us as we walked. There is no rehearsal for a wedding here. So, during the first round the nervousness leaves the body as those family and close friends positioned at the corner coax you along with a soft pat on the back as you pass by.

It reminded me of trying to keep step in a parade and while you were definitely headed for the 'finish line,' you couldn't seem too eager or lag behind. For the beat on this path was steady and we were propelled along the course of life with our Guru at the center, and our family and friends, there to support us. Given my own spiritual journey, these words made me relive my own travels so far and raised hopes that marriage would not take me away from God but in fact was part of the course I had to complete on my path to stay connected to the One I was so deeply in love with.

As we cleared the last turn on our fourth round, flowers began to rain on us from all quarters. All the guests were given handfuls and the term wedding 'shower' took on a new meaning. By the time we bowed and sat down, we were ankle deep in petals. Then came garlands and cash gifts, and sweets shoved in our mouths. It was certainly an overwhelming experience.

After the ceremony, my father spoke, sharing not only a father's feelings for his son, but sharing a bit of what it meant to be Jewish and married. Manjit Singh spoke from the Sikh side.

127

And then Maharaj ji told me to speak. I couldn't imagine how a newly wed groom could share his inner most feelings at that time, but Maharaj ji was so kind that they automatically took form.

"I want to thank you all for coming to support us at this wonderful time in our lives (or some such beginning). You have just stood witness to our commitment which while symbolized by this ceremony far transcends it in time. It is lifelong, and we are bound as we were by this cloth which we grasped on our way around, in the presence and with the blessings of our Guru, and with the love and concern of our family and friends. We will always remember your commitment to us, and as we pass through life's difficulties, be buoyed up by your love and support. Thank you again and God bless us all."

The photos at the reception showed the joy that had spread through the community. Maharaj ji held us as any proud parent would his children. We were so smothered with love and affection from everyone that it was really hard to take. But we enjoyed every moment. It was the uncertainty of what lay ahead and the weight of the commitment and responsibility that had us both a bit shell shocked. This was totally new for both of us and we had a lot to learn.

Adjustments – Merging Two Paths
For both of us who were totally in love with Maharaj ji, and devoted exclusively to His mission, married life was a hard adjustment. Joginder and I both had work schedules. I left with the roses or milk early in the morning and she left for her office. We each returned tired, tried to find time for each other and still maintain our prayer/spiritual life. Often I would be away in Punjab on a lecture tour for months at a time. In fact, I was not able to reach Delhi in time to witness the birth of our first son, Chetan. He decided to come a few days early, so Joginder had to get to the hospital, in labor, by herself, enduring the bouncing of a scooter and the bus. I only arrived the next morning.

We began our married life in my room in the corner of the dera, but Maharaj ji soon allowed us to build a house on one corner of the hill. Compared to my room it was palatial: one spacious bedroom with attached bath, living room, dining area and kitchen.

It had a nice veranda overlooking the entire fields and dera below. There was a 'deck' on top of the well which offered a nice private place to sun the baby.

It was a short walk across the hill to the dairy when I worked with the buffalo and took a little longer to get to the main compound for our prayers. Walking the dirt path while keeping the barbed wire fence to my right allowed me to reach safely even in the dark. Today part of Maharaj ji's house stands on the spot where we used to live. As we walk from room to room, we try to envision our early life there.

Our commitment was stronger than any of the difficulties we faced, and today as I write we have celebrated our 35th anniversary, and have raised two wonderful young men, Chetan and Tegbir. We've been blessed and I mean truly blessed to have them as children. Chetan is married to Sukhpreet (our new daughter according to Indian custom) and they have brought Budhivali (the princess of wisdom) into the world to start the next generation.

Double culture shock – Honeymoon in the U.S.

Returning to America from India in those days was always a significant culture shock. Coming out of one small room with a long walk to the bathroom into a New York apartment or house was always the easiest part. It was everything else. Like which toothpaste to buy. In India we had about 5 boxes on the shelf. It was hard to look down an isle of brands and determine which 'flavor' Crest I used to use. When I left there were only two varieties.

But now I had a wife with me who had no experience at all of America. I used to joke with Joginder to take a good look at the roads, cars and trucks. "You're about to see something that will absolutely amaze you." While Joginder, an architect by background, was not overwhelmed by the space, or the sheer scale of things, it was all the little stuff that was most difficult.

Take food for example. While I had grown up with meat all around and was not uncomfortable with foods sharing space, Joginder was incredibly sensitive as she had never eaten meat in her life. We would stand for what seemed like hours reading labels on everything from bread to beans making sure there were no eggs or meat products in the ingredients. I felt like a food inspector rather than simple shopper. We soon found that just walking into a pizza place where fresh pepperoni pizza had just come out of the oven was enough to nauseate her. What was more, even the benign grilled cheese sandwich was often cooked on the same griddle as the bacon or burgers, and sandwiches were cut with the same knives as the turkey clubs. As we criss-crossed America on the Greyhound bus, we finally got the hang of what to order, or keep our appetites in place til we arrived in a city where we invariably stayed with a Sikh family we had been introduced to.

The Eggless cake

Then friends invited us to dinner. Everything went well until they put the beautiful home cake on the table that was baked just in our honor. After all our care in shopping, we couldn't help asking, "Does it have eggs in it?" "Of course, it's a great cake." They replied enthusiastically not realizing what that meant to us.

"We're sorry, we can't eat it," I managed to blurt out. It was one of the most uncomfortable moments between friends I can remember. "Please, just pretend the eggs are not there," they pleaded.

Today as I look back, especially since I do eat eggs now, I understand how tough it was for me with my new bride by my side to cross that barrier.

On our return to India we asked Maharaj ji about eggs. His answer was quite typical as it was humorous. "Eggs these days are like potatoes. There's no rooster involved. Go ahead and eat them if you feel like it."

Too bad we hadn't had that conversation before our dinner. Our friends would have felt a lot better.

Holding hands openly

In India even married couples didn't hold hands openly. So when Joginder would see kids hugging and kissing in public she was appalled. It was really offensive to her. For me, having stepped out of a culture of promiscuity into a spartan lifestyle, it was hard not to see this as a sign of societal decay. While I didn't want to

130

be judgmental, seeing things through Joginder's eyes increased my sensitivity as well.

Getting lost in the crowd

There are many Americans who like the idea of getting lost in the crowd. Especially on bad days, having your identity swallowed up by the mass of New York humanity appealed to them. However it was nothing less than terrifying when Joginder lost my hand walking up the crowded steps to an office building and found herself in the middle of people with me not in sight. With heart pounding and shouting out for me, she was in quite a panic until I was able to look down from a vantage point on a higher step and spot her. I quickly descended into the sea of people and rescued her.

Watergate and the Great American Divide

While we were learning to overcome our cultural divide, America itself was deep in the throes of its own divisive identity crisis - the Watergate Hearings. The media was dominated by the escapades of President Nixon's men and the extent they had gone to maintain power. We arrived in Washington and spent a day in the Capital. We asked everyone, "Is this going to make the American people more responsible?" It seemed the obvious issue to us. Howard Baker and Lowell Wykert, both key Senator's on the committee, greeted us cordially and responded that they certainly hoped so. Wykert remarked, "Nixon may be President, but he has to put his pants on one leg at a time just like the rest of us." But many people looked at us as if we'd just arrived from a different planet.

We were waiting in the hallway of the old Senate Office Building for our turn with Sam Ervin (the Chair of the Committee) when a reporter came up beside us with his recording equipment strapped over his shoulder. He had just climbed the worn marble stairs and was catching his breath before his interview when I asked him the question. He retorted, "Responsibility! What's that got to do with anything? You mean if I see a banana peel on the stairs and an old lady subsequently comes up and slips on it, I should feel responsible?"

"Well... yes," I responded.

He just shook his head. Apparently he was able to project his perspective more effectively, for later that night, with makeup in place and glasses removed, he was under the bright lights in the rotunda filing his report for the evening news on a national network.

Go to Toronto and meet the Sikhs

Despite being away from Gobind Sadan, the training in what I like to call "distance learning," began while Joginder and I were staying with my Grandmother in Syracuse. She had gone next door to stay with a neighbor so we could have her apartment to ourselves. I woke up to meditate in the morning and Maharaj ji told me, "Go to Toronto." "Maharaj ji, how can I get to Toronto?" I asked. It was over two-hundred miles away across the Canadian border. I had never been there, and I didn't know the bus or train schedule. Besides, it was 4 a.m. Maharaj ji answered matter-of-factly, "Take your Grandmother's car."

Well that was great!

She would be still sleeping when we pulled out of the garage with her car. As soon as I thought she might be awake, I called her from a rest stop on the way to let her know what had happened. While she wasn't too pleased, she was a loving and understanding Grandmother who would do and had done anything to make her only grandson happy. In Toronto, we asked where the Gurdwara was and were directed to Pape Street (the original and sometimes infamous) Gurdwara housed in a small two-story brick building in a working-class neighborhood. We were late and even had missed *langar*. But the reason for Maharaj ji's directive soon became apparent. There was a meeting in progress. Sikhs had come from all over to discuss educational issues. Through that core group, including Kuldip from Detroit, we were introduced to the leading Sikhs in North America, many of whom are still friends. Among whom were the legendary farmer Didar Singh Bains who hosted us in Yuba City and the internationally famous scientist, Dr Narinder Singh Kapany known as the father of fibre optics, in Palo Alto. Didar Singh started with a small peach orchard bought from his former boss and has grown into one of the largest farmers and most successful businessmen in California.

132

Dr. Kapany has his patents surrounding him on his office walls much like we would hang art work. As a young student in Cambridge, he felt that he could make light bend and not long thereafter actually achieved his goal. From there he founded and took two companies public and maintains a faculty position at Stanford. He is a patron of Sikh art and literature and a kind friend. Ishar Singh, his son Sher, and brother Phulel Singh, kindly hosted us in Toronto.

The first thing we'd do when I'd reach a new town was open the phone book to Singh and call the first or 'most promising' name on the list. "Sat-siri Akal. My name is Ralph Singh. We're here on our honeymoon and would love to meet you." This is how our friendship with Surjit and Helen and Buffalo started.

We spent 3 months, roughly the summer of 73, criss-crossing America, and when we returned it was like re-entering through a time seal. The day after we returned, we were helping to dig some new septic systems along the road outside Maharaj ji's dera house. It was September already, but we had gotten soft and out of shape. Besides, neither of us could take the heat. It took us a while to readjust but soon found ourselves back into the routine.

13

Preaching is your Life not your Livelihood

In addition to my work in Gobind Sadan, Maharaj ji would send me to Punjab to lecture in Gurdwaras, schools, and colleges. While I had actually failed public speaking in High School, as the only American who had adopted Sikhism who was fluent in Punjabi, my talks were in great demand and I often gave up to four lectures a day, throughout the Gurdwaras, schools, colleges, and universities of Punjab (and Haryana). I was the featured speaker at major holiday functions, and my articles appeared in Sikh newspapers. My themes always based on Gurbani and laced with quotes I had memorized for the occasion, mostly dealt with spiritual themes of meditation, and seva. But underlying everything was the stress on values and the challenge posed by modernization to traditional life. And to hear a young American tell students or villagers that drinking and drugs or too much materialism weakens their society had a decided impact.

In the major areas of Amritsar, Ludhiana, Jalandhar, Chandigarh and Ropar district there was scarcely a major Gurdwara, school, college or university where I did not have the privilege and pleasure to lecture. Maharaj ji had said, "You've learned about the Sikh tradition, now go live among the Sikhs and learn their culture." And so, I was free to accept any invitation, though I usually checked my itinerary with Maharaj ji.

Becoming part of Sikh history
The first time Maharaj ji had me speak publicly was at the now famous historical *Singh Sabha Shitabdi* celebration on Vaisakhi 1972 at Anandpur Sahib, Guru Gobind Singh ji's famous

historical Gurdwara and one of the five seats of Sikhism. When Gyani Gurdit Singh, who was organizing the occasion came to seek Maharaj ji's blessings at Swaranjit Singh's Defence Colony house, Maharaj ji introduced him to me. Gyani ji asked Maharaj ji to send me to Anandpur Sahib so he could introduce me to the *Panth*. Maharaj ji then turned to me. "Not only will you go there, but you will speak there and speak in Punjabi."

I had barely been in India a year and my Punjabi was broken at best. But he gave me a message to deliver, and put me under the care of Manjeet Singh, now a senior Sikh leader. It was at Anandpur Sahib that I met most of the Panthic leaders and luminaries. Following my lecture, I was invited by Gyani Harbhajan Singh, a retired teacher from Kharar, to speak throughout Ropar district. I told him that I would first have to take Maharaj ji's permission and returned to Delhi. Unlike others who would only want to keep their students in their own schools, Maharaj ji on the contrary wanted me to experience the Sikh tradition through the eyes of the Panth. From the villages to the cities, from the leadership and high command, to the students, I had the privilege of being welcomed by and enjoying the hospitality of some of the great Sikhs of the day. From Sirdar Kapur Singh to Muskeen ji, Bhai Jeewan Singh and Bhai Mohinder Singh (SDO) to Bhai Ripdaman Singh Bhagrianwale, Sardar Atma Singh, Gyan Singh Rarewala and many others too countless to name. Suffice it to say there wasn't a leader I hadn't met, from Tohra to Talwandi and Longowal, to Bindrewale both Jarnail Singh and Kartar Singh, and his son Amrik, and Badal Sahib all who have played such central roles in the recent history of the Panth.

The hospitality of the Sikh community is unrivalled. We sometimes joke that one needs at least one extra stomach if one goes into the villages. Each home wants to greet you and by that I mean "feed" you. So it was not uncommon to be given large glasses of whole milk and sweets at each stop or at least tea and a variety of snacks before your host had you sit for your full meal.

I clearly remember lecturing in a village Gurdwara near Ludhiana. I was supposed to have dinner at the home of the village leader, or *sarpanch,* before I spoke. But the man who had arranged the lecture was late and we had to go directly to the

Gurdwara. I didn't return to my host's home until 10 p.m. But that didn't lessen the hospitality. A tray was placed in front of me and the food began to appear. The dal had almost a ¼ inch of ghee floating on top of it and to wash it down I was given a full *gharvi* (small jug) of warm whole milk (cream and all) followed by a dessert of *halwa* which again was laced with ghee. I could barely walk to my bed.

Riding with the Nihangs

I had become friendly with families from Patti, the historic village North of Amritsar which was the home of Bhai Bidhi Chand, a famous Sikh of Guru Gobind Singh ji, and was visiting around Holi (the festival of colors). In the Sikh world, Holi is celebrated as Hola Mohala and the place to be is at Anandpur Sahib. And the people to be with are the Nihangs, the modern day remnants of Guru Gobind Singh ji's army. Divided into Dal's these proud warriors wear their blue turbans high on their head and sport a varied array of steel, from swords slung across their bodies to quoits wound into their turbans.

It so happened that a group were leaving from Patti to go to the celebration at Anandpur Sahib and they offered me a ride. I happily accepted and was given guest accommodations, riding atop their truck on the 5 hour overnight trip. We arrived shortly after sunrise. Anandpur Sahib rose like a shining cliff from the planes below. Every street was clogged with horses and people joyfully celebrating the day.

The fields behind were the site of the games, and I watched in amazement as one man managed to ride three horses at once, where two was easy, and others performed more remarkable tricks on the horses. During a break, they offered me a horse. Now I had ridden as a child but that was different. This was bareback on an Arabian with a very sensitive mouth which reacted to the slightest knee pressure. I was off in a flash holding on as best I could. The problem was that the tighter I gripped the faster the horse would go. I knew I had to relax to slow him down, but I would find myself slipping off and suddenly have to grip again and off he'd go. If riding in the truck wasn't enough of a thrill, that horse was in total control and how I turned him I'll never know. But Maharaj ji was kind enough to have the horse turn around and gallop me back to the waiting crowd who had gathered, I'm sure, more in amusement than appreciation. There were kind words for me and my 'bravery' but I was simply happy to be back on the ground.

More conveyances

I traveled on bicycle, motorcycle, truck, bus, train, and even by tractor from village to city to village again, never once feeling out of place or threatened. Once I was speaking on *Sangrahan*, the traditional opening day of the month celebration, at Bhatta Sahib, a historic Gurdwara of Guru Gobind Singh ji near Chandigarh. There was a large gathering of over ten thousand people and many politicians took advantage of the stage to speak against the government or put any other points they wished forward. Following my talk which was strictly on Sikh history and spirituality, I was summoned by a policeman to a room where he and his colleague politely but firmly interrogated me. "What are you doing at this political gathering?" I replied that my understanding was that this was a religious gathering and that as they had heard, I only spoke on Sikhism and had no political agenda at all. After a few more perfunctory questions about where I was staying and where my next talk was to be held they thanked me and let me go.

I was a bit puzzled but not at all shocked. Politicians had turned religious gatherings into their personal platforms and in the places where one should only hear praise of the Guru, they would typically pour out their venom against the government. I began walking back towards town when one of the officers who had interviewed me rode up on his bike. "Hop on," he called, "let me give you a lift." He was all smiles. "I hope we didn't insult you. We have heard a lot about this Ralph Singh, the American Sikh who spoke Punjabi, and wanted to know what you were like." It seemed my presence and movements in Punjab were well-known to the Indian government. It actually made me feel quite honored and even more comfortable. In fact, by that time I had become as comfortable walking into any town or area of Punjab as I did coming to my own home.

137

The Gobind Sadan 'team'

Whenever we could, the Gobind Sadan team of Major Sahib, Bibi Kirtanwali, Harpal, and me would plan programs together. Major Sahib would speak on history, Bibi Kirtanwali and Pal would sing, and I would speak on that same theme mixing the Gurbani and History in the way that Maharaj ji had taught me. It was not uncommon, especially when we lived together in the dera outside of Chandigarh, in what is now Sahib Zada Ajit Singh Nagar, to have Mukhand Singh take Bibi Kirtanwali, with Pal holding the *vaja*, and me sitting on the back of his scooter to preach in the surrounding villages. We still laugh about it.

If I hadn't gained enough bona fides from my lectures in Punjab, or met enough of the Sikh leadership, I was also invited to tour the United States and Canada with the famed Sirdar Kapur Singh and Sadarni Nirlep Kaur in the summer of 1974. Being in their company and speaking along side them to groups, raised our visibility even more. Maharaj ji used to joke, "We should have had you run for office." Dr. Amarjit Marwah was a kind host during the trip. A dentist to the stars by trade, Dr. Marwah epitomized the early civic- minded Sikhs, who while founding the Gurdwaras, also stepped outside the confines of their narrow community and contributed to the community at large. He served as Chairman of the Los Angeles Cultural Committee and set up sister cities programs between LA and cities in India.

Sikhs and Sikhi

Perhaps my most memorable talk was given at the All India Akali Conference in Ludhiana in the summer of 1978. There had been a clash between Sikhs and a group of Nirankaris in which some of the Sikhs had been killed and the Panth perceived that Sikhism was under attack. The cry was "Sikhi is in danger." The rally attracted almost a million people and there wasn't a leader who wasn't on the stage. I still have the photo of me standing in my tie delivering my talk. Maharaj ji had instructed me to tell the gathering that "Sikhi could not be endangered as it came from God." So I crafted that into the words that He taught me so well:

"Sikhi ek atul sachae hai"

Sikhism is eternal Truth and Truth can never be threatened. But Sikhs can be threatened if they do not follow that path of Truth.

Choosing between Sikhs and Sikhism came up several more times in my life. And since my early talks and writings it has become a common refrain that others have adopted to title their talks and books.

While I loved the Sikh people, I had some real concerns about their leadership. Much of my concerns were realized when the conflict with the Government came to a head with the attack on the Golden temple in 1984, something that should have been entirely avoidable.

Preach but don't accept anything in return

Maharaj ji was very strict about separating our preaching and our community service, from our livelihood. Never were we to accept any payment for preaching. He himself had worked in the fields and considered himself a farmer. Once early on when asked to come to Punjab to preach, Maharaj ji answered, "Until I can afford to pay on my own to fill my own tank with gas, I will not be able to come." He was outspoken and unrelenting on this point.

His instructions to me: "You can't take anything (even a shirt) for preaching. That is your love, your life, to share God's love with everyone. It is not for sale. You must work to earn your living to support yourself and your family and then from the earnings, take time to preach."

In fact, it is your life that becomes the sermon. Maharaj ji often said that the impact of preaching is not through lectures but through the character of the one who speaks. Our conduct must become our message.

139

BOOK II
A LIFE TO LEAD

PATH V

Lessons from Life – American Experiences

"Now go and live it"

14

Amulee Jeevan – The Exemplary Life

While I knew my training period would end at some time, there was no clear timetable and while the tests continued to come almost daily, I could never have said I was nearing graduation (I still can't). While the house on the hill was clearly meant to allow us the experience of independent living, I could have stayed there indefinitely. But that changed abruptly and unexpectedly.

I returned one day from delivering milk and was greeted by Joginder at the gate, "You're leaving tonight and you're taking the baby with you!" I don't know which was more of a shock. I wasn't expecting a graduation ceremony or a diploma, but I did think in my heart that Maharaj ji would call me to Him and tell me Himself when it was time to leave.

"Your grandmother's had a heart attack and is on her deathbed. She wants to see the baby before she dies," Joginder blurted out the rest of the story. "Maharaj ji has already said to go." The message crashed through any nostalgia I might have had. This was real. And as for the baby, I had barely ever changed his diapers let alone given him his bottle. But Joginder couldn't get her visa fast enough to leave with me so she had to trust her first born to the inexperienced hands of her husband and pray that Chetan didn't wake up on the flight.

What followed was a whirlwind of legal clearances needed to leave India, not to mention getting a ticket for that night's flight. No easy task. But what normally took days was over in minutes as Maharaj ji opened every door for my departure. Before leaving me at the airport Joginder had the baby changed, fed and fast asleep. I was well equipped for the trip, with bottles and Pampers, last minute gift from Embassy friends. Everything was in order.

When I returned to Gobind Sadan, Maharaj ji was waiting for me in his courtyard. I bowed deeply at his feet, feeling like holding on to them. One part of me didn't want to get up. "You have spent all this time in training, now go live it. Remember, you can't sell the Truth, and don't work for anyone else." With these cautions, He blessed me and told me that He would always be with me and that He would call me back often.

Saying goodbye to Joginder was not quite as hard. Though naturally there we had to deal with the separation, we both had faith that we would be together soon, and the power of the moment didn't really allow us too much time for reflection. We had been catapulted out of Gobind Sadan into the world without even a second's notice.

At the airport, check in went smoothly, the baby was sound asleep in my arms. But, as I approached the final security check point, the policeman asked me for my passport. I had been checked twice before and had already put my papers away. I screwed up my courage, and looked the policeman straight in the eyes, "If you want my papers *you* hold the baby." The sympathetic crowd around me laughed, the policemen conceded, and I made it on the plane with Chetan still fast asleep.

He traveled well with help from the stewardesses, and was greeted in N.Y. by my Aunt who had driven fifty miles to the airport to bring the baby a blanket for the cold journey to Syracuse. My Grandmother hung on to life long enough to feel her great grandson next to her. While almost comatose, one of her last conscious acts was holding her finger out for the baby to play with. She died a few days later.

My mother helped me care for the baby until she had to return to New York a week later. While my grandmother's nurse stayed on, I was in essence alone with him for about 3 weeks, until Joginder's papers finally cleared in January. It was a great time for bonding. At four and ½ months he was just beginning to recognize me. I never knew I could compose baby songs. But I had a captive audience for whatever tunes – on or off key, and the words generated lots of smiles and coos.

After Joginder arrived, we set up the house. Maharaj ji called me back in 1977 and again in 1978. But I had in essence been left to learn to stand on my own two feet, establish myself and raise my family in the world I had left. This was the way of life I had rejected as false. Now I had to learn to find and live the Truth within that falsehood. It was not easy, but Maharaj ji has been with me in every step of the way, guiding my every move. Although I was no longer in His physical presence, as if to inspire me more, His spiritual presence actually seemed to increase.

Distance Learning – Guiding our movements not just our lives

Maharaj ji finds our house for us

My first experience with Maharaj ji "touring" the U.S. was while I was still in India. I was inquiring about my mother's apartment and Maharaj ji started telling me where things were. He literally took me through the rooms (now I should not have been surprised. After all if He had taken me on a tour of the universe, what was my mother's apartment in New York in comparison). Maharaj ji often tells us that God always visits our home. To show me how present He has always been in my life, he began to describe my Mother's New York apartment down to the details of the clothes hanging on hooks behind the bathroom door. "See I've told you that I come to see you even though you may not be there to welcome me."

After my Grandmother's death, we maintained her apartment until her lease expired and then bought a small house in the city. When Maharaj ji called me back in 1977, I asked him whether there was a house in the country He would prefer, since we were sure He would someday bless us with a visit.

In response, He drew a verbal map. "Here is your office (downtown) and here is some water (Onondaga Lake). Go past the lake out in the country and you will find an old couple with an old car in the garage who wants to sell their house."

Most of our time had been spent on the East side of town, we had never even been the route He was describing. But when I returned, Joginder and I would spend many weekends driving out

147

in the country looking for the house. We finally met a real estate agent who took us to the house. Sure enough, the car was in the garage and the couple was very happy to sell their house to us. And more importantly Maharaj ji has blessed the house by staying in the room Joginder had made for Him on five separate occasions, and walking the boundary lines of the cornfield behind the house, almost to bless every inch of the ground He Himself had chosen. It is a shrine to His love and His greatness. We feel greatly blessed to be allowed to live there.

There must be a better way
Maharaj ji always had His ways of showing that He was always present, especially, when we were lost. A notable experience with directions actually happened not far from our house in Elbridge. I had just finished a business meeting in a remote and somewhat unfamiliar area and was running late for my next appointment. I knew that if I had to retrace my path and go the way I knew I would be 15 minutes late. I was driving along thinking to myself, 'there must be a better way,' when Maharaj ji said, "Take that road to the left." I glanced left but continued a short way up the road when He said more emphatically, "What's the matter, don't you trust me?" That was it. I slammed on the brakes, backed up and took the road. It connected to the expressway that I needed to take and I was 5 minutes early for the meeting, whereas I would have been late if I had gone the original way. Maharaj ji is always with us. He goes wherever we go.

I don't know whether I learned from Chand or just felt it myself, but I always sensed He was sitting beside me in the passenger seat. He was always there to talk with or consult whenever I needed to. I mention Chand because the passenger seat of her car was always occupied with a life size picture of Maharaj ji. While we put a sheet on the seat when He actually has graced our cars with His presence. She would drive to all her meetings, classes, whatever, with Maharaj ji occupying her passenger seat. A real testament to the great faith of a great lady indeed.

While Maharaj ji guides our major decisions, He is concerned about even the smallest detail: "Don't forget your umbrella," He'll caution on a perfectly sunny morning. By afternoon it will definitely rain, especially if we ignore His precaution and don't take our umbrella!

He may explain a scientific or philosophical issue

When speaking before a large audience, often comprised of preeminent scholars or scientists, Maharaj ji would start by saying, "I'm not a lecturer, I'm a simple farmer, with no education. I can't read or write, but whatever I've experienced from God I will share with you." Then He will launch into the most eloquent discourse leaving the audience totally mesmerized. At the end, He will welcome and answer even the most complicated questions with ease.

He often told me, "I can't go everywhere. You will have to represent me at various places." My response was simple, "Maharaj ji, I can physically stand there, but it is You who must speak." He laughed and blessed me.

While no doubt I had a wonderful education, I had no advanced degrees. So when Maharaj ji did send me to conferences with some of the best minds present, and had me engage them in debate or just simple dialogue, He would always put words in my mouth that I would never have thought of myself. True to form, the other person would always want to know how I learned these things. My reply was simple, "From His Holiness Baba Virsa Singh ji of Gobind Sadan," of course.

A case in point occurred at a nationally televised seminar about God and The Human Mind. It was held at an historic old church in lower Manhattan and the huge Satellite dish transmitting the event occupied one side of the close. A famous neuropsychologist was pontificating on the mind as a receptor for the material world. He claimed that he found no difference between what some people claim to be spiritual experiences, and the psychotic episodes of his patients. Maharaj ji immediately told me to go up and tell him that if he tuned his 'dish' to God, perhaps he would be able to perceive the spiritual dimension. So up I trotted to the front, the only Sikh in the place, and put the question: "If you think the mind is only meant as a receptor of the material world perhaps you have your 'dish' tuned to the wrong coordinates." Needless to say, both he and the moderator were stunned and had no response while the 'audience' was quite amused.

He heals and blesses

While I've mentioned many miracles that Maharaj ji has done, it is only appropriate that I mention two noteworthy ones where, without my even thinking or asking, Maharaj ji chose to help friends of mine in need.

It is common courtesy to ask about a friend's wellbeing. And in the course of the conversation I found that her mother was hospitalized and in danger of losing her eyesight. Immediately Maharaj ji said, "No problem – give her *jal.*" All right I thought, but how to put this diplomatically. I began to tell her how at Gobind Sadan many people had been blessed and that if she wanted me to help, then I could take some 'holy water' to her mother. She said that would be very kind and told me the room number.

Now I had never met this woman before and when I arrived at the room, she sort of just looked up at me as if to say, "Where did you come from?" I simply said, "I've brought some Holy Water for your eyes," and without wasting a minute she took the bottle from me, opened it and poured it on her eyes. She thanked me and I left.

The next time I saw her was in her daughter's living room and her eyes were fine. The old woman looked up at me and said, "What did you expect? When God sends Holy Water He knows what He's doing."

The two sided cross and the gift of a child

I was visiting a friend from high school whom I hadn't seen in at least 25 years. They had no child of their own and were hoping to adopt one. On the wall in their hallway were three beautiful Coptic Crosses. Two very large ornate brass ones bordered a smaller one in the middle. It was comparatively rustic and made of stone. My host told me that it had been carved out of the rock of the ancient churches in Axom, Ethiopia, which were some of the first to be built after Christ. "But that's not what makes it so unusual," he continued, taking it off the wall.

"Have you ever seen a two sided cross?" he asked, knowing my interest in religion. I held it studying it closely. On one side, the face he had displayed, was carved the Crucifix with the Holy Mother at Jesus' feet. The other side had a diamond in the center with what looked like rays of light emanating and Mary was beatified (with angels' wings). Maharaj ji suddenly said, "He is the Light." Of course! immediately you could see that in ancient ceremonies, they would hold up the cross and say, "I did not die on the cross, I am the Light" and flip the cross over.

I shared that with Chris. We put the cross back on the wall and continued our conversation, catching up with each other. Over dinner I had told him and his wife that many people had been blessed with children in Gobind Sadan and that Jesus had appeared there and given a boon as well. Turning to her husband she said, "Maybe we should go there." I responded that while they were welcome to go to India, God is with them and can bless them anywhere. We went to bed early since I had to leave first thing the next morning.

When I woke up and sat in mediation, Maharaj ji spoke to me: "Tell them I want to give them a Christmas present. Have them take the cross from the wall, dip it in water and drink it and then put it back with my real face out (the Light)." Imagine my position. I hadn't seen my friend for such a long time and now I have a very important message to share with him. But, how would he take it? It wasn't like delivering a letter.

So when Chris joined me for breakfast I told him, "I don't know exactly how to tell you this but I have something important to share." I gave him the message exactly as Maharaj ji had told me. He immediately asked when he should do it and if he had to wake his wife up too. I said, "No problem. Let her sleep and give it to her later." So, he took a glass of water, gently lifted the cross from the wall, and dipped it in. He drank from the glass being careful to leave enough for his wife, and then returned the cross to the wall as instructed. That was the end of November. She conceived in January and a beautiful son was born the following September. When I visited them next, the cross was still Light side out.

151

Maharaj ji shared this story with the *sangat* at Gobind Sadan USA, saying that God can work through anyone He chooses. Again emphasizing that it is not the person that does anything. Maharaj ji can assume any form we wish to see and speak in any voice that we wish to hear. He is all forms. In this case, it was Him speaking as Jesus.

Our neighbor who had no children themselves, loved Chetan very much and expressed a wish to have a nice child like Chetan. So we told Chetan, then only three years old , to pray to Maharaj ji that they be blessed with a child and indeed a wonderful baby was born.

We were in California visiting a young couple who this time had admired Tegbir. The wife said, "He is so sweet, I wish we could have a boy like him." We told Tegbir to pray to Maharaj ji for them and next year a son was born.

Maharaj ji saves my life – Be Fearless not Foolish

Several years ago, a man came to Gobind Sadan who was blessed with a special gift. Simply by looking at a person (perhaps the lines in his forehead) he could tell his future. He also would foretell events for people and countries based on the letters in their names. Now this is nothing unusual. All the greatest *pandits* and astrologers come to Maharaj ji to seek His blessings and guidance. The great Pandit Gyan Chand of Delhi once told me: "I tell people what is written for them and then tell them to come with me to meet the One who can change what is written." When I met Mota Ved, the famed *Hakim* of Delhi who was once whisked away by Maharishi Mahesh Yogi on his private plane to the White House to treat President Reagan, he said holding up Maharaj ji's *janam patri* (horoscope), "Have you ever seen such a beautiful thing as this. This is very rare and only a true Avtar can have this configuration."

This man began by telling that certain countries such as America and Canada would have problems that year. Then turning to people he said that someone very close to Maharaj ji whose name has "Ra" in it would be killed in an accident. I wasn't paying that close attention but suddenly it struck me, perhaps he was talking about me. As I

152

saw him out to the gate, he looked at me strangely and then left. Joginder reminded me that she was sure that he had meant me.

I returned home to Syracuse and forgot this prophecy. That winter we had a very bad ice storm, and freezing rain covered the roads. I waited until later in the day to go out so that the roads could be properly salted and the ice would melt. I had hardly gotten three miles from my house when I lost control of the car on a hilly section of a three-lane expressway. I was going 50 to 60 mph and the car swerved to the left and then spun completely around. As soon as the car swerved, I looked at Maharaj ji's picture that hangs from my mirror and felt a complete calm come over me. There was actually no fear whatsoever. I felt that Maharaj ji Himself was holding the car. Everything passed in slow motion. The car veered toward the right side of the expressway and slammed into the guard rail. But rather than hitting it head on, Maharaj ji had turned the car completely around so the full impact was taken by the rear bumper on the drivers side. While it nearly tore the trunk off the car, the gas tank was not punctured and I was fully cushioned from the force of the blow. The car then slid slowly off the guard rail and came around facing in the right direction. More amazing than the position of the impact was that there was absolutely no traffic while the car was spinning across the highway from the left lane to the right. But as soon as it came to rest on the shoulder, cars started speeding by in all lanes. I sat for a minute making sure I was all right. Braced against the seat, I had barely been shaken. While naturally some minor whiplash and back pain did follow, I was completely unscathed. Moreover, I got out of the car, inspected the sizeable damage to the rear end, but noted that the wheels weren't impaired. I turned the key. The car started immediately and I drove it to the nearest garage. They checked for any gas leaks I hadn't seen, cleared it and I drove first to register the damage with the insurance company and then home. I thanked Maharaj ji continually for his kindness. When I spoke with Him, He simply said, "The one who was to do his job has done it, now he's gone. Let him go and don't think of him again" He was referring to *Sunichar Devta*. For the uninitiated in Indian

153

astrology, Saturn, as fascinating as its rings may look, is known for its ability to "run rings" around human beings, literally disrupting their lives in every way possible. Unless one is saved by the hand of one's Guru or able to appease the force behind the planet.

The *Grahas* are Real

If there is any question in anyone's mind of how I can talk of the impact of spiritual beings on our life or the existence of the "gods" of the planets let me share the following with you:

When Maharaj ji was in our home, a hukam came that we should deliver a bottle of wine and a warm coat to someone on behalf Rahuji. We don't drink so we bought the wine and got the coat but were not able to follow through on delivering it. The person deputed was not ready to make the trip at night into the neighborhood where it had to be given to any person on the street. The next morning Maharaj ji said that He had been troubled all night by someone looking for his belongings. "Maharaj ji, we beg your forgiveness, we did not deliver the wine and coat as you had directed." He just looked at me and said, "That's the reason. No wonder. Don't worry, you're forgiven." I bowed with deep regret, apologized again, and left His room. I was walking downstairs, when a very deep and threatening voice spoke. I'll never forget the words, *"Guru ka maf, mere ta saraf"* (You get forgiveness from your Guru but you will be punished by me). I rushed upstairs and told Maharaj ji. He said Rahuji was angry with me. Maharaj ji instructed me to not go anywhere and told me to leave my keys where they were, and not to think of driving that day. Thankfully, the day passed with me sitting in Maharaj ji's presence. By evening the curse was over and I was free. The following weekend on the appointed day, I took the wine and the coat to the area as I was directed. I saw a man crossing the street and Maharaj ji said, "Give it to him." I made a right turn and stopped the car. "Excuse me Sir, I would like to present you with these gifts." The man gratefully accepted and I was on my way home.

Flight Tracking – Maharaj ji's style

Long before we had web-based flight tracking systems, Maharaj ji would let us know whether the flight was on time. And even now if the computer indicates the flight is ready to leave, Maharaj ji may tell us otherwise. Often we would be throwing last minute items in the suitcases or rushing out the door when He will say, "Do a Jaap Sahib," or "Go to Baba Siri Chand ji's shrine."

"But Maharaj ji, we'll be late," would be the common thought. We have learned that if we do rush to the airport, the flight will invariably be delayed.

The whole lesson revolves around which clock we pay attention to. Which order are we going to follow? The order of the world, or God's order. And while they may at times and on one level be concurrent, the fact that Maharaj ji teaches us to hear and hopefully listen to His Voice makes all the difference in the world. For it is His orders which are the constant driving force for good.

15

Setting up Shop – Integrating a Spiritual Life with Work in the U.S.

Dhan jio te ko jag mai, mukh te har chit mai judh vichara
Great are the ones who keep their minds attuned to God while
fighting their worldly battles.

Guru Gobind Singh

When Maharaj ji sent me back he gave me a simple directive: "Don't work for anyone else." It was clear that I was still under His orders and I must somehow find a way to earn a living while remaining in His service.

I had left the U.S. six years earlier and said goodbye to any thoughts of a career. Now with a young family to support, it was time to pick up this thread again and weave work into my spiritual life. Wherever it would lead I knew Maharaj ji would guide me.

My family was a professional lot – scientists, educators, doctors, and lawyers. But after leaving the family fold and giving up my opportunity to become part of the family business, a research laboratory, I was hardly in a position to ask their help to go to law or medical school. Sales seemed the most natural profession. Since I had spent the last several years marketing roses and milk in Delhi, I felt I could sell anything. Typewriters or pharmaceuticals weren't exactly what I had in mind. Neither was life insurance. On the surface, it seemed diametrically opposed to my spiritual groundings given the caricature of the unrelenting insurance salesperson.

I had a much older family friend, Don, in the business with MassMutual, a prestigious company, in arguably the most respected agency in Syracuse. Insurance agencies are always hungry for new blood. Anyone willing to be rejected hundreds of times, miss family dinners to make calls to prospective clients, and cold call on people who would have preferred anything but to talk to an insurance salesman, were always welcome to try. I passed the licensing and aptitude tests with flying colors. Then came the interview. I put on one of my hand tailored Indian wedding suits and a silk tie, got Joginder's final approval and a kiss. The shoes were a little tacky but all in all I was presentable. But the suit and tie, and even shoes were not the focus of my attire. There was little doubt that mine was the first turban to cross the threshold of this sanctum of the business world.

Forbes, my boss to be, had a large corner office on the 12th floor of MONY Towers, one of downtown's tallest buildings. His assistant, Shirley, professionally and perfunctorily waived me in, steno pad in hand, and Forbes invited me to join him at his long cherry desk. Once I was seated, Forbes picked up a remote control, pushed a button and the door slammed shut behind me. With little time for platitudes, Forbes smiled and looked directly at me, "Do you think you'll be able to relate to the American businessman?" "Of course," I replied without a minute's hesitation. And that was the end of the interview. I was free to try my hand.

Behind the scenes, one of the senior agents told my trainer, "You're not going to hire him with a turban on his head?" To his credit, Henry, a strict Christian retorted, "If ever he comes to me complaining that he can't sell insurance I might suggest that the turban could be a problem, but otherwise more power to him."

And more power ruled. Maharaj ji gave me great success in my first year and even had me win the sales contest. Actually, He had called me to India just at the beginning of the annual contest and the General Agent was not at all pleased that I was under someone else's command. I politely explained that I had a commitment to Maharaj ji and whenever He called, I was obligated to go regardless of the consequences. Though I left in the first week, I still had enough business to win. While I may have suffered financially at times, Maharaj ji continually rewarded me by building my practice. I still remember His words: "We'll make you a businessman."

157

With that blessing, I would feel as comfortable walking into corporate board rooms as I did gathering with a couple over their kitchen table to discuss their dreams and needs. I enjoyed challenging myself with larger and more complicated cases. Sometimes to keep focused on the simple day-to-day things I would put a little sign in front of me 'Stop swallowing whales.' Yet despite my caution, I would always end up trying something new.

Walking into offices with a turban often did make heads turn. It was instant recognition. Corporations pay consultants 'big bucks' to develop a brand and all I had to do was tie five yards of colored cloth on my head every morning and not cut my hair or shave my beard. When I would call a person who I had met casually all I had to say in answer to their query, "Who's this?," was "The fellow with the turban," and I could hear the smile spread through the receiver.

The Whole Person, Goal Setting, and the To-Do list

The business allowed me to develop financial and organizational skills I never would have dreamed of, among which were time management and goal setting. Juggling personal, family, and community commitments with business was critical to success.

The 'whole person' concept was just coming into vogue. Our company fully endorsed the idea that while business was essential, if we didn't live a balanced life our business would ultimately suffer. Further the stress from business often destroyed a person's health and family.

From the minute I joined the company I was exposed to a constant stream of guest speakers sharing their secrets and systems. Our annual goal's manual included sections on personal, family, and spiritual growth, so I felt very comfortable integrating, at least on paper, how I would allocate the time I spent in each of these dimensions.

Then we were introduced to the tools of the trade, from 'Day-timers' diaries to databases. These evolved with technology from alphabetized punch cards, sorted by hand with a long skewer, that we recorded in paper journals, to more sophisticated computerized solutions. But at the heart of it all was the 'to-do' list which I was taught to keep diligently. Moreover we were always conditioned to make the list the night before and review the tasks for the next day so that when we woke up in the morning we would be focused on the day's work, not wondering what we should be doing next. This was a fascinating habit. We were literally programming our minds to focus on the tasks at hand and having to prioritize what was important in each area of our lives. But for me it was much more.

Since Maharaj ji was directing every minute of my life, I saw the 'to-do' list as either His orders for me for the day, or my appeals to Him for help on my work at hand. At times the lines would blur. It became hard to tell whether He was driving my agenda or whether He was so kind to fulfill my wishes. In reality it was both. For He put the thoughts in my mind and then answered them. Knowing Maharaj ji was behind each intended action certainly eased the pangs of procrastination. Once it was on the 'to-do' list, we shouldn't back off. No matter how difficult or lofty the goal, He would take care of it.

Even when I had a computer, I would always keep a yellow legal pad on my desk. Early on it was divided into three columns – business, community, and personal (family). Even today a yellow pad is my constant companion and whatever I write down, Maharaj ji gets it done. Sometimes it is amazing that a full page of tasks is completed in the blink of an eye. Or Maharaj ji may tell me that I will have to put aside a particular task as it is not yet time. There was nothing that He couldn't accomplish. But of course if I put 'too-much' down, I am exhausted by the end of the day. When we set goals according to His orders then He himself pushes us, or drags us across the finish line, despite our limitations.

I came to regard *hukams* as God's to-do list, how God orders and runs the cosmos. Of course that system was in place eons ago. After all what is time management for the Creator of time and the Ruler of Universes. It is merely for us human beings to understand how to order our lives according to His will.

Public recognition

Strolling through malls, in the grocery stores, just being around town, the young children usually responded with great curiosity and if I waved, which I usually did, their faces lit up and smiles would spread across their faces. Sometimes their parents noticed and smiled as well and sometimes, the adults just missed it entirely.

We were walking through a store in an Albany area mall, and were just passing an area where some games were installed for children. Before video games hit the market, pin ball, fortune telling, and grab a prize, were popular. There was a young boy, standing tip-toes on a stool, eyes glued to the glass, staring intently at a turbaned fortune teller. Just as we passed, the boy turned around, and looked at me. Instantly he turned back to make sure the fortune-teller was still inside the game box, then turned back to look to see if I was real. We laughed and waived. And the poor boy looked back at his game once more before it sunk in that some real people wear turbans too.

But older kids, who have lost their innocence, teens and some young adults who have learned to be threatened by differences, saw us with turbans on our heads, and the laughs would come, fingers would point, heads would turn and sometimes, only sometimes, epithets – 'towel head, rag head,' would follow. This was harder on the kids than it was on me. They got fighting mad. They wanted to teach them a lesson. I taught them to ignore and engage. I would ignore the insult, but confront the people. I would smile and say hello to the kids if they weren't in a passing car. Wave at them too. Give them a thumbs up or something to acknowledge that they had acknowledged me.

At one of our early agency meetings, I was met at the reception desk by a colleague with a big smile. "Hey where did you park your carpet?" Everyone wanted to sit next to me at lunches so they could get the meat off my plate. Since they couldn't get any reaction out of me, they let me settle in.

One night at an agency retreat, a drunken group of new youngsters who had never even talked with me, decided to publicly make fun of my turban. I took it in the spirit of the evening and waited for Maharaj ji to teach them an appropriate lesson.

The next morning when the entire group of 70 or so had settled down for business, I asked for some time to respond. I folded a

160

wire coat hanger and put it on my turban and began by telling them that I pick up all sorts of information. The audience applauded. Then I told the gathering, as Chair of the Human Rights Commission, that their behavior was not acceptable, but more importantly as human beings, God does not like us making fun of His diversity.

In contrast to those brash youngsters, one of our guest speakers, a nationally known senior agent from Chicago, came to me the evening before his presentation. "I've enjoyed visiting with you. Would you mind tying a turban on me for my presentation tomorrow?" I couldn't believe it. "I mean no disrespect. If you don't mind, I would really appreciate it." As he was Irish, I dug out a green turban and he stood patiently in the hall outside the conference room while I wound the cloth on his head. Then he walked out to a stunned audience and began – "You have some very convincing people in this agency."

Sports stadiums – The baseball games
Surprisingly enough, while TV often showed rowdy fans, we found that the sports stadiums both in the U.S. and Canada never presented a problem. People were polite. We cheered they cheered. Our kids brought their gloves and scorecards to get autographs and stood in line to meet the players. Even walking through tailgate parties we never aroused much interest, we were all fans. And given the costumes and face painting that goes on we were not necessarily the ones who stuck out in the crowd.

I believe that Guru Gobind Singh meant to have us stick our necks out. We were meant to stand out in a crowd. Why else would He have given us such a distinguished look. Not everyone is comfortable with nonconformity. It was our job as parents and citizens to let people know what we believed and what we stood for. If we kept silent and let others form their own opinions then we were more likely to get into trouble. A lion who doesn't roar, hardly deserves respect; like the story of the donkey who put on a lion's skin. When everyone ran away, the donkey was so happy that it began to bray. When the town's people understood the ruse, they beat the donkey to death. If you look like a lion you can't be weak. This too I've experienced.

Public appearances

One of my first public leadership roles was as President of the United Nations Association of CNY. With our interest in alleviating world hunger we were one of the first sponsors of the Food Bank of CNY and I had to appear with other community leaders at the opening.

My public speaking skills, honed more in Punjabi, came easily in English and my remarks were appreciated. But one of the other leaders came up to me later and confided as he gestured towards my turban, "You spoke very well, but you have a definite advantage over us in your instant recognition." Sure enough, the media tended to key on me.

People often asked, "Wasn't it difficult being different?" And as I taught our children, who early on often were teased mercilessly in school for their appearance: People are always going to tease you for something. If you're too fat, too slim, wear glasses, laugh a particular way, are too bright or too stupid. For whatever reason society demands conformity and conformity tends to mean mediocrity. So we have to distinguish ourselves. Both in our behavior and in our appearance. So I always used to like to say, "We are not different. We are distinguished members of our community."

Show and tell

As with most American schools, our children had a 'show and tell' period every year from Kindergarten through 2nd grade. This was the time when teachers encouraged them to bring in something which interested them or they liked and have them present it to the class. I always had our kids bring me. Tegbir, our youngest, especially thought it was fun to bring his Dad for show and tell. "Hi kids, I'm Tegbir's Dad," and the little kids would laugh. "This is my turban. I have a beard. Tegbir doesn't cut his hair either." Do you have any questions?" Lots of hands went up. "Why don't you cut your hair?" "This is our way of showing our belief in God." "What's that thing on your head for?" "So people who are in trouble can find us easily."

Later teachers would ask me to come in each year and speak about our beliefs or life in India. So through grade 7, I would speak to the classes at least once a year. Joginder was active in supporting

162

all the activities. The bake sales, being a "room Mom," helping out the teachers, volunteering for field trips. So between the two of us, we were highly visible around school and the community. That helped overcome much of the teasing. But as we learned, it was not the 'good kids' who were the problem. Usually trouble came from kids who were troubled themselves, those who were always looking to take out their problems and frustrations on others. And as we've seen throughout our lives, these kids grow into intolerant adults unless they are counseled early on.

Having said that, it behooved me to work twice as hard and become even more successful than others because I was maintaining and representing particular values. No doubt there was pressure. But Maharaj ji was very kind. Whenever the well was about to run dry, and at times you could even see the rocks at the bottom, He would send such a flood that we could never think of ever wanting for anything again.

Digging up the back garden

While we were still on Nichols Avenue, money had become so tight that I couldn't think of how we were going to make our next payments. I didn't want to ask my family for any more help as they had already been very kind to us. I remembered a story that Brig Sahib had told me. He had been posted to a remote area and his men were not properly equipped for the terrain. He prayed to Maharaj ji and was directed to go to a particular spot, dig, and he would find the needed provisions. Following the orders, his men dug at the site and uncovered a buried supply of boots and other paraphernalia that was exactly what they required.

Taking the cue, I prayed to Maharaj ji and took out our shovel. Next to the garage we had a sizeable vegetable garden. I was more than willing to sacrifice the vines and plants for what I was sure to be the solution to our financial woes – buried treasure. Joginder, while usually totally supportive of my faith-based initiatives, and often way ahead of me in her commitment, couldn't help herself. She laughed and pleaded with me not to proceed. But I was not to be deterred.

163

Soon, I was standing 2 feet deep in a hole and still nothing. But I was not willing to concede. Finally when the hole began to reach a serious depth of 3 feet plus I realized my folly. Maharaj ji wanted me to work my way out of this one and not expect Him to rescue me miraculously. Throughout my time, He always exacted difficult tests but in the end rewarded me. To date Maharaj ji has never given me anything without working for it. But sometimes that just meant listening to his directions and asking the right people. Many times the largest cases simply came from asking people I had met or knew at the right time.

But that is what business, and all of life's successes are all about. Not just being at the right place at the right time, but recognizing the opportunity that it presents and acting. If we don't take the proper action, whether asking the question or talking to the right person, the opportunity may well be wasted. We can always talk about getting there and the experience of being there, but only a few times will we be able to say we were able to 'score' our goal. More often than not, our shot goes wide or is blocked. But we still play for the sheer joy. Maharaj ji has always taught us to play the game of life the same way.

Values in Business
The business provided an opportunity to cultivate many wonderful lifelong relationships, provide a valuable, often invaluable service to families, provide my family with a comfortable lifestyle and me with the freedom and income to support the many community projects I loved and of course to serve Maharaj ji whenever needed. It turned out to be totally consistent with my values, and the professionals were some of the most principled individuals I'd ever met. As they had to provide leadership to the wealthy in areas of charitable, estate and business planning, many were leaders in their own communities and practiced their values.

It was at my very first agency event that I was introduced to one such individual. From the minute we met, still standing outside on a snowy porch at the exclusive country club, Tom and I bonded. He had just flown in from California to be our guest speaker and his smile was as broad as his warm sense of humor. A Mormon Bishop, recognized as an industry and community leader he kindly served as an early mentor to me in business. Tom has since become a lifelong friend, a committed leader in the Interfaith movement, and has visited Gobind Sadan and been blessed by Maharaj ji.

A Life of Relationships

I realized early on, without any nudging from marketing companies, that all life, not just business depended on relationships. And it was out of good relationships that everything positive in life sprung. This was a very spiritual concept. All people are inexorably linked in an endless chain, so the goal was to figure out how we were supposed to interact together.

I had an extra large white board in the office that I loved to draw on. It hung over my small conference table. So during a meeting I would write, 'Relationships,' on the board. Then I would say: "I have only one wife, and no one else is going to fill that relationship. But, I am involved in a variety of community projects and I also do business. Many of the people I do business with join me in my community work and many in the community work chose to do business with me. It is all a matter of how the relationship develops." That made people very comfortable and in fact it was true.

Meditation and work

Maharaj ji had told me early on that people would remember me for my work not my visions. Now that I was in business I was told again by a successful young business mentor, John, that while he felt that I really had much to offer people spiritually and philosophically, they would only take me seriously if I were successful in business. I didn't realize how true this really was.

Then I had a relatively spectacular year. By company standards I ranked in the top twenty-five nationally and my colleagues began to take notice. Suddenly everyone wanted to know my 'secret'. It had to be meditation or some 'mantra'. So we would gather in my office sit on the floor and recite *Nam*. How

165

much they stayed with it remained to be seen, but no doubt, Maharaj ji helped each of them. On a recent trip to the office, Andy, one of my colleagues smiled and said, "I'll always remember, '*Ek Onkar Satnam Siri Waheguru.*' Whenever I get in a tough situation, I just sit back and close my eyes and recite it and everything is all right."

16

Balancing Community Service and Work

Khal kai kich hathon dehi, Nanak ra pachanai sahi
Earn an honest living, share with those in need, and you will
recognize the True path.

As students in the 60's, we had always debated how to change the world. It was a time of political turmoil and many felt they must actively protest against the war and the Powers that Be who perpetrated it. But in the end the answer lay in transforming yourself. A new society lost in ignorance would soon fall prey to the baser human tendencies and the cycle of corruption and oppression would start all over again.

But did we have to wait until we were enlightened? That might take forever and in the meantime the world and those who wanted to control or destroy it would have long since come and gone. Was the spiritual solution a complete disconnect? Did the fact that the material world was transient mean that it required no attention?

Maharaj ji's way was full engagement. It was a simultaneous process. Clean your mind and clean up the world around you. The world became the classroom and its challenges your tests. So it was for me to take the experiences I'd had at Gobind Sadan and apply them.

I had left America with the goal of learning ways to link with God and then re-link the broken pieces of our society. By the time I returned, our society soon reached the stage where programs for youth competed against the needs of senior citizens – arts and culture were vying with education for funding, and healthcare was not universal. In some areas, including my own, infant mortality rates were higher than in some third world countries and our education system was in shambles. Despite our wealth and power we had ended up a more polarized and politically divided nation.

Building Community – Connecting the Dots

"Everyone is part of my community, I see no one as outsider."

Guru Nanak

Maharaj ji provided a vision that was so inclusive that it was hard not to find ways to serve.

It was also through these programs and this shared vision that we all were in community together that Maharaj ji drew many of those who would ultimately serve Him.

Having spent my time in India focused on the needs of others, it was hard for me to simply put blinders on and earn a living. My first year back I had to do this. But, by the second year, Maharaj ji proceeded to lead us into a maze of projects out of which emerged an amazing network of people. It was like connecting the dots of a child's drawing book to watch a beautiful new picture of the world emerge. Life was all about what my friend Bud called 'Guided Discovery'. God has placed all the resources to solve even the most intractable problems right under our noses. If only we'd open our eyes. I often asked myself and others, "If we could put a man on the moon why couldn't we overcome poverty?"

Maharaj ji had me focus on several key areas: Teaching values to youth, working with the poor and disabled, building Interfaith Understanding and being an advocate for Human Rights.

A Lion among the Lions

A friend, Pali, one of the few Sikhs in Syracuse, invited me to join the Lions, the prestigious international service club. Given that Singh means 'lion' it seemed a natural thing to do. What amazed and impressed me was that these businessmen, mostly mature, if not elderly statesmen of Syracuse opened their luncheon meetings with a prayer. I had been in academic settings where prayer was anathema to intellectual freedom, but it was alive and well in the business community. Moreover I realized that the U.S. Congress

168

opened with prayers as did our local City Common Council. Somehow there was a disconnect with the school systems and the public-private debate.

After a few meetings, I was accepted as a Lion and soon found myself out on the streets of downtown collecting money for the blind. Lions Club led me to the United Nations once a year, in dialogue with senior officials, as two local members of our club had been the International representatives to the United Nations. There I was able to meet the likes of Robert Muller, the popular Under Secretary General and build a relationship with the United Nations Association that continues to this day.

Everywhere I saw Maharaj ji's hands at work, laying out game plans for uniting existing organizations to focus on solving major problems. Through my association with Lions, I was able to focus on drug awareness projects with the city and county middle schools, and work with the visually impaired helping to start a 'beeper-ball' league. I remember the first practices inside an ice-rink in the park. As the team began to travel, other club members, mainly Dave and Cindy, who had more time, took over.

I was then asked to Chair the Community Service committee of our Insurance Trade Association. This way I could link resources of different organizations to highlight problems and find solutions. We were weaving the threads of the human family together, rebuilding a sense of community that had been lost to the divisive politics and prejudices of American society.

Cub scouts and the local country fair

Elbridge, is a quiet farming community that had grown into a bedroom community for Syracuse. It lies about 15 miles outside the city and one mile beyond the western-most suburb of Camillus's town line. Our house is on the main route between the towns. As a matter of fact Route 5 was the original East West trade route in Upstate New York between Buffalo and the Great Lakes and Albany and the Hudson River.

Being out in the country left Joginder quite isolated. I worked in Syracuse and she had little contact with Elbridge itself. But all that changed when one day at the library she ran into a wonderful new friend, Ellie.

169

Through Ellie we were pulled into the community and ended up working on the "Elbridge Country Fair," the main annual fund raising project which supported many of the areas volunteer programs. I was asked to help with publicity. Though this was my first contact with the media, it was fun to "sell" a community and community spirit. So we had a design donated by Kathy, a noted stain-glass artist, put it on T-shirts and sold them, and wore them wherever we went, used it on our advertising placemat, and in general created wonderful visibility for this tiny village and its great people. Joginder and Chetan helped out with booths and displays and cooking.

One thing about America is that once people see that you're willing to volunteer you are called on for all sorts of opportunities to serve. Here we were the only visible minority in this small farming community. I'm certainly the only person with a turban and beard they had ever met. And what happens? They asked me to be Cub Scout master and entrust their children to my tutelage. This allowed me to bring Chetan and Tegbir up in an atmosphere of respect. It was really humbling and great fun. But such are Maharaj ji's ways. His love always shines through.

Cub scouts are at an age when everything is new and exciting. And parents are anxious to help and watch their children progress. So from "pinewood derbies" where the kids made model cars out of a block of wood and raced them down ramps, to marching in local parades, the group stayed together and supported each other. This was positive peer pressure at its best.

But as children in America grow up they face a myriad of problems, and without the spiritual roots to hold them they are buffeted from all sides. And as in all countries drugs were a major symptom and a major trap.

Drugs

While in India, Maharaj ji used to call me out of the fields and send me to preach among the villagers in Punjab. One main theme was always overcoming drugs and alcohol. It had become and still is endemic.

We had always heard stories of governments themselves introducing drugs to control unruly populations. But drugs and those who use them don't discriminate. They have crossed all borders, not simply between countries, but between social classes. And in all countries of the world it is the youth who suffer most.

There was a time when drugs and Sikhs were an oxymoron. Now it has become more of a synonym.

History shows how even the most powerful personal ethos can be eroded if we don't maintain strict vigilance. Sikhs were so strong no one could conquer them. Their only focus was on God and defending the people against continuous terrorist invasions.

The Durrani King, Ahmed Shah Abdali, who regularly pillaged India, when told that the Sikhs sleep in their saddles, eat corn from the fields, and have no homes, determined that he could never, indeed no one ever could conquer them in battle. Rather the only way to weaken them was by enslaving them to drugs.

Guru Gobind Singh created a code of conduct which would specifically keep Sikhs from becoming enslaved by any habit. The only habit he linked them with was unceasing prayer – reciting *Nam* wherever they were.

An American, sharing these stories seemed to have a great impact on Punjab villagers. Back home I wondered what the impact would be of an American with a turban on the youth of America.

While there were many successful models for drug education, most were used among the wealthy and well-educated, while the poor, where drugs had become a violent way of life, were left to their own devices. Besides drug programs and money were being divided between, education, law enforcement, and treatment, and seldom if ever were all elements united in their approach to the children or the community. So the first challenge was finding people within each sphere willing to come together for the program. As I had access through both Lions and business associations, out of this network of the top Law Enforcement agency (John, the District Attorney's office), the top treatment center (Otto from Crouse) and the schools (Arnie) and Len (AA), the **City-County Drug Awareness Poster-Essay Contest** was born. With Maharaj ji blessings, we were able to put together a consortium of all the agencies dealing with both treatment and enforcement to jointly address students at a middle school (ages 11 to 13) when they most needed help to resist peer pressure.

The participation was tremendous. We got all kinds of great art work and the essays often reflected the kids' own reality of living with drugs in their communities or families. On the day of the awards ceremony the auditorium of Crouse Hospital, which hosted the program, was packed as the buses arrived. The students' eyes opened wide as they came in and saw their posters displayed on the walls. For many it was the first time they had been in a formal setting outside of school or church.

The second year, I got a note that Le Moyne College wanted to get involved. A Jesuit by the name of Roy had tremendous experience with drugs and alcohol on campus. Roy himself a recovering alcoholic, was a nationally and internationally known lecturer on recovery through the 12 step process of Alcoholic Anonymous which has been replicated by self-help groups throughout the world. And with Roy's commitment and Le Moyne's involvement we were not only able to expand the contest, but Roy and I would end up expanding Maharaj ji's mission to many new areas as well.

Living as a Sikh

Guru in a Sikh context

Koi jan har sio davay jor
I long to find the one who will lead me to God.
While I am well-known in the Sikh community, even internationally, and have lots of friends, many do not share my spiritual path.

Within the Sikh community there is a sharp divide, and an even more strident voice: the use of the term Guru for anyone or anything other than Guru Granth Sahib, the Holy Word of God is considered taboo.

Maharaj ji never claimed to be Guru, and in fact, no one held Guru Granth Sahib in more reverence and taught everyone of all religions reverence for it, as witnessed by people from all backgrounds at Gobind Sadan waving chauri sahib over it day and night. In our

172

home, we allocated one bedroom as a special prayer room where Guru Granth Sahib presides. We pay proper respect and take God's order daily. We taught our children that this is where their day starts and ends. They still as adults go to their respective prayer rooms before breakfast and before bed to offer prayers. And I, as you shall soon learn, have even seen the power of Guru Granth Sahib to survive undamaged the flames of arson and the tons of water used to douse the fire. To me it is alive and speaks to me constantly. It is no doubt Guru.

But the argument remains: Can there be an enlightened being in the world today, and what would you call him/her? I chose the term Guru. I suppose I could have opted for Spiritual Master or Teacher, but as I clearly state that to me in my personal experience Maharaj ji embodied that Light of God which is Guru. For Guru Granth Sahib as all scriptures teach that God exists in Spirit, in the Holy word enshrined in scripture, and in the body of those who become merged with Him. Besides, before I knew Guru Granth Sahib existed and before I had even seen a Sikh in my life, I was called through no possible thought of my own to the feet of Baba Virsa Singh.

For those who think one doesn't need a person as a spiritual guide, that spirituality is a subject absorbed through osmosis or that religion is one's birthright, consider the analogy of apprenticing oneself to a great artist. If one seeks to become a doctor, you go to medical school, then intern, and do a residency. You owe your skills to those you study under. After law school, a lawyer may clerk for an esteemed Supreme Court judge. We apprentice ourselves to one who has achieved what we would like to become. And, we hold them in the greatest esteem for they have transferred their skills to us. While medical and law schools are many, master artists or goldsmiths are few and far between, and a True spiritual master is even more rare. And the tests He puts us through are much harder.

Havan – the eternal sacred fire

If using the term Guru is not controversial enough for many Sikhs, try talking about havan. Immediately you'll hear, "Havan is a Hindu thing. No self-respecting Sikh would do havan." The havan long before I arrived on the scene became a line of demarcation between Hindus and Sikhs. And, the more strained the politics became between the majority Hindu and minority Sikh communities, the more Sikhs became concerned that their identity was being threatened and their practices adulterated. So they began drawing the line tighter and tighter around who was a Sikh and what were their practices.

But this couldn't be the sacred fire before which I would sit and meditate each day, bathing in its spiritual glow. This could not be the sacred fire whose eternal flame is represented in all traditions all the way back to Leviticus where early worship in Judaism revolved around offerings on the sacred fire. Moreover, Baba Siri Chand ji was always pictured with His sacred fire burning before him, and he was following Guru Nanak Dev ji's orders in his prayers. This too, as it turned out, had become a political issue for the Sikhs, one too long to go into the misconceptions of the last 150 years. Suffice it to say, that Baba Siri Chand ji and his spiritual order, the Udasis, were blessed by Guru Nanak Dev ji himself and had been and are officially recognized as part of mainstream Sikhism. To me it simply says that God and spirituality is core to a Sikh and means more than the politics of the day.

Besides Maharaj ji always saw havan as a unifying and healing force. "This is the eternal flame which has existed in all traditions since time immemorial, and is still represented in many ways today. Its power is undeniable."

Raising Sikhs – The Camp Movement

We were relaxing at home towards the end of the summer of 1978, when the phone rang. It was Harbans. Dr. Harbans Lal, who had been presented the Bhai Sahib award for his dedication to spreading the message of the Gurus, had become a close friend was a master net-worker. "Ralph, they have just finished the first Sikh Youth Camp in Racoon Creek State Park outside of Pittsburgh. The closing ceremony in tomorrow and you have to go." We had never driven to Pittsburgh let alone heard of the Park. But this was clearly a calling, not just a call. So we packed up Chetan, who was just 2 years old, and headed out on the 7 hour drive. We arrived in time to witness the birth of a movement. Balwant Singh and Ujaggar Singh were giving awards to those dedicated group

We were hosted by Sarjit and Ranjit, local physicians and key camp organizers in their Weirton, W.V. home and immediately bonded.

The next summer we received a call from Sarjit. The camps had split. Would we be willing to run the Pittsburgh camp. And so it began. We helped develop the Northeast Regional Camp with Ujaggar Singh and Balwant Singh, Kuldip's Detroit Camp, and the North Carolina camp with Gumukh and Sukhi Harmohinder Singh, and Parminder and Tejpal Dhillon. In the process, Sarjit and Ranjit, Tejinder and Surjit and many of the Pittsburgh/Ohio *sangat*, the Tri-State New York sangat, the Detroit/Windsor *sangat* and the North Carolina/Virgina *sangat*, A.J. and Dilpreet, and the Washington sangat. and their children became our lifelong friends. Suddenly we had hundreds of nieces and nephews, as the tradition requires children to call their elders, Uncle and Auntie. To this day, some of our favorite young adults will still address us as Ralph Uncle and Joginder Auntie.

Even though I am a bit dismayed that much of the political rhetoric has spilled over from their parents, I can honestly say that children who have experienced youth camps, have more knowledge about their heritage than most of their counterparts in India. The generation of Sikh youth in the U.S. are an exceptional, distinguished group of young leaders in their fields. The country and the world is better for them.

We must maintain our character – against all odds

My experiences in India together with my experiences with summer camps, as both camper and counselor gave me a cross-cultural perspective through which Maharaj ji was able to guide me in developing novel approaches to teaching values through religious stories and history. Joginder and I, with the children, spent our entire summers for almost 10 years, helping develop the camps and helping the youth bridge the culture-gap.

Growing up Sikh – How to be a Sikh in America

While culture may be linked to Punjab, values are universal. If the kids could understand that the symbols represented their values, they would soon learn that individuals who stood for virtues were actual a very valuable asset in US, or any other country for that matter.

175

As a matter of fact there were many Americans who appreciated that Sikh children did not date or drink or smoke. They made an excellent peer group. It was important to see one's identity as positive, distinctive, and that they were distinguished members of our community.

In class the dialogue went something like this:

You are all good students aren't you? Yes!

Then you work very hard to get 'C's' right? No!

Why not? What's wrong with a C? That's average. We don't want to be average.

You mean you want to excel? Yes!

So you want to distinguish yourself from the average student and stand out among the class?

Of course.

Then being a Sikh is no different. Guru Gobind Singh ji wanted us to distinguish ourselves by our conduct, by our character, and be recognized as people who stood to defend positive values for everyone. We are here to serve everyone. We must maintain the highest sense of business ethics, and do our best at everything we attempt.

How is that different than what you personally want to achieve? It's not. But why do we have to wear a turban or why not cut our hair?

Ah, but you just said that you wanted to distinguish yourselves. Keeping your hair or wearing a turban is instant recognition. But you must then live up to it. Sometimes people are scared to make a commitment. Scared to stick their neck out. But that's exactly what our Gurus expected of us: to be strong enough to constantly stick our necks out.

Sticking your neck out may mean doing the right thing. Speaking up for those who can't. Speaking up when you see something wrong. Working harder and smarter than the next guy.

Companies spend millions on logos, trademarks, and branding. You come with your brand. Live it. But once your brand is recognized, you must maintain your quality. One slip and the name is tarnished.

Through the work with youth, I was able to develop a useful introductory lecture: **Sikhism – A Course for Life,** using the metaphors of curriculum, campus, uniforms and mottos to explain the teachings, core values, sacred places and scriptures of a Sikh. I was honored to be invited to present at the Smithsonian Institution, and such prestigious private schools as Phillips-Andover, and Hockaday in Dallas. Soon my lectures in churches began to rival the number I gave in Gurdwaras.

1984 – Sikhs or Sikhism – The Human Rights Issue
1984 – The Orwellian year of Big Brother. Summer had come and it was still business as usual. There wasn't a ruffle of anything amiss. I was relatively unaware of events in India and the level of tension that had surrounded the Golden Temple. I was focused on community work here, always feeling that the Sikhs in India could take care of their own political problems and I should continue to educate people about Sikhism, do Maharaj ji's sewa, and run my office.

But July changed all that. I happened to be in Washington on business when the news hit. The Indian army had invaded the Golden Temple and tens of thousands of innocent pilgrims who had gathered for a major celebration (the 400th anniversary of Guru Arjun Dev ji's martyrdom) were killed. The troops then fanned out and "cleaned-up" villages in the surrounding area. Reports were coming in about random killings of any youth with a beard and turban and the Sikh community was understandably outraged and in a panic.

Sikhs from all over the country converged on Madison Square Garden. While there were many talks of outrage there were few constructive suggestions. I tried to offer a human rights approach but the emotions were too high to gain audience. So using my experience with the local Human Rights Commission, we set up our own group.

177

Sikh Human Rights Group

I established a coordinating committee with the leading International Human Rights organizations, Amnesty International, Asia Watch, Human Rights Internet, and the Minority Rights Group. At the outset we were able to maintain our focus on human rights violations and steer clear of any political issues, and provide unbiased information to the world community. Our briefing booklet, *The Turning Point*, which used high-profile photos and supporting testimony was in high demand. But human rights and politics are inextricably mixed, and when we held a briefing for Congressional aids in the Annex, the story was intentionally sensationalized in major Indian dailies and periodicals. And when some pseudo-intelligence groups became involved carrying the disinformation, it was a first hand lesson in international intrigue.

International Human Rights Commission

I was all set to go to Geneva to represent the case before the International Human Rights Commission. I had a ticket in hand and sponsorship at the commission by the Minority Rights Group. As I was meditating reviewing the process, it became clear that my path did not lead through Geneva. Again, I had to choose between representing Sikhs or representing Sikhism – the teachings of the Guru. Even though I had devoted 2 years of my life to the cause, there were many people equally or more qualified than me to present the Sikh case. I had been chosen and trained to preach the Guru's mission. As soon as the day began, I picked up the phone and cancelled my seats, called and explained my decision to several disappointed supporters, and in essence from that point on stepped back and allowed others who wanted the stage to come forward. I have never regretted the decision.

Character Education

What is the character of America without a visible standard?

The Material World: Consumerism at its best

Values have price tags. Our values have been debased. We were, and still are, the ultimate consumer society. But what we don't realize is that we are the ones who are being consumed. Material existence can best be defined as I am what I have. Who I am doesn't matter. We define ourselves by what we have, not by who we are. The label is everything. Image is everything. Our brand. Everything is external and we depend on external stimuli to make us comfortable and validate our very existence, as witnessed by the constant need to entertain ourselves. We have to be plugged into something all the time.

Just as all values were being questioned, the taboos about pre-marital sex seemed to fly out the window in a period which was referred to as 'free-love'. Boys and girls immediately began to focus on sexual relationships (a trend that continues today at alarmingly young ages). If sexual attraction and 'compatibility' was not the main issue in a relationship, it ranked near the top.

Moreover, children were validating their identities based on these relationships with one another. They were only valuable or desirable if someone else 'desired' them. And once again that desire almost always had sexual connotations. If you were not in a relationship then you were not a desirable person. This proved very dangerous emotionally for many a youth. There was no stability in that form of love. And no real sense of self worth.

We all need a course in character development. It could be subtitled: 'Accepting Responsibility and the Consciousness to use it wisely (controlling the mind).'

Character is not only central to Maharaj ji's course, it is at the heart of almost every single one of His discourses. It is the one thing that distinguishes a student and the one thing that actually transcends Truth in the philosophical sense. He often quotes Guru Nanak Dev ji

Sachai urai subh ko – Upar Sach Achaar
Truth is supreme – but higher still is truthful living.

Our character is not only the expression of Truth within us but the way in which God's order and values are reflected in the world.

But how do we bring character back into focus in the modern education system which is so concerned with pumping facts into students that it has been accused of 'teaching to the test'? The tests of life are clearly not in the curriculum.

A Community is built on people of character and visible standards

Values in Public Education – Schools of Character

While talking with Roy after another successful poster-essay contest, I lamented that we were still just dealing with the symptoms while the spiritual root causes and lack of values were so pervasive that we hadn't even begun to address them. Roy chuckled, "Funny you should mention that. I'm part of the Central New York Education Consortium, made up of all the public and parochial schools, private and state Universities from Oswego, to OCC, Syracuse, and Le Moyne, and we've just convened a new task force on values in public education. I'll recommend your name. Go see what you can add."

The first meeting took place in the old administration building of the East Syracuse Central Schools, and was chaired by Fritz the former superintendent. There was Scott from SU, Mary from OCC, Don from Le Moyne, the superintendent from FM, and several area principals. They were all well-known, some even nationally known, educators. I was the only 'lay-person'.

The discussion opened with a challenge to define what we meant by values and to name the project. I had some experience talking with groups and raised my hand, "Being a newcomer may I ask a few questions?" "Of course." "First whenever we speak of values in a public forum, the word has become so politicized, that the question we'll invariably meet will be 'Whose values are you talking about?'

Once we've crossed that hurdle and been able to present values as universal, not belonging to any group, we will inevitably face the next: 'Which one of your teachers is capable of teaching my kid values?'

So my feeling is that if we start with values, we're putting ourselves in a hole to begin with."

That was much appreciated and they then asked for some alternatives. So Maharaj ji naturally had me ready with the answer: "Aren't we talking about character education. Isn't the real purpose of education beyond imparting knowledge, is to develop character in the students. And isn't it a goal of each community to have their schools be a showcase of the character of that community. So let's call it 'Schools of Character'.

They loved it. It would be school based. Meaning that it was a grassroot program developed along certain guidelines and provided resources and training by the university specialists. But each district could choose how to participate, down to which buildings and what themes they would develop. The program would therefore hinge on the initiative of the principals (who were the building and community leaders) with support from their superintendents and boards of education.

At one of the annual workshops at Syracuse University, Scott had invited me to address the group. I remember one of the questions were, "How can we really teach values to little children?"

"That's easy, just tell them Bible stories," I responded without a second thought.

"Well we can't do that, given the separation of church and state."

"Of course you can. Just tell them 'Bible stories' from each tradition." Well that was new ground that they weren't quite ready to tread.

MPH and Exploring Spirituality

When I read in the Gunnery bulletin that Baxter, who had been a class ahead of me, had been appointed headmaster of Manlius Pebble Hill, the premier local private day school, I invited him to lunch and subsequently recommended him to the task force.

Shortly thereafter, Manlius Pebble Hill sponsored a community wide day on Values in Education featuring the famous Harvard psychiatrist, Robert Coles. Knowing my involvement in the issues, I was asked to present on the role of spirituality in character development.

Subsequently I was asked to develop a values-based curriculum which could be taught using the stories and scriptural teachings from the world's religions. We wanted something other than simply a comparative religions, or world religions survey course. If we could find a way to use spirituality as the core and use the spiritual truths of all traditions to teach ethics in high school, it would be unique in modern secular education. And Baxter was enough of a maverick to make it happen. After a brief discussion about his desire to allow kids to experience a sense of spirituality in the school, I suggested the name, "Exploring Spirituality." As the name suggested, it would help kids connect with the Truths of all religions and provide a framework for their development. While it was a source of great pleasure for me, I can't say that it was the most popular course in school. I can say that most kids who took it benefited (by their own admission). Some of the greatest accomplishments were in helping children who had clearly rebelled against their own traditions find their way back or children who had rebelled against society find themselves again.

What God don't you believe in?
Quite often early on in class, at least one student would express their doubt of God's existence.

"I don't believe in God," they would declare, almost as if to challenge me to convince them. I'd simply ask, "Which God don't you believe in?" That would always make them pause and think, of how to express what they do believe. If they came up with a common misconception, I'd respond, "I don't believe in that either. God is way beyond that."

Losing touch with the Message
"In each tradition there is someone who hears the Voice of God. Let's call them the Messenger. Then when the message is recorded or shared, it becomes scripture and is passed on to the people as a guide for them to live – a road map for this path of life. But somewhere along the path, people lose their way, and forget the message. Then God has to send another Messenger to remind them."

182

To demonstrate the process I used a childhood game.

"You all remember the game of Telephone?

For those of you who have never had the pleasure. I whisper a word to the first person, who then in turn whispers it to the next and so on. The word is passed around the room and the last person repeats it out loud for all to hear."

We played, passing a phrase around the room. Predictably when the last student repeated it, the message had totally changed. I asked what happened.

"Either we didn't understand the message."

Or, "It got lost in translation. Someone changed it."

Perfect.

"Isn't that what happens to religions today? We get in the way of the message. Putting our thoughts before the teachings of God."

Standards and Standard Deviation

One day I walked into class and announced, "Would all the nonconformists move to the left side of the room." Everyone got up and moved.

Conformity is a very powerful force. We all conform to something. No matter how rebellious, we all have some standard or something that we think sets us apart. This is how clubs, cliques, and even gangs are formed.

I would draw a straight line across the board and proceed to draw a squiggly wave along the line. "Does anyone know what this is? The line is our standard. It is the basis against we measure everything. Like an axis in a graph is our base line. Now do you know what we call the wavy line?

That is 'standard deviation.' It is a scientific concept used in everything from engineering to financial models to account for the amount of error which will naturally come in our equations. If we apply it to life, it means we are all deviants. No one is perfect. No one is always on that line.

Standards define us, define our family and our work. And they define our communities.

183

The question for each of us and for our communities to ask, is how much deviation is acceptable. This is where the walls that divide us are built. Even among co-religionists you can't take communion in another church even though you're all Christian because you don't adhere to the same standards. Fundamentalists take it to an extreme and suggest that anyone who doesn't conform to their strictest literal interpretation can't be part of their community and they set about imposing their order on everyone else.

So who can be part of your community? How far will you allow yourself to stray off that line. These are critical questions as you begin to define your integrity and find the strength to maintain it."

This would always spark great discussions about drugs, pre-marital and extra-marital sex, race relations, gay-rights, religion and beliefs, and even political parties. In the end, the kids usually concluded that people who respect each other's rights and act out of love regardless of what beliefs they profess could be part of their community. They wanted to exclude those who act out of hatred or violence towards another.

That first year I was asked to offer the invocation and benediction at Commencement. When I looked at the program, I found they had listed me as School "Chaplain." It took me a long time to dry my tears. As Maharaj ji had blessed the school with his visit, He always gave me poetic pieces of His love to share:

A Parent's Prayer

As you turn this corner, don't turn and walk away from our Love

We have been there when you took your 1st breath – some of us saw your head emerge and cut the cord to keep you in this world–

Love gushed and overflowed.

We watched as you began to crawl, then walk.

You took a few steps but always turned and looked back at us.

We were on the sidelines of the sports fields, the courts, the rinks, and in the audience cheering for you

You have always been our pride and joy.

Now we release you to follow your dreams

Bring that same pride and joy to all you meet

It is our prayer that you always turn back – don't turn away

If we failed to always model the path we hoped you would follow please forgive us – for we are all too human

We will always be there for you – from a distance

Know that all the love and support you felt will always be with you

For as you are God's gift to us and the world

We as parents are God's way of reaching out to welcome you – and nurture you

You are God's children not ours – and always were

It is our illusion that we can or should control your life

You were born for a purpose much greater than to be our child –

To bring pride and joy to the world

That people who see your work will benefit

Now go swiftly lest we try to hold you

Know that God's love – the love you felt within us

Will always be with you

Cultivate it – talk with it

Like you did with us

Listen for it extends beyond your conscience

It will empower your dreams

And for this we pray - Amen

185

The Adult Ed Version

The course attracted enough attention that the school decided to offer it as part of their adult education series. Parents, faculty, and even grandparents came the first year. By the second year, the word had spread throughout the area and many people came from outside MPH as well.

It struck a chord among those who on one hand felt a connection to God but were disenchanted with institutionalized religion. They warmed to the metaphor of the Light, for God, and boxes for religion. From then on the theme was 'You can't wall up the Light,' and much discussion revolved around 'un-boxing'.

When questioned about the difference between spirituality and religion, it was easy for them to understand that spirituality defined and developed their connection with God, and unfortunately, organized religion as practiced today, for the most part defined their connection with the 'church,' or other institutions. It was the external man-made form which they saw as corrupt or at least a corruption of the pure Spirit of God.

In the end, they concluded that what I termed 'spiritual existentialism,' meant spirituality without a belief in God, was not valid. Maharaj ji offered me the phrase, "You can be spiritual without being religious – but you can't be spiritual without God."

To those who connected spirituality with a 'new-age' movement, I'd say, "Spirituality is not a section in your local bookstore." It is the way you live and the way you see yourself and the world around you. It is the basis for your commitment to the environment and people's rights.

Ritual, or the way it was enforced, was like using ladders to reach God. The clergy instructed us to climb up when they had never been there themselves. Maharaj ji always taught that all ritual done with love can lead to God, but without love, ritual was merely for show.

The Trellis and the Vine

How often do we hear that the youth of today lack discipline. It's not that they don't have discipline but they call it attitude. It's the way they like to structure their own time. They have rejected imposed authority. But in the process they have discarded the very structure which supports their growth. So in order to teach the children that self-discipline is critical in providing a framework for values to grow on Maharaj ji gave me a children's story that the parents appreciated as much if not more than the children: "The Trellis and the Vine."

One fine spring morning, a vine popped out of the ground and was greeted by the trellis.

"Oh how beautiful you are. I've been waiting all winter for you. Come climb up on me."

But the vine was indignant. "Why should I climb up on you, I want to go out on my own."

So the vine set off across the lawn, very proud of itself. Until someone stepped on it. "Ouch," cried the vine. Then (as one student added) along came a lawnmower and cut the vine.

As quickly as it could the vine retreated to the trellis. "May I climb up now?"

And as it wound itself around the trellis it began to bloom and all the neighbors stopped to admire it.

We all need a framework for growth. And for values, it is our spiritual roots and traditions which give us support. If we jettison them completely we lose the very strength that we need to maneuver through the difficulties of life.

Including those whom other's have cast out

Community meals and the Black community

One who doesn't serve those in need will not find salvation in God's court.

Maharaj ji had early on told me to think of ways to help the poor out of poverty. While in India abject poverty was widespread, in the U.S. poverty was clustered in the inner-cities where people are trapped because of race or lack of work, or spread out in rural areas where poverty remains hidden from view in the back woods of the country. While the rural poor remain an under-represented and often undeserved group the urban poor are both visible and vocal. In the United States, the majority of urban poor happen to be Black or

Latino and drugs and violent crime among them is epidemic. It's safe to say that the jails of the country are filled with young black men. No doubt there are white men in jail but the vast majority of prison populations are racially imbalanced. We looked at the problem and felt that there was a lack of access, not just to power, but to the basic steps that lead to power. It seemed the only way a poor black man was allowed into the halls of power was in handcuffs.

One way we felt we could contribute was helping bring the people together through community meals, our version of a *langar*. There were many programs which fed poor people. And they were good. But we thought it was necessary to serve and eat with the people. We would invite community leaders and hospital or school executives to come to the community meal. Once the people had met someone who worked in the hospital, it wasn't so intimidating for them to go for medical treatment next time, because they had met Miss Daisy or Mr. Bill and they were kind. It made all the difference.

Ray Baird

"This is your brother speaking," was Ray's way of announcing himself on the phone. People may have found it strange to see this seasoned Black civil rights veteran walking arm in arm with a Sikh, but our love and mutual admiration was boundless. When others asked Ray what he had to do with me, he just answered, "We feed the hungry together." It was through Ray that Maharaj ji introduced us to the community leaders and we began the *langars*. But Ray stayed with me every step of the way. When Maharaj ji first visited Ray, through his office as State Superintendent of Buildings, he arranged for His reception at the airport. And amazingly enough, of all places, Ray lived only 5 miles away from Gobind Sadan, USA and together we spent many hours fixing frozen pipes or doing other odd jobs together in the early days.

The Mullicks

I had been invited to speak at a gathering at a friend's (Kirpal Singh) home in Corning. As I finished my talk following the kirtan, I naturally mentioned Gobind Sadan and Maharaj ji's work. Suddenly a thin man thrust his way forward, through the crowd. "Maharaj ji, Gobind Sadan, you're that Ralph," he was almost in tears. "We have heard of you for years but didn't know how to find you. Now Maharaj ji has brought you to us." Satinder Mullick and his family were old devotees of Maharaj ji who had been blessed through Gurcharan Singh Randhawa. Along with his wife Mohini, and children Tarun and Deepa, he soon welcomed us as part of his family. Satinder, Chief Economist for Corning Glass, became a lifelong friend, a mentor, and supporter of all our work to further Maharaj ji's mission. With his help and guidance, we established Gobind Sadan Community Services as the first arm of Gobind Sadan to extend our seva to those in need. Every month Joginder would cook for 100 or so people in the various community centers or churches.

Sherman Cummings – the ruby throated deep voice of Praise
I was at a funeral for a major Black civic leader and was on the pulpit to offer my tribute, when a tall man stepped up to the microphone and began to sing. He quickly filled the church to the rafters with the most beautiful deep sounds that I have ever heard. Sherman and I quickly bonded and began planning ways in which the Black Churches could create economic programs for their community. When Col. Sahib visited, Sherman invited him to address his church and later he asked Joginder to cook a community meal at his church.

Laveda – my sister
If Ray and Sherman were brothers, Laveda was my sister. An old time community organizer, she worked with us on the meals to help develop community based programs. Together we developed what we termed an "empowerment survey" which not only assessed the community's needs and access to services from Education and Transportation to Medical and Legal, but encouraged the people to get involved in planning and coordinating their own services at the block level. With Laveda's help we had more than a 95% participation, which is literally unheard of in surveys.

189

Community Workplaces – an idea whose time had come but we weren't quite able to put it together

We felt no matter what we did to raise community consciousness, that unless people had access to employment there would never be an end to the cycle of poverty. We didn't want people to have to go to prison to find work. Maharaj ji clearly felt that someone who didn't work, should not be considered poor. Rather those who worked hard but couldn't make ends meet should be given help. So we tried to develop a model, which would put employment and training in one center in the neighborhood, and encourage people to work their way off welfare. We were a little ahead of our time, and couldn't quite get it off the ground. Today the idea of 'workfare' is a popular part of community development.

Celebrate Together – 1000 points of light – Breaking down barriers between able-bodied and people with disabilities

One of the projects I inherited as Community Service Chair of my professional association was 'Celebrate Together'. In conjunction with the City of Syracuse Department of Parks and Recreation, we would plan and sponsor a picnic in the park for the disabled community. The problem was that it was not interactive. The disabled were brought on buses from their various group homes or institutions, seated and served and sent home. It was a nice outing but not much to celebrate. I found that many people with disabilities were in fact very active. The blind, or visually impaired, had their own version of softball, and many confined to wheel chairs had started their own basketball league. So we began to convene the groups and their advocates, notably Jim and Sally Johnston, and retool 'Celebrate Together,' into a picnic with a purpose: to break down the barriers between the able-bodied and disabled communities. It was great fun. We had music 'signed' for the hearing impaired. Full sighted players put on blindfolds and played beeper ball. Able-bodied members sat in wheel chairs to play basketball, and we put together a wheelchair obstacle course that was a terrific educational tool. You had to take a wheelchair over gravel, up and down steps, in and out of a phone booth or toilet, over deep carpeting and up a curb. By the time the day was over the kids had learned the difficulties that the

190

disabled community faced and next time legislation came up regarding accessibility for the 'handicapped,' everyone there was more sensitized. Moreover they had made great new friends. At age 5, first Chetan and then Tegbir began interacting with visually impaired players. Helping people from their homes to the car and helping them onto the field. Joginder supervised the shopping and the cooking and all had a great time. The fact that the project was nationally recognized by then President George Bush, Sr. as one of the 'Thousand Points of Light' was really icing on the cake. It is a project that is, low-cost, high impact and easily replicable.

City County Human Rights Commission

Through our work with the Black and Disabled Communities, I was approached to serve on the City-County Human Rights Commission. This was a Mayoral appointment considered quite an honor. After a short tenure on the commission, I was offered the position of Chair. This was indeed an honor. I served through 3 Mayors (a ten year period) until it was time for me to leave. Throughout my tenure, I tried to use our good offices to further access to employment, and education, and inclusion of the undeserved. We were the main body to monitor minority participation in all government contracts, maintain supervision of law enforcement agencies, and monitor and train for diversity in the workplace.

United Nations Association – adding a world view

In high school I had participated in MUN (Model United Nations) conferences, so when I was invited to join the UNA-USA by a Lion who had actually been present at the charter signing in San Francisco, Harold Curran, Maharaj ji again gave me the opportunity to merge my love of international issues with a local program. Within the first year the long time President stepped down and this group of distinguished citizens asked me to take over. We became a model chapter expanding our presence and programs, and Joginder would cook for over one hundred people at our annual meetings. Given our Chapter's success, I was asked to serve on the National Council which put me in the company of leaders and opinion makers of our country, many of whom are still good friends. When Maharaj ji wants to raise our visibility He finds paths we could never imagine. The Spitzers, Maryann Winters, Fred Fiske, Michelle Ulm all figure prominently in our lives today.

CNYMUN

2008 marks the 25th anniversary of the Central New York Model United Nations. Students, almost 1000 strong, now come from throughout the Northeast and Canada. But it started with a phone call from two students with a dream. I was sitting in my office when I received the call from two young ladies at Fayetteville-Manlius High School, Amy Allen and Jenny Nagel, who wanted our sponsorship to start a local MUN. Lois Spitzer and I met with them and Barry Miller, their faculty advisor, put them in touch with my friend, Ambassador Goodwin Cooke, at Syracuse University, and the rest is history. From 200 students from area schools it now is a major winter break event.

Interfaith Understanding

"Unless we break down the barriers between our religions how can we expect peace on our borders".

Maharaj ji's message to the Millennium Peace Summit

SAIC – Syracuse Area Inter-religious Council

I was in line during a U.N.A. friend's funeral and began a casual conversation with the person next to me. Terry was in charge of the Chaplaincy program at SAIC, and the more we talked about faith issues, she said, "You've got to meet Dorothy Rose." This was Maharaj ji's way of introducing me to the local inter-religious council. After a cordial lunch with Dorothy, the Executive Director, she invited me to make a presentation to her cabinet. In the synagogue, where my mother was confirmed and my Grandmother's funeral service was held, I presented 'Sikhism a Distinct Universal Religion' (which later became a small tract for education material in Wichita at the founding of the NAIN and other interfaith functions).

I can still remember the then Chair, Msg. Ron Bill, who also served as a General in the National Guard, sitting directly across from me and maintaining eye contact throughout the presentation.

As a result, The Sikh Congregation of Central New York, was voted a member of SAIC. And despite claims by others, this was the first local interfaith body to invite a Sikh congregation as members. When Maharaj ji first came to the U.S. in 1986, SAIC was one of the major sponsors of his visit.

NAIN and the Family Reunion

I had earned a reputation in the Sikh community for my oratory and knowledge so I was asked to join the coordinating committee and the delegation to the 1st North American Assisi, in Wichita, Kansas. While this would be the historic founding meeting of the North American Interfaith Network, it actually was more like a spiritual family reunion. I have always felt that wherever Maharaj ji sends me, I will meet those I've been connected to before. And NAIN has always attracted more than its share of wonderful brothers and sisters.

As those traveling from across the country converged on the small Wichita airport, several of us found ourselves waiting for transportation. Among them, Pam Blair, an interfaith minister from New York, Butch Mazur, a Catholic Priest from Buffalo, and an author from Connecticut doing research for her college textbook, *Living Religions*, named Mary Pat Fisher. Mary Pat and I kept crossing paths throughout the conference and promised to stay in touch. She had come to our room and spent time in meditation surrounded by relics and rare manuscripts brought by Deol to display at the conference. It struck me that unlike most authors, she was mainly interested in the practice of the religion and less about the history or politics of the people.

Editor Sahib, Gurbachan Singh, had just arrived from India so I brought him along to introduce him to the Interfaith movement which was where Maharaj ji clearly had "positioned" Gobind Sadan, USA.

He immediately recognized Muni Sushil Kumar (who had become a leading Jain teacher in the U.S.) as an old contemporary from Punjab and the two of them had a grand time.

After the opening ceremony, I had the privilege of presenting the Sikh perspective on "Justice," to the entire body under the watchful but benign eye of the very Reverend James Park Morton, Rector

193

of the Cathedral of St. John, the Divine and President of the Temple of Understanding. This provided me with some bona fides to approach other key speakers and leadership. So following her keynote talk, I tracked down Diana Eck, the well-known Harvard professor, and invited her to lunch. Over that meal, I asked her how someone who was so knowledgeable about interfaith dialogue and India could ignore Guru Nanak. I recounted how my education, which had included a summer at Harvard, and the years at Rochester and Columbia, didn't uncover a trace of Sikhism nor a mention of Guru Nanak. Her initial advice was to encourage the Sikh community to endow a chair to draw attention to Sikh Studies. While this was a common approach, I thought of a simpler method. "Diana, why don't you just include Sikhism in your course?" Happily, later that year, I received a note that she had done just that.

Much of the benefit of any conference occurs after or in between the formal sessions, and late evening one always finds a group of die-hards locked in conversation. Most areas in the hotel had closed down, but as expected the bar was open. So I ended up in a booth with Chuck White and Elizabeth Espersen. Chuck, who soon would be selected as NAIN's co-chair, was from Buffalo and along with Butch Mazur whom I had met on the way in, ran BAMM (the Buffalo Area Metropolitan Ministries).

Elizabeth, also originally from Buffalo, had left the life of a Nun, to reach out into the interfaith world and was notably the Executive Director of Thanksgiving Square in Dallas, Texas. As I explained the teachings of the Gurus and Guru Granth Sahib, Chuck leaned forward, "If I understand this correctly, we should thank the Sikhs for bringing forth this sense of pluralism?"

*Gobind Sadan, USA – Babaji's Gift and
My Dream Fulfilled*

Gathering His Flock

I am convinced that Maharaj ji only travels when and where He is called, sent by God, or called by a devotee from this life or past. Sometimes people have no idea of their connection until He appears and suddenly the switch goes on and they fall in line to serve Him. There is nothing random about His movements. But for us the path is revealed with each step He takes.

Just as a father, Maharaj ji travels to meet His children and gather his flock. When they are all assembled His real mission will start. He often says we haven't even started yet. "I'm just building the base." He often will welcome someone 'totally' new with a rousing, "You've come." Or say, "I had to come here, you were calling me with so much love."

17

Maharaj ji Visits the U.S.
"The Face of Peace"

"Peace is as elusive as a unicorn," began the reporter, "but today I came face to face with peace. His name is Baba Virsa Singh."

Vince Golphin in the Post-Standard Article.

It had been almost 9 years since I had been with Maharaj ji, though His presence was always with me. It's hard to imagine how I got along, as in my first years in Gobind Sadan, I couldn't stand to be away from Him even for a day.

We had tried to bring Maharaj ji to the U.S. several times. Inder had even purchased tickets and visas had been prepared. But the time wasn't right and the trip would fall through at the last minute, something quite common when one stays around Maharaj ji.

Before He goes anywhere, He will stand in prayer and literally ask God's permission. And if the answer is "No," then it doesn't matter who's waiting, He won't go. Once the whole government of U.P. (the most populous state in India) was waiting to receive Him. They had organized a special car on the train and had the route of his arrival decorated and the stage all set up. The cars were packed and ready to leave for the station, but the order came "no" and Maharaj ji cancelled the trip.

Maharaj ji Himself once said to me half jokingly, "Don't worry, we'll call you when we reach New York." So I'd gotten in the habit of preparing everything and then telling myself and others, "We're never sure until He is actually on the plane."

But by the end of August 1986, everything was in place, and the *hukam* was "Yes". He was on the plane and when He did arrive, it was like the Light descending on earth.

The Seeds are Planted

After Maharaj ji's triumphant arrival in New York where He stayed with the Chadhas on Long Island, and was hosted by the Chatwals, Kahlons, and Ahluwalias who gathered other leading area Sikh families to hear His message, Maharaj ji flew to Syracuse. He was accompanied by Bibi Nirlep Kaur, and joined by Harvinder Singh and Bibi Jaswant Kaur. While there He was welcomed by the Mayor, Tom Young, and the Country Executive, Nick Pirro, who issued proclamations in His honor, and He met with many community groups. After his dialogue with the religious community at the SAIC offices, Sandy Reyes, a local doctor and community leader, asked Maharaj ji if He would bless her nationally known drug treatment unit. Not only did He bless the unit, but also accepted her invitation to ride in her car. Later Sandy hosted a large gathering at her home for key people, which Bibi ji did an excellent job translating. To this day, Sandy talks about it and keeps that spot in her house, "sacred."

Aside from the meetings, Maharaj ji also enjoyed taking rides into the beautiful countryside along the lakes and into the mountains. On one such trip, we stopped for a snack at the Howard Johnson's in Lake Forge, a scenic community which serves as the gateway to the Adirondak Mountain Park region. Overlooking the water, Maharaj ji laid out the main points of his plan to heal America:

Overcome drugs

Overcome poverty

And heal people's minds of the disease of worry

Maharaj ji selects the site for Gobind Sadan, USA

Before He left for the airport in November, Maharaj ji was sitting in Dati's living room in Westbury, and turned to us. "Standing at your garage – look 40 miles north-west. There's a widow who's very depressed. She wants to sell her farm. A real estate agent will help you. Go and buy it."

After Maharaj ji left, I had no choice but to refocus on business. It was one of our busiest times of year. Since I was way behind, I picked up the phone and called an old friend whom I knew was doing well. In the course of the conversation, I did something I've never done before. I simply asked how much insurance he had, and when I heard the nominal amount, I counseled, "Someone of your stature should have $10 million at least." He asked me how much it would cost. I gave him a ball-park figure and he agreed. Now we had the money, but we still had to find the farm. Of course, Maharaj ji had that detail covered as well.

With winter approaching, Joginder contacted as many agents as possible who dealt with farms. She traveled all over the area but couldn't find any that met the description. The snows descended and we felt we would have to wait until Spring to begin our search again. So we went about our other business and waited. One night toward the end of February we were sitting home when the phone rang. "Hello, I understand you're interested in a farm". I asked who was calling and how he'd gotten our name, then turned to Joginder and asked if she'd ever heard of him. "Not at all," she replied. He was not one of the people she had contacted. He continued that he had gotten our name from a friend and was just about to list a farm in the town of Hastings (which is northwest of us). I asked who owned it. When he said a widow, my heart skipped a beat and I asked when we could see it. We made an appointment for the following morning. Fortunately the day dawned clear and we drove up to Mexico (NY) to meet the realtor and then on to the farm and our meeting with destiny and Marion Graves who indeed wanted to sell the beautiful 270 acre dairy farm. As we walked the well-built farm roads lined with stone walls, and looked across expanse of beautiful fields, we were absolutely sure this was the farm Maharaj ji had chosen. So we drove back to the agent's office and made an offer. Then we drove home as fast as we could and called Maharaj ji. "Yes this is the place, buy it," He confirmed. And that was the end of the deal. It took several months to incorporate Gobind Sadan, USA and make sure the land was properly titled in the name of the corporation and we finally closed in September 1987.

Fortunately, Mrs. Graves had the privilege of meeting Maharaj ji and getting His blessings on his next trip before she passed away a few years later. She confided how happy she was that her land was being put to such blessed use.

Replicating a model

It was not a matter of Sikhs or Sikhism and it was not a matter of simply maintaining the sanctity of the place, but cultivating the Power of the gift that Maharaj ji had blessed us with. To the extent we were able to communicate this, and keep our focus based in meditation and prayer we were successful.

This was the fulfillment of my dream. As I look back I read the words on my sketchpad – '...to build a spiritual-based community,' I still get the shivers. All our community projects blended into G.S.USA, and we began to capture people's imagination. One early write-up in a local paper invited people to 'spend a day in the country building community'.

Editor Sahib and Colonel Sahib arrive

Maharaj ji always showed great respect to anyone who held any position in the world. And so an army officer, regardless of how long he'd been retired was still Colonel Sahib, and the retired Editor of a major paper was Editor Sahib. Maharaj ji wanted to send not only trusted people but people whom he had blessed to develop Gobind Sadan, USA. Editor Sahib, Gurbachan Singh, was blessed with great vision and healing power as our friend Ray found out.

Ray's bad knees

Ray was an amazing character. He was known as the psychic plumber, not just because he could locate pipes behind walls without any meters, but he would regularly publish his dream casts in the papers. Now while predicting the weather is considered a great science in the U.S., many cities joke about their resident meteorologists. They are always off by a day or so and sometimes completely wrong. But not Ray. He would dream about the upcoming weather, and then take out a small add in the local paper, stating that on Wednesday of the following week there would be severe flooding or the next Friday we would break a new record for cold or heat. He was never wrong.

Ray had met Maharaj ji at Sandy's clinic, followed him to her house, and soon became one of us. Whenever Gobind Sadan, needed a plumbing or water problem solved Ray was quick to respond. And whenever Maharaj ji came he would make an effort to see him.

But Ray had an extremely bad knee, which was not good for a plumber who had to lift things or spend long stretches kneeling. So he was counting his days before his next and final chance to have his knee operated on and called me. "Ralph, would you pray for me. This is my last chance. I need my knees to work."

No doubt, I offered a prayer, but Maharaj ji had blessed Editor Sahib, so I called him and apprised him of the situation and asked him to offer a prayer at the *havan* and let me know what he sees.

It wasn't even 20 minutes when he called me back. "Call Ray and ask him if he ever showed disrespect to the Bible? Jesus is saying that he doesn't respect the Bible."

Well that came as a shock. Now I had to call Ray, who was deeply spiritual and confront him with this order. But Editor Sahib was not wrong.

So I dialed the number and waited impatiently for Ray to answer.

"Ray, I hate to ask you this, but did you ever show disrespect to the Bible?"

I could feel the hurt and disbelief shoot across the line. "Ralph, you know me, I love God and the Bible. But wait." Slowly his voice lowered and became more hesitant. "You're not going to believe this, I'd totally forgotten. But when I was a kid, they tore down a church in my neighborhood, and while I was walking through the rubble I kicked a Bible that was lying there. After all these years. It's amazing."

I explained Gurbachan's gift of vision and then hung up to relay the message to Editor Sahib who had been totally confident that we'd find some such event. But Editor Sahib was amused to think that Jesus was telling him about something that the man himself had not remembered for over 50 years. Anyway, Ray came and offered prayers as instructed and his surgery went well. Needless to say, his respect for Gurbachan and for Babaji continued to grow.

Col. Daya Singh – the Kind Lion

Col. Sahib and Mrs. Baweja were some of the earliest residents in Gobind Sadan. When I arrived they were my neighbors. He was one of the few people who knew English, and being as kind as he was would often help me whenever any problem arose, from simple things like shopping, to scooter repair.

He was not only an upper classman, he was a model of humility and discipline, rising every morning at 2 a.m. meditating and then arriving promptly at 4 for *Asa Di War* kirtan, with his dedicated wife. He would then take his scooter to his army office and return in the evening to begin the cycle again. He had 5 terrific children and yet had room to adopt me as one more. At the end of every month we would compare class notes to see who did worse on their exam.

When he visited Syracuse before Gobind Sadan was established I held a press conference for him. His name Daya (kindness) and Singh (Lion) couldn't escape the journalists and the headlines read, 'The Kind Lion, roars a message of Peace'.

So when Maharaj ji sent Col. Sahib and Mrs. Baweja to be permanent residents at Gobind Sadan USA I was ecstatic. Along with Editor Sahib's spiritual blessings and his wife's (Manjit) help, Col. Sahib's warmth and Mrs. Baweja's kirtan would round out the team.

And that's what happened. The word got around and people would begin to drop in to meditate and share their spiritual experiences with Col. Sahib. Mrs. Baweja ran the kitchen and began to teach kirtan. The place began to hum.

The Canada Connection

There's a wonderful story from the life of Guru Nanak Dev ji:

As He and Mardana, His faithful servant, were traveling they stopped at a village for the night and townspeople were so rude that they didn't even offer them a decent meal or comfortable quarters. In the morning the Guru stood on the edge of the village and prayed: "Oh God grant these people great wealth that they stay here and prosper for generations to come." Mardana was a bit perplexed but didn't dare question the divine guidance of his Guru. The next night they stayed in a town where the people outdid themselves to serve them. They offered the best food and saw that they had the most comfortable accommodations for the night. After such a wonderful reception Mardana expected the Guru to grant great blessings to these good people. But he was shocked, when the Guru stood and prayed: "Oh God, may these people be uprooted from this village and scattered to all corners of the globe."

Mardana gasped, he couldn't help himself, "Great Guru, your ways are certainly strange. You have cursed the people who have shown us love and blessed the ones who abused us." Guru Nanak laughed, "The people in that village were so bad that I didn't want them to torment another soul. So by blessing them, I made sure that their spite would never leave that place. On the other hand, the world needs good people. So I have sent the other villagers forth to share their love wherever they go."

And so it was with Maharaj ji's Canadian *sangat*. Long before there was any thought of a Gobind Sadan USA in Upstate New York, the children of the Mehrauli *sangat* who had built Gobind Sadan, were family by family settling in and around Toronto, Canada. So when Maharaj ji came and the farm was purchased, this dedicated group of devotees would make the five hour drive, work all day, stay up all night in prayer and song, and then drive back the next day. It was amazing. Month after month, through some of the worst winter storms the Grewals, Anejas, Capt. Sahib, Bhajan and family, Karnail Singh, Suresh, Sarbjit and Prakash, Sheri, Preeti, and Biba, Prof Sahib, both Sukhis, Sajjan Singh and family, were prominent among the many others who never missed a weekend. The entire physical plant was built and maintained by their efforts, and still is.

The Akhand Paths
Surinder, Gurbachan's son-in-law had a dream. He saw Maharaj ji doing *chaur sahib* over Guru Granth Sahib while the *sangat* continued *Akhand Paths*. Maharaj ji was very happy with everyone. Aside from the dream, it made sense. The continuous reading of Guru Granth Sahib brought many blessings and brought the

community closer together. So in the small first floor room we had our first *Akhand Path*. Friends from out of town came to help (Surjit from Buffalo, Kirpal from Corning and several Syracuse *sangat*). With Maharaj ji's blessings and Editor Sahib's, Manjeet Bhenji's, Col. Sahib's and Mrs Baweja's and the rest of the *sangat's* hard work they have continued monthly ever since.

Jesus and Guru Gobind Singh walking side by side

Maharaj ji showed me that Gobind Sadan, USA was being developed by Jesus and Guru Gobind Singh walking side by side. While I knew this to be true, it was fascinating as always to watch how Maharaj ji wanted it to play out. Roy and I were driving back to Le Moyne in his truck when Maharaj ji said to me, "Ask him to be on the board. Ask him to be Vice-President." The order was clear and unmistakable. "Roy," I said, "You're putting in more time than anyone you should be on the board." He was a bit amused. "Can a Catholic Priest be on your board?" "Of course, and moreover Maharaj ji wants you to be Vice-President." Now he knew I was serious. "I'd be honored but I have to ask permission from my order." Permission was granted in short order and Roy became our official Vice-President.

G.S.USA: The Dedication November 21, 1992

Maharaj ji stood in the field next to the barn. The local reporter held out his mike for the first question. "Tell me about your beliefs?" With the fall foliage as a fitting background, Maharaj ji explained that God is omnipresent. "There are not two Gods. We should learn to see God in the trees, the flowers and fields, and in the water. And that the more we meditate we will learn to see God within ourselves and then see Him wherever we look." The reporter was pleased. This was an easy story. Then on to the land, "Babaji how does it feel to have such a large farm?" I could see the smile spread. "Actually this is the smallest of our farms," He replied modestly. The reporter was duly impressed and we moved into the barn where Maharaj ji gave an impromptu talk about the sanctity of marriage to those gathered: "This country is plagued by divorce. How can Jesus be happy when every day couples break their vows? When a young

204

man came to Jesus and asked, 'I don't get along with my wife, may I divorce her.' Jesus replied, 'When your marriage was made according to my father's order why do you seek to break it?' And so I tell you, control this bad habit. There are many difficulties we suffer in life, but that doesn't mean we should divorce."

Having given His informal messages outside, by the time the formal dedication started, Maharaj ji wanted to again focus on the universality of God. The havan was bursting at the seams and people overflowed into the barn where close circuit TV was placed. The light from the *havan* flashed across the walls, and the *kirtan*, echoed across the fields. From across Central New York, friends from 8 religious communities joined Maharaj ji to dedicate Gobind Sadan, USA. Each one brought a sacred object to grace our altar and shared a message of hope. Maharaj ji spoke of God's love and the power of the Light to sweep away the darkness.

"Until you meditate you won't be able to recognize God. But, once that Light arises within you through *Nam* and prayer, you will see the light dancing all around you, in every person and in all nature. Then you will not be able to see anyone as an enemy and your anger will diminish. Let us put aside these divisions that we've created and celebrate God in all His wondrous forms."

The event had such a powerful appeal that it was featured as part of the Christmas Special on local television.

Should I come in uniform?

Apparently, the publicity from the dedication had raised some suspicions and I received a call from the Town Supervisor that a group of trustees would like to meet with us to discuss their concerns. I asked Editor Sahib and Col. Sahib to prepare for our guests and invited Bob and Roy to join us. Roy's question was simple, "Should I come in uniform?"

You have to know Roy to understand the question. Jesuit priests in the city usually appear in public with their black clerical colors. But at Gobind Sadan, Roy was usually seen in his shorts or jeans and a T-shirt working harder than anyone else in the fields or buildings.

Since this was an 'official' meeting, I naturally accepted his offer. So we gathered on the floor of the living room awaiting our guests. Along with the photos of Guru Gobind Singh, Baba Siri Chand and Maharaj ji which graced the wall, there was a beautiful luminescent picture of Jesus etched in copper that literally radiated light to all who entered through the main doorway.

So, as the Town officials entered they were greeted by 2 Catholics and 3 Sikhs, and beamed on by Jesus's photo hanging from the opposite wall. Like any group, there was one strident voice who had insisted on checking us out. But when Roy was introduced in his official capacity from Le Moyne the man was visibly perplexed. He had come ready for a fight and was greeted not only by love but by his 'own' people. His children were students at Le Moyne. Still there were questions about land use and what would happen if we, the current administration of Gobind Sadan were to change? We assured them of our commitment to the area, served them some tea and snacks and saw them off. With Maharaj ji's blessings, a negative became a positive. Dan, a Japanese American who had been interred during WW II, knew prejudice, and was open and happy to have us as neighbors.

The Bishop's Cap
One day Roy showed up with a crimson cap (yarmulke) to don for meditation at the havan. As I admired it, he laughed heartily and told me that the local Bishop had given it to him. I knew Tom Costello, a saint of man, dedicated to helping the poor, and one of the founders of the Syracuse Inter-religious Council. When Roy told him that he went up to Gobind Sadan to meditate and that we traditionally cover our heads, Tom took his cap and tossed it to him. It was more of a kind-hearted gesture, but to us it signified in some small way, that Roy had the Bishop's blessings.

Roy had use of Le Moyne's vehicles, their shop and equipment, and garnered all the resources and even a small contribution for the work at Gobind Sadan.

More uniforms – The Air National Guard
If there was still a question in any of the local community's mind as to where we fit into the American landscape, it was dispelled when

a contingent of Air Force volunteers many in uniform driving vehicles with US official insignia on it rumbled up the country roads to Gobind Sadan. Through one of my community boards I had become friends with the base commander, and the Colonel liked what we were doing. He had Gobind Sadan adopted as one of the two community projects that his base undertook that year. More than a dozen men with their equipment helped fix our roads, put in culverts, and lay an irrigation line under the road so the green house and vegetables could get water. It was a wonderful sight of cooperation.

Dick Bose, Bob, Roy, Col. Sahib, Jeff and Editor Sahib would gather Tuesday evenings for Jaap Sahib and then come into the house for a cup of tea or coffee and share their spiritual experiences.

Mauford and the tractor

As we began to establish ourselves, a neighbor stopped by to ask whether he could hay our land. He was a tough old character with a heart of gold. From there, our love affair with Mauford just grew. When we set up the greenhouse, Mauford got equipment for his tractor just so he could help us in the fields. Whenever we needed any help he was always around.

Roy and the greenhouse – Grow your own food

One of the more creative and community building projects revolved around a greenhouse. We had determined that to follow Maharaj ji's example of providing food for the poor, we should not only cultivate it ourselves but also offer opportunities for the poor to grow their own and market it.

Though we spent a weekend dismantling and trucking back an old glass greenhouse a client of mine had donated to us, by the time it reached much of the glass had broken. So we approached and received a grant from the local Community Foundation, with which we bought a new greenhouse and state of the art irrigation supplies. Next Roy found a clearing house that donated seeds to projects such as ours. We then enlisted the help of the local school's horticultural program who germinated the seed for us and gave them back as seedlings. From there our volunteers repotted them and when they were hard enough, planted them in the raised beds carefully made with a brand new tiller that Roy had driven all the way to Troy to bring back.

Once the vegetables were ready we set up Farmer's Markets in the poor communities, and opened an upscale stand in our office park. While we didn't make much money and the weeds often got the best of us, the project captured people's imaginations and to date there are farmer's markets throughout the communities.

You're all our children – Marsha, and the Alternative to Incarceration kids

One group which benefited greatly from the atmosphere of Gobind Sadan were inner city kids who had at a young age already been in trouble with the law. We let them come out for a day of work and some meditation. When the kids arrived you could see the tough looks on their faces, but by the time they were out in the woods or driving the lawn mowers they were laughing and having a good time. It was only when the day ended and they had to go back into their home environments that they put on their tough facades again. We could see that if we ever could develop a residential program there would be many children who would benefit.

Steve and The Unity Connection

"There's a doctor who doesn't believe in death and he's talking all about Indian philosophy. You go see him," the younger agent came into my office stammering in frustration. What to others seemed like a waste of time was Maharaj ji's trademark for a spiritual connection and lifelong friendship. And so it was with Dr. Steve, a local chiropractor who had a great spiritual network. After our initial meeting, where insurance was quickly left for later, Steve invited me to speak about Gobind Sadan at Unity Church where Daniel the pastor was extremely supportive and ultimately invited me back for several more talks.

From Unity came a dedicated group of volunteers and the folks who would gather with Col. Sahib for his spiritual sessions. The work, prayer, and gatherings continued until Sept. 11th changed the script.

208

18

Arson, Forgiveness, and Healing in a Post 9-11 World

September 11th, 2001 instantly redefined how Americans viewed the world. And soon after how the rest of the world would come to view America. The landscape had changed forever. And while the mountains and the prairies and the oceans still stood as a lasting tribute to God's bounty, we the people, had changed. Perhaps forever. And the media's images of the planes crashing into the Towers, the terror it created and the turbaned Bin Laden, were so all pervasive that when CNN erroneously announced the "First arrest" (the picture of the handcuffed young man in a turban pulled off the train in Rhode Island), and sent it around the world almost overnight Sikhs became the target for revenge and the perception went from Alladin to Bin Ladin. But I was rooted in a broader community that needed my support.

MPH and the Poem

The halls were packed with students waiting for their first classes to start. I had just entered the class room when the news spread. "We've been attacked," Liz's face was laced with panic. But somehow, the words sounded false, as if someone was playing a prank. Attack on America was almost an oxymoron. But as the panic spread through the school and the scenes continued on TV there was little doubt it was true.

We gathered the students and tried to keep them calm. But it was difficult. That afternoon trying to make sense of it all, a powerful poem came. As we gathered the students around the flagpole the next morning, Baxter, now openly referring to me as the school Chaplain, beckoned me to share the words:

A Nation Mourns
9-12-01

I mourn the loss of Liberty

Torn from Eagle's mighty grasp

That held secure our boundaries of this our Promised Land.

I mourn the loss of humanity

Dashed in one fell swoop

To watch our Spirit smote by evil billow up in smoke

What hatred minds must harbor, to bring their ships crashing down?

On what milk were they weaned? That love of fellow beings

Never coursed through their veins.

I mourn the loss of innocence – of others' lives and of myself

For in this moment of disaster, I sense my own remorse.

For what I have called security has come at someone else's expense

What I value, has a cost oft paid with others' lives

Now I must face the Nation and the World

And determine what price am I to pay

To restore my Freedom and Liberty if hope is not to fail.

For Hope will always rise above the ashes of despair

A hope borne on a Prayer that carries o'er the world

That out of grief and mourning a new promise will appear

A Promise of God's presence among all peoples

For Goodness and Compassion to prevail

So Peace may Dawn and reign supreme for all eternity.

Let us pray!

Memorial service at Clinton Square

Through my position on the Inter-religious Council, I was invited to speak in Clinton Square at the huge public rally, one of many held around the country to show our support for the country and thank those who had given their lives in New York.

While it was a great privilege and important for me as a Sikh to appear and speak in pubic, I must admit I had some trepidation about wading into an expected crowd of 10,000 or more patriotic Americans with a turban on my head. With Maharaj ji's grace I'd developed a public prayer using Jaap Sahib and ending with a hopeful quote from Maharaj ji's letter to the people of America. I knew it would have a great impact. But I had to get there first. I said my final prayers in Maharaj ji's room before Guru Granth Sahib and took Baba Siri Chand ji's blessings. Then I called a friend and asked him to meet me for dinner at a nearby restaurant, and left the house assured that everything would go well.

The restaurant was packed, but we were able to find a booth quickly. It was right near the door so anyone coming or going or even walking by on the street could see me. There were veterans with caps on, everyone had flags, and the spirits were flowing. We had just gotten our food when an older man with a veterans cap came up to the table,

"I want you to know that if anyone in any way insults you, this is not the America we fought for!"

I was overwhelmed and thanked him profusely. Buoyed by that experience and clear sign from God, I waited my turn patiently and then climbed the ladder to the stage. There in front of me stood over 10,000 people packed wall to wall in the open public square. The TV live trucks were stationed around the perimeter and the broadcast booths were set atop platforms built for the occasion. It was a beautiful sight.

"All I see is light. Let us stay in the light," I began. And the people cheered.

"Tonight as we gather to ask God's blessings to overcome our fear and our grief, let me share a prayer offered some 500 years ago when India was under the torch of invasion: Guru Nanak turned skyward and asked: 'Oh Lord – the world is burning, from whatever door we call to you, please hear our prayer and bring peace.'

Now as we all gather as one community from different traditions, let us pray –

Eternal One whom we know by many names
Be with us now to quench the flames of our fears and grief
With every breath let us Praise You
With every breath – let us drive out the pain of loss
Breathe in Your love
With every breath – drive out the anger
Breathe in Your mercy and forgiveness
With every breath – drive out the hatred and thoughts of revenge
Breathe in Your peace

Let us breathe in God's love together as I pray.

Jaap Sahib
Fount of all virtues, generous and merciful
Infinite is thy glory
Eternal Thy existence, incomparable Thy grace
Self resplendent and ever indestructible
Infinite is Thy might
King of Kings – Sun of all suns
Lord of all angels – incomparable is Thy Glory
Lord of all heavenly kings – Greatest among the great
Poorest among the poor – Annihilator of Death
Beyond physical elements
Ever resplendent with light
Infinite speed beyond any measure
Generous fount of virtues and treasures
Worshipped by sages without fear or desire
Mighty radiance – indivisible and immeasurable
Thy actions spring from Thy Nature
Thy laws from the noblest ideals
Thou adorn and fulfill the universe unbound and unchallenged

God of all creation – Lord of our minds
Fill our minds with so much Love

That your Peace overflows and spreads across the world
So if we are to spill anything let it be peace.

Let me close with a message of hope from the great Seer from
India – His Holiness Baba Virsa Singh ji. Speaking of his vision
Babaji tells us:

> The great solution is to pray to God, to seek God's
> blessings, and to sit down together peacefully. Thus there
> will be peace everywhere. Come together and go forward
> lovingly. I see that people are not uniting, and that is the
> source of the whole conflict. Once people come together,
> everything will improve. Evil-mindedness has always
> developed. Satan always works through human beings. But
> human beings can be blessed, and then Satan flees. When all
> our countries will sit together, God will be there in that
> gathering. People's minds will definitely change and war will
> be averted.'
> And to that let us say - AMEN."

After the prayers, I waded into the crowd to be surrounded
by the sea of people. It was an amazing feeling to be caught up
in a sea of humanity who could have been swept up with hatred,
but instead a prayer service brought them together.

At the airport – Is that you Ralph?

Tegbir, our younger son, had just flown home from Boston, after a
nasty confrontation with an untrained security person. The new recruit
told Tegbir to take off his turban and submit to a check if he wanted
to get on the plane. He let the man know in no uncertain terms that
it was offensive to him and refused. Fortunately, a soldier on duty
calmed the security person and offered Tegbir the option of a pat
down which he accepted. As he passed through security, the soldier
told him how much he respected him for maintaining his values.
Perhaps they were stricter because Boston had been the launching
site of the attack. But I had heard about Sikhs being stopped at
airports around the country and given a hard time, and again being
told to take off their turbans for the search.

213

Now it was my turn. It was the first flight I'd taken since 9-11. I was booked to fly to North Carolina for the wedding of two children I'd known since their childhood. Both the bride's and groom's families were close friends and I really had to go. It was still dark when I reached the airport and I was not sure whether there would be curb-side check in or not. I stopped in the outer circle, got out and peered across the dividers to see whether anyone was on duty. Suddenly a voice rang out, "Is that you Ralph?" I couldn't believe it. Now I travel frequently out of the Syracuse airport and Steve, the man on duty had worked with me in the past. But the chances of this happening that morning were so slim, that I knew Maharaj ji was welcoming and guarding me. Here I was worried that the turban might bring unwanted recognition and once again Maharaj ji showed me wherever you do good work, that turban will remain a positive symbol for all.

Fulton Community Memorial Service (9-30-01)

Once again I was invited to participate in a public service, this time in Fulton the small city closest to Gobind Sadan. The local papers had just publicized the local school's adaptation of the Dr. Seuss's poem, 'The Grinch Stole Christmas,' in which the 'turban' was vilified. It was essential to clear this misconception.

"Thank you for welcoming me into this wonderful community. It is an honor and privilege to be with you. For those of you who read the Brinch poem –Let me assure you that this turban is not 'screwed on too tight'," I began.

"This is the turban of a Sikh, one who loves God and all God's creation, and it stands for Truth, Justice and the American Way. To help the poor, the sick, and the elderly, those with disabilities and others we've disenfranchised, feel part of our community. To defend the rights of all people to gather in prayer – publicly or in private according to their own beliefs without fear of persecution."

Then I followed with the prayers from Clinton Square.

Standing among the police and firemen, being accepted as part of the local clergy I felt secure. Little did I know that my talk and all our community building efforts had not reached everyone. The fear and the fires of hatred that raged beneath the surface were about to burst forth.

Arson and the Triumph over Evil

Guru Granth Sahib Survives Untouched by Flame or Water

I was awakened at 2 a.m. on the morning of November 18th, by a call. "Someone has set fire to Gobind Sadan!" It was Gurbachan Singh. We arrived on the scene to see our blood, sweat, and tears up in smoke. While the hundred-year-old, wood-framed farm house which served as our Gurdwara was gutted, Guru Granth Sahib, the Holy Scripture, didn't burn. To us this was a miracle and a great sign of hope that the message of love for all people, respect and reverence for all those who bring God's message triumphed over evil – That the Power of God's Light does indeed overcome darkness. A Methodist minister friend brought her 12 year-old daughter to offer support. As the mother pointed to the charred remains of the building and she explained that the scripture had survived, the girl's response: "Mommy that must mean that God is really present here." If only we could see God's presence in each other's places of worship the conflict we experience could be overcome.

Forgiveness – gateway to healing - As we gathered around the charred remains of the building, Jean Polly one of our members, suggested we offer a prayer of forgiveness before we leave that day. So we prayed that the ignorance that led to this senseless act be taken away. That immediately cleared the air. The smoke-filled atmosphere of hatred lifted. We had risen above the ashes. Now it was time to help unite the community.

The media soon arrived. The microphone was stuck in my face and the reporter asked as if to question why we'd chosen this spot in the first place, "Are you going to rebuild?"

Maharaj ji had me say: "This provides us with an opportunity to rebuild the broader community based on love and understanding so the ignorance and hatred that led to this senseless act can be taken away and when that happens the building will automatically be rebuilt." These words were carried around the world. I received a card from

Roy Drake from Singapore where he was conducting a retreat and Diana Eck read about it on a trip home to Bozeman, Montana and used it as the basis of her Sunday sermon at Harvard on her return.

The story continued to be covered extensively locally and made national and international news. And soon 4 youths, aged 17-20, were arrested and charged with arson. They had associated our turbans with the media's image of the terrorists, thinking that our name Gobind Sadan was Go Bin Ladan.

Maharaj ji had blessed a very powerful statement which I had the privilege of reading first at the press conference following the arrests:

"We have offered a prayer of forgiveness that the ignorance or hatred that lead to this senseless act be taken away. However, there is a distinction between forgiving a person and forgiving the act they committed. There is no doubt that the act was terribly wrong – no matter what the motivation. Laws exist to hold people accountable for their actions – and we will not interfere in the process of law.

Yet we know God is all forgiving to those who seek His forgiveness. And the Sikh tradition like all others calls on us to forgive others (forgive us our trespasses as we forgive those who trespass against us) so they may seek forgiveness from God, and learn not to commit acts of violence or hatred again.

For if we show hatred to those who act against us then how will they ever understand that God whom they can't see is forgiving. And out of our hatred we will only perpetuate the cycle of violence that exists in the world.

By forgiving our enemies we have the opportunity to create peace."

The 20 some odd hard core law enforcement personnel – from the D.A. to the U.S. Attorney's office – the State and local Fire investigators – the Sheriff's office – FBI and ATF – literally applauded.

But for me one of the most emotional moments of my life, was to cross the bar at each of the court hearings, stand face to face with these children, ask the court for mercy and read this powerful statement.

While the boys were still serving their three and four year sentences they corresponded with us:

216

Josh wrote – 'I wish I would have learned or known a little more about your religion and your beliefs before I decided to get a little tipsy and take part – I would have done things differently.'

Billy, "As hard as it is for me to stay focused I do believe that good will come out of this. With the kindness your community has shown, to Cassie and Jayden, has reassured me that we are all brothers and sisters of God's family."

Shortly after the arson, I was approached by Richard Breyer, Professor of T.V. and Film at the Newhouse School at S.U., to make a movie about the arson and the impact on our community and the community at large. It was entitled, "North of 49", after the state route which to Dick's colleague David, who helped with the script and filming, was the line of demarcation between the more educated and the rural America from which the seeds of arson had arisen.

A year later the film was completed and I was asked by Diana Eck to share our story with the Interfaculty Working Group at Harvard on Immigration, Religious Pluralism, and American Civil Society.

I needed a title appropriate for a Harvard presentation. Maharaj ji in his greatness gave me one.

19

Towards a Theology
of Community

My Harvard Talk – 29 October, 2003

A Story of Intentional community building
Educating a Civil Society: Nurturing a socially conscious/
responsible citizen of the State of Virtue
Behind our actions, everyone's actions for that matter, is a view of
the world shaped by our values (innate or learned) that I'd like to call
a 'theology'. How we respond to each other and our environment is
determined by our view of God or whatever belief system drives
us. And it is the collision between these 'theologies' which is at the
heart of most of the conflict we see in the world today – from
interpersonal relationships to international conflict. Whether we chose
to recognize this problem and how we chose to resolve these
differences may well determine the future course of civilization –
whether we continue in the downward spiral of endless conflict or
take the higher road to world peace.

But just as the act of arson was intentional and based on certain
assumptions, because of our appearance we posed a threat that
must be driven out of 'their' community, so too our response of
forgiveness was equally based on our understanding that everyone is
part of 'our' community. Both are based on 'theologies' one exclusive
and the other inclusive. We were both products of our education.
We all learn who is part of our community, and which elements we
need to purge ourselves of, in one way or another. To some the
message of love and compassion for all people which is at the root
of all our traditions is suddenly twisted to mean loyalty to a political
cause or ethnic group, and hatred for all those who are different.

While in the Sikh tradition, Guru Nanak whose birthday we celebrate next month, declared: "Everyone is part of my community – I see no one as an outsider." And in Gobind Sadan, to break down the barriers to peace, Babaji teaches us through meditation and prayer to purge ourselves of hate so we can overcome our differences, has us celebrate each other's holidays to learn reverence for all those who bring God's message, and work to alleviate poverty as a source of conflict.

Specials Moments and Lessons

Both from a scriptural and historical perspective we can observe the art of community building. From its opening word of "1 God" to its revelations of not just the Sikh Gurus but of saints born in Muslim or low caste homes who saw God beyond the confines of their parochial religions, Guru Granth Sahib sets the tone for openness.

One of the Key messages - *'Don't criticize any Scripture as false: the Vedas, Bible, Torah, Koran, are all true – false are those who misinterpret their message.'* Throughout his life, Guru Nanak traveled on foot to Baghdad and Mecca – through Tibet to the southern regions of Russia – to the East and the South – carrying a message of one God to a strife torn world. His first institution was a community kitchen where all who sought his blessings must sit and eat together breaking both caste and religious barriers.

Guru Gobind Singh restates the message: *"Recognize all people as one human race - (that in God's eyes) - the Prayers of the Hindu and Muslim were the same – to see the Masjid and Mandir as the same."*

Sing the praises of the 'ever-greater God' – the Formless Eternal One who is beyond any worldly boundaries and cannot even be claimed as the possession of any religion. To those who claimed Truth as their own, he responded: *"The Truth is that only through Love can one reach God."* Love was the only unifying factor necessary – love of God and love of all Creation.

The Sikhs changed the face of the continent – sealing off India from what some like to call the 'Afghan terrorist' threat of the time, and encouraging those who fought against them to settle and live peacefully. Prior to partition Hindus, Muslims and Sikhs commonly worshipped together at Gurdwaras. One could view the entire Sikh history as a story of community building in a world divided by religious ethnic and class conflict.

Gobind Sadan and the Sikh tradition

To me this vision is alive today because of the landmark work of His Holiness Baba Virsa Singh, the great modern seer, who is fast becoming recognized as one of the world's greatest leaders and who has created a living model of community. Gobind Sadan translates as God's House without Walls, and Babaji continues his work breaking down the barriers to peace. For newcomers to Gobind Sadan it's often astounding to find a life-size image of Jesus standing in a pristine garden in what one thinks of as a 'Sikh' community. Every night as the sun sets, 125 candles are lit and the Lord's Prayer is recited in as many languages as those represented there and usually there is not a Christian in the group.

I remember showing Jesus's place to a Minister friend who was visiting for the first time. After we paid our respects we were standing reflecting on the experiences when 3 Sikhs, obviously villagers from the way they were dressed, approached Jesus with hands folded and bowed reverently before Him. The minister was amazed. I suggested he ask the men why they as Sikhs would bow before Jesus. Their reply – and this is from 'uneducated farmers' – "Because our Guru loves Jesus and we do too. He teaches us to see Jesus with the same love as we do Guru Gobind Singh." This is what some have called 'practical religion'.

A large Menorah stands nearby, (soon to become the Sch'ma place) its Candles illuminating the darkness. Behind Jesus's place a Mosque has been lovingly constructed by community members and the hauntingly beautiful verses of the Holy Qu'ran waft through the air. One of Gobind Sadan's gardeners, a deeply spiritual person, serves as Imam, lovingly sharing stories and teachings from the life of the Prophet to the enthrallment of all present.

Prayer continues 24 hours a day at the sacred fires which have been burning continuously for over 30 years. Paths are lined with Mandirs to Lord Krishna, Durga Mata, Lord Shiv ji and Hanumanji. And throughout the time, in the main compound, reading of Guru Granth Sahib goes on day and night.

These places of worship are not to make guests of varying backgrounds feel welcome – but rather for all of us to stretch our understanding of God. This is not some synchretic approach to religion or attempt to dilute the richness of particular practices – but rather a celebration and lesson in appreciation of the fullness of God within each of His Magnificent Paths.

This is the Sikh tradition – a spiritual path that not only honors all sacred paths but through which, one learns to find God in each, and to enter Gobind Sadan is to experience the Sikh tradition at its best – experience the presence of God to learn reverence and to grow in your personal faith drawing ever closer to that which is God in your life.

This is how reverence is taught and community is built and this is the foundation on which G.S.USA was started 15 years ago.

Building Bridges – Classes and Groups to India

In addition to my regular class, the school asked if I would teach an adult-ed version. At the end of the first session the class greeted me with: "We want to take a field-trip. I thought they were talking about local places of worship. Instead they floored me with: "India! we want to visit India with you next time you go." So that was the beginning of our 'private tours' Since then we take anywhere from a half-dozen to a dozen people with us on our trips in September and February. We stay in Gobind Sadan, participate in the prayer life – visit the farm and take some side trips to the Taj or Jaipur and forays into Delhi. Last year we took a diverse group of youth and adults to participate in a seminar and spent time with the Director and staff of the NCERT – understanding the new "faith based" curriculum and the politics it raised. Each time our friends have come away with a new understanding of the world and possibilities for overcoming our problems.

We shared pulpits at churches and spoke at community gatherings in the surrounding community. Following 9-11, I spoke at several major memorial services – both televised, wrote editorials, and we even held an interfaith service at G.S.USA called 'Preparing for Peace'. But it was none of that audiences who set the fire. They rallied around us.

Community response

Area churches have volunteered to help us raise money and rebuild. Manlius Pebble Hill, a local private day school raised $1100 in a "dress-down" day. A local Catholic parish raised $800 at a pancake breakfast: Why? Because they know that Gobind Sadan stands for the love of all.

We began to reach out to the schools. We got such a positive response that every school in the county wanted to participate as they all recognized that they lacked diversity and they needed to find a way to supplement their curriculum. It was determined that Mexico – the school closest to Gobind Sadan, USA, and where two of the culprits were enrolled should have the first chance. When we met with the superintendent – the school board president joined the meeting. Not only were they excited about the proposal but saw this as an opportunity to allow the community to heal from the wound of the tragedy. So committed was the board president, Mark Lichtenstein, that he accepted our invitation to visit India with me and share the concern of his community and become an ambassador between Mexico, New York and Gobind Sadan. He was warmly received and deeply touched, and returned to begin paving the way for the exchange program with a commitment that his students and community would help rebuild G.S.USA.

Using the media to build community

Our son Chetan who was then in school for TV communications said, "Dad do you realize how big a story this is? This is the first instance of arson against a Sikh house of worship in the country." He used his contacts and called all the local stations. When they showed up asking whether we felt this was a hate crime; we tried to keep them focused on the positive aspects of the story, what it meant to us and what opportunities it provided. We knew that 'hate crime' would be a constant refrain anyway. We wanted the media to carry our message, and not for us to simply become grist for their mill.

Thankfully we received and continue to receive excellent coverage on all aspects of the story. BBC called and did a piece, then Maryknoll

Radio – Voices of Our World did a feature on forgiveness. Whenever we have an event, local TV and press give extensive coverage. We are covered on the Web by Beliefnet and the UPI wire.

But if Forgiveness opened the door – the film took us through, and has become a major medium in spreading the message. The film and filmmakers actually became an extension of our message, both in the actual filming and also reaching out to areas of the community that we ourselves had not penetrated and at the showings.

Before they went public, Dick and David invited all of us who were in the film to the university to view it. Most of us had never met, let alone all been in the same room together. It was an overwhelming success. And it was followed by a pizza party where we all just got closer – ending up with kids sitting on my knee or gathered around sharing stories. It was a wonderful experience.

Here is one student's impression: "Beyond the technical stuff, the film touched me and I came away admiring the Sikhs and feeling uplifted that the young girl was able to learn and grow from this awful experience. When the lights went up in the back, one of the men from the temple was holding the baby of the arsonist who burned his church – wow! What a sweet moment! That small gesture pretty much summed up the whole film – forgiveness, acceptance, unconditional love. Bravo!"

We've been featured on 3 local TV programs – and have had 3 local showings (4th will be at the Maxwell School at SU) – one in a community theatre, one at the Mexico High School, and one at the local art museum sponsored by the Cultural Resource Council. In each case over 100 people showed up on short notice and stayed to dialogue with us for up to an hour after.

It was shown to the U.S. Department of Justice division of religious discrimination and because of Joginder's treatment that week, I had to be tele-conferenced in for the Q & A.

It is starting and will be shown in schools and we hope to have an interactive forum on the site where people can post how they are using it and their questions. The film-makers and myself will be available for speaking.

223

Rebuilding – an ongoing story

For many years those of us who have met Maharaj ji here or in India would gather in small groups. We are people from many backgrounds and religions. Many clergy come to share prayer and stories on spiritual themes or just share spiritual experiences. One person said: "Gobind Sadan is the one place where we can come and just talk about our relationship with God without being judged." Similar gatherings occur in the NY area and in Canada and I'm sure wherever people are together. And the extended community continues to gather every month at Gobind Sadan for weekends when Guru Granth Sahib is read (the same scripture that survived the fire).

Last year we had a 'Gathering around the Light' to commemorate Nov 18th. Once again we wanted to focus on the Light and not the darkness of the arson. Some 100 people braved an ice storm to join us but the highlight was clearly having Cassie, one of the kids who the year before had set fire to the place, and her new born son came with her family to be with us. When I saw them step through the door it was just an amazing feeling. You can see the picture in the article in your packets and if you come tonight at the close of the film. It's worth the price of admission.

The new building has created more opportunities for people to come together. The logistics of getting volunteers on the same schedule as the construction hasn't always worked, and it's not like a single Habitat project where the volunteers are already together and trained. We've had kids from a church group one weekend and a few local people the next; but all in all it's an amazingly rewarding experience for everyone who has come and once again the media has done an excellent job with coverage.

This year we hope to celebrate our anniversary in the new building. Though it's not fully completed it will be done enough to serve as a symbol of this rebirth – the phoenix rising from the ashes. That means it will be enclosed, insulated, and heated.

It was burned out of fear that we were not American. It will be rebuilt out of the understanding that this turban stands for Truth, Justice, and what some might call the American way to help those in need – the poor-sick-the elderly and those who have been disenfranchised feel part of our society again. To stand for everyone's rights, to pray privately or in public according to their own beliefs without fear of persecution.

Other Gatherings – Local showings
Charlie McDougal, a local dairy farmer who is featured in the film has a daily ritual. Every evening regardless of the season, he lights a fire under his favorite tree, lights his pipe and sits in his rocker that was his mother's favorite and invites anyone near to a good conversation. Since the film came out, he's hooked up his VCR and brought 4H kids and an assortment of neighbors to see it as he himself narrates the story.

New Beginnings
The impact of this story is just beginning. I am confident that the rebuilding of Gobind Sadan, USA will create an example of community and religious harmony for the country and the world to emulate. As one local man, someone we might have mistakenly branded a redneck said at the end of one of our talks to a district of United Methodist congregations, "We are pioneers, we're going to show the rest of the country how to live together in peace the way God wants it."

And if we can all reach out and embrace each other and realize that it is indeed the same light of love in all of us no matter how it is expressed then we really can overcome the hatred that we see everywhere, and I'm confident that no matter how dark the world may seem it is just a backdrop for the Light to play upon and we are not far from seeing in our lifetimes that peace which has long been promised. That evening we showed the film and took questions about our future and the future of America.

The arson was a defining moment – Guru Granth Sahib triumphed and its power manifest, our position and Maharaj ji's statement of forgiveness helped galvanize a divided community, and the rebuilding efforts provided opportunities to involve the broader community.

Once again the question remained, were the volunteers helping Sikhs rebuild their place, or were people coming together to realize the potential of Gobind Sadan as a place where different communities come to work and pray together.

This question was never totally clear and the line effected both the Sikhs themselves and the volunteers.

The answer came once the 'temple' was rebuilt. The focus necessarily being the temple – a Sikh temple – further defined Gobind Sadan as a place for Sikhs. While this was not intentional, it took more than all our resources, and more than all our time just to rebuild the temple. The ability to develop 'Jesus's Place' and other places of worship as we have in India are still just marks on the site plan.

I have full faith that once the image of Jesus and the Mosque are standing, as is Maharaj ji's order, the whole nature of G.S.USA will be transformed. The power of *havan* and Guru Granth Sahib will take on new meaning, as not just for Sikhs but for all people. And the healing will spread as it was written in the original order (excerpts):

> *"If you do havan 24 hours a day, any person coming into that area will be healed. The spiritual power will be very powerful in that area of Gobind Sadan. The Power of the Holy Spirit, the Father's power, and Guru Gobind Singh's power will be very strong and clear. The light of love from recitation of Jaap Sahib and the havan.*

> *This letter is not just for one time. This message is forever. What is the eternal rule for this place:*

> *Love God – see God in the flowers, the trees, the animals, the earth and seas.*

> *Know God's Light also exists in places that you can't see.*

> *See God's Light in yourself and see it throughout creation.*

> *Make no distinctions between an enemy or a friend. See all as one.*

> *This is the mission of Gobind Sadan.*

> *Whatever is written here should be practiced from this day forth. Don't consider it theory. This letter is a blessing for you all. If you follow it, you will feel the presence of God. Then God will make the commitment to look after all the problems."*

In the mean time we continue to pray and work and serve.

Lessons in Forgiveness

Forgiveness is not holding a person in a particular time. If we don't forgive, we freeze them in the moment that they hurt us, physically or emotionally, and what's more important is that we ourselves or a part of our selves will be frozen there as well. Forgiving loosens their grip on us and allows both 'them and us' to move forward. In fact, the moment the event was over they have already moved on. But we may not. We say 'don't dwell on your problems'. We end up dwelling in the moment of pain.

Neither of us are the same people. We are two particles colliding in space. We may carry the scars of the collision with us or let them go. If and when we meet again we may be able to interact in a totally different way. If we are in close orbit we will definitely meet. It is best to let the pain drop. Otherwise, our speed will be forever diminished. While the other who hurt us may have long forgotten the act or even not have been conscious of it to begin with.

If a friend or colleague or spouse offended me and I don't forgive them, the grudge will weigh me down. Each time we meet the resentment will carry forward to undermine any new project we can do together. With forgiveness transformation can occur and we both move closer to God.

Apologies aid in the process. But even if they are not forthcoming we should forgive. People ask, "What if they are not repentant?" I would reply, "To us or to God?"

For us, the lines of the Lord's prayer is like a conditional phrase: "Forgive us our trespasses as we forgive those who trespass against us," reads more like: "If you don't forgive others, God will not forgive you," or spoken more softly, "How can you expect God to forgive you, if you don't forgive others?"

Being at one with God, not having anything stand in the way of your relationship with God is the single most important goal in life, both in our personal and spiritual growth.

Maharaj ji teaches us that even hurting another's feelings is a sin. How tender God's heart is that He 'feels' every action. I sometimes am ashamed to think, that God is sitting right on the other side of the curtain. There is a real confessional in our minds. Every thought, let alone every statement be it a blessing or a curse, and every action parades before God like a movie on a screen. Maharaj ji sums up God's presence so beautifully, "God is sitting inside you. He is closer than your hands and feet."

Those who are ignorant of God's presence may perhaps be judged less severely. Hence Jesus's powerful act to ask forgiveness for those who crucified Him, "Father forgive them for they know not what they do."

Yet we who claim to have some knowledge of things spiritual, continue to defile that screen with our anger, lust, and greed. How can we be forgiven, if we are not willing to forgive others? Thus as Maharaj ji repeats again and again, "The Guru's say, first look within yourself. Don't you have the same weaknesses? How can you be angry with someone else when you haven't controlled those weaknesses yourself. First, get control of your self."

As Jesus said, in confronting the angry crowd prepared to stone a woman to death, "let he among you who has not sinned throw the first stone." And all the stones dropped. Let us all drop our stones. Forgiveness becomes the path to salvation. The one way we can atone and be at one with God.

So when we forgave those children it raised us above the general public. It distinguished us. Here were people who actually stood for what they believed in. To this day people who see our turbans say, "You are the people whose Holy Book didn't burn, or you are the ones who forgave those kids."

A Catholic friend of mine summed up his feelings over lunch shortly thereafter. "Ralph," he said, looking me straight in the eyes, "You did a very Christian thing forgiving those kids. Truth be known, we probably would have killed them."

228

20

Baba Siri Chand ji Comes
to Elbridge

As Joginder tells the story, she and Chetan were meditating in the living room. When she opened her eyes, Chetan was looking around very concerned. When she asked him what had happened, he replied, "Mommy, I saw Baba Siri Chand ji walking in our backyard."

While wondrous for him to appear to Chetan, we were not surprised. We had felt this force always present in our home. Joginder had prepared a beautiful *gaddi* in our prayer room and the children always paid their respects. As a matter of fact, after Tegbir was born and came home from the hospital we laid him at Baba Siri Chand ji's feet.

During Maharaj ji's first visit, Joginder had made a chicken sandwich for Nirlep Kaur. She could only finish half and told Joginder to give the other half to me. Dutifully Joginder first asked Maharaj ji. He looked directly at me and smiled: "If you eat this chicken sandwich Baba Siri Chand ji will leave. The kids can eat it, but not Ralph."

I was at the opening of a local Home Depot, a huge hardware and builders supply store covering an acre or more. At the entrance was an unusual sight. Dozens of animals, some life-size eagles and bears stood carved out of wood. In the middle with chainsaw buzzing was a small man, head phones and goggles concealing his face, cutting away at a tree the way a wood carver would whittle a stick with a pen knife.

It was amazing to watch the figures appear out of tree trunks within minutes. Dennis it turned out was a chainsaw champion of North America and on hand for entertainment at the store opening. During a break in the action, it occurred to me to ask whether he could carve people and he directed me to his display book where he proudly exhibited photos of life-size Native Americans on horseback. "Yup, I can do people." I thanked him and tucked his number away.

I could see the pieces coming together. We were to build a shrine to Baba Siri Chand ji in our backyard. Before my trip to India in 1999 for Maharaj ji's birthday we had asked and received approval from Maharaj ji. And I took several pictures of Baba Siri Chand ji with me for Maharaj ji's approval. Maharaj ji was sitting in his downstairs home on his couch and carefully studied each picture. Closing his eyes briefly He chose the classic of Babaji sitting beneath a large tree with falls in the background. "He stands over 6 feet tall," Maharaj ji emphasized, "and has a very strong body." I asked Maharaj ji whether Dennis was the right person and He blessed him saying Baba Siri Chand himself will guide him, and have Dennis make him the way he wants it to be made.

On my return I mailed the photo to Dennis, as he lived over 200 miles away, in the PA hills and our discussion began.

The spring of 1999, we drove down and Dennis took us out in his field to show us the large section of the tree he had selected. It grew near water and could withstand cold temperatures without cracking. These days it was rare in the U.S. He shared that he had been keeping it for a special order, and when he had seen Baba Siri Chand ji, he felt this was just what he had been waiting for. He felt from the photo, the grain would also favor Babaji's likeness. We gave him a deposit and left totally satisfied.

Meanwhile, we had forgotten to ask Maharaj ji where Baba Siri Chand ji would like to stay. We thought we can't leave him outside and we can't put him in the barn. We wanted to see him and have people visit him, but couldn't decide what was best. While we were arguing over the correct place, we called Maharaj ji.

He knew why we had called and without our even asking his response was direct, "Baba Siri Chand is not for display. He likes his privacy. Make him a special place behind your barn under the big tree."

So while Dennis was carving Baba Siri Chand ji's image we found Bob and Tim to build a pond complete with falls and a beautiful shrine. They staggered 20 foot slabs of slate on top of each other to form the steps and platform on which Baba Siri Chand ji would sit and constructed a strong cedar shake roof which was hoisted onto supports by crane to complete the shrine. (We later enclosed it and added a wood stove for the *havan*)

We drove down once to check on his progress and took some flowers. When we arrived Dennis was still in the house, but we could feel Baba Siri Chand ji calling us. As we opened the barn door where Dennis had been working we were swallowed up by this huge spirit and there sat Baba Siri Chand with a broad smile. Dennis had done an amazing job.

By that time Dennis had joined us, "I had my brother-in-law who's 6'2" sit cross-legged so I could get the sense of how big to make him. How does he look?" He looked wonderful. Dennis proceeded to show us the stain and finish he would use. We visited for a while and then proceeded home.

Towards summer Dennis called saying Baba Siri Chand ji was ready to come home: "He wants to go home, the flowers are dying, and he wants to get out in the fresh air. He doesn't like being cooped up in the barn any more."

We still had a few weeks to go on the shrine, but hurried things along. Finally on Thursday June 10th (the date is still emblazoned in Scott Shaw's mind) everything was ready. We rented the biggest van we could find, but were still concerned who would help us bring him back. I felt very strongly that Maharaj ji would send help, and Joginder and I left with Tegbir as Chetan was still in college. Halfway there, as we crossed Binghamton onto 81 south into Pennsylvania, I noticed a Chevy Suburban full of kids. "It's the Shaws!" We couldn't communicate too well at 65 miles per hour, so we had Tegbir hold a paper with our cell number to the window and within seconds Jeff was on the phone. "Hi Buddy — this is amazing. Let's stop at the next rest stop." They were taking Scotty to the national track meet and couldn't believe we were there. I asked if they were up for a "mission" on the way to the meet. I explained we needed help loading Baba Siri Chand ji and they were excited to gain the blessings. They happily followed us 2 hours out of their way.

231

On arrival, we again paid our respects to Baba Siri Chand ji. Joginder took out the Chauri Sahib she had brought and placed the bananas for ardas. With a wonderful light moving through the space, Baba Siri Chand ji just radiated his blessings.

We asked Dennis whether he had something to cushion the rider. Without another word, he went in the house and emerged with large swath of new red carpet. "I had the house re-carpeted several years ago and this has been lying there just for this occasion."

We laid the red carpet in the van, then the men lifted the 200 plus pound carving and set him on his carpet.

Joginder and Tegbir took turns doing Chauri Sahib and we all recited Dhan Dhan Baba Siri Chand Sahib all the way home.

By the time we reached Elbridge, the sun was starting to set but the pond team was waiting patiently. We drove the van across the backyard behind the falls as close as we could get to the site. Then the men helped us lift him to his place on the top stone. As dusk fell, the light from Baba Siri Chand ji still filled the area with a warm glow. He was home. The water gurgled happily from the falls into the pond and Tegbir just wanted to sit with Babaji. We all found a favorite rock and enjoyed the scene late into the night. It was a moment to savor and to share.

Many have seen him and many serve him
As part of my Exploring Spirituality course at Manlius Pebble Hill, I would take the class on a 'field-trip' to various places of worship around the Syracuse area (as the class was predominantly Christian they wanted to visit places they were less familiar with and could squeeze into the half-day allotted to them). In addition to the Synagogue, the Mosque, and the Zen Buddhist center, we would always come out to the house for snacks to show them how we actually lived in an interfaith environment. One of the highlights was always 'meeting' Baba Siri Chand ji.

It was always surprising to see which one of the students was most impacted by the visits. On this particular trip there were about a dozen kids and Paul was brining up the rear. I enjoyed Paul but no one could honestly say that he was especially focused on the class, and while he took part in the discussions, anyone observing the group would say that there were others more 'spiritually' inclined and more active participants.

Paul was chatting with friends as we walked down the stairs to the shrine. We were still a good 15 yards away, when about halfway down the steps, he looked up and almost shouted, "Who's that?" He had seen Baba Siri Chand ji. His eyes were riveted on the shrine as he covered the rest of the ground. The first group of kids had already entered the shrine and paid their respects. The closer he came the more confused he got. There was no doubt in his mind that he had seen a 'real person'. But now on entering the shrine, and coming face to face with what his friends were telling him was a wooden carving he couldn't figure out what to think.

When we called Maharaj ji to share the news, he just laughed: "What do you expect. He's really there."

Joginder's dreams

Joginder hadn't gone out to the shrine because of the snow for a long time. In her dream Maharaj ji was with us at our home, and was about to come to see Baba Siri Chand ji. He told her to go ahead and start the *havan*. When she went there, she didn't see him at first. Then he appeared lying down on the stone moving his legs. "I'm hungry and tired of just sitting here." When she called Maharaj ji, he said it was very good that Baba Siri Chand ji was asking for food. "Feed him twice a day."

And so the privilege of feeding Baba Siri Chand ji began. Summer or Winter, rain or snow. We and a dedicated group of those who had been to Gobind Sadan or come to love Babaji would come out with their offerings spend time in prayer, sometimes noting their experiences of joy and love.

All year long, the wood was split, the fire stoked, the stove maintained and the shrine cleaned or decorated as the spirit moved everyone. They'd add Christmas decorations, a Buddha, an image of Mother Mary who needed shelter, and of course seasonal flowers and plants. It was more than a labor of love and they all have their stories. Some of which they'd share in our gatherings.

21

The Family Gatherings

Marylee called it a gathering. Those souls who had always been united, coming together to share in their love of God. Two ministers, several Catholics, and a sprinkling of others sitting reading Jaap Sahib, verse by verse, (a practice started by Sue) all bound together through Maharaj ji's blessings and their desire to serve Baba Siri Chand ji. As we went around the circle, our spirits bonded, soaring higher with each line. Until the room was so full of love, that it literally got up and hugged you.

There was Jean the internet-famous librarian, Larry, her husband the tech genius, Bud and Donna, old friends from MassMutual, Judy, the Methodist Minister, Jeff the insurance corporate executive, Robert the electrical contractor, Sue the teacher, Sara the pediatrician, her husband Bob the attorney, Joe, private school educator, Dick, the filmmaker, and of course Marylee. How Maharaj ji wove us together is much of the early story of Gobind Sadan in the United States.

Jeff: I couldn't leave

Jeff had just joined my office a few months before Maharaj ji arrived in 1986. I can't say that we had ever engaged in anything more than a passing hello, until I hung the notice in some prominent places around the office inviting staff and colleagues to our home to meet Maharaj ji. When I entered the kitchen, Jeff had just read the notice, and greeted me. "Is this open to anyone. Can I come too. Can I bring anything?"

"Of course."

Joginder was coordinating the food as it was typical for people to bring dishes to pass on such occasions.

On the appointed night Jeff came early and stayed late. Maharaj ji went around the room asking each one present what they believed in and the answers went, "I'm a Catholic, an Episcopalian, a Methodist, a Lutheran." By the end, Maharaj ji simply looked at them and said, "Yes but you all believe in Jesus don't you?"

When it was time for everyone to leave, Jeff just kept hanging around. I had to shoo him out.

Next morning, we got a call. It was Jeff, "Can I come over again? What time?"

And so it went. His young wife Hillary was afraid she was going to lose him. Joginder asked him, "Jeff, why are you coming so often, you can't even understand what Maharaj ji is saying." "It doesn't matter, Jeff replied, "I just want to be in his presence."

He brought Hillary and his children. Maharaj ji lifted Alex and the boys onto his lap and blessed them and told them when they grow up they must come and visit him in India. Alex and Joel have already come.

And he assured Hillary that the love that Jeff feels will help him be a better husband and father and be able to share it with all he meets.

From that time, Jeff kept *Nam* with him and even had it tattooed on his arm (in Gurmukhi). He would rise early morning and call his friends 'Nam-buddies' who would meditate with him or come to Gobind Sadan.

Maharaj ji accepted his invitation to visit their home and blessed them greatly. But Jeff's faith and devotion and commitment were something to be marveled at.

Maharaj ji on one of their visits told them that God was going to bless them with another child. They looked at each other. Hillary laughed nervously. They already were raising 5 children. "No thanks," she said. But Maharaj ji said, "This is a gift that God wants to give you." And so it was.

Several months later she was pregnant but the amniocentesis brought some bad news. "This child won't be normal," the doctor told them. "It will be retarded. You have the right to abort the child."

Jeff without even thinking, replied, "This child is God's gift to us and however she comes into the world is fine."

We told Maharaj ji the story. He was so happy with them that in fact the child was born with no problems at all and out of gratitude they named her Angela (God's angel) Mara (*mehar* for blessings). And what a blessing she is.

People often spoke of the messages that Baba Siri Chand ji would give them, but sitting with Baba Siri Chand ji, Jeff took enough notes to finish a few novels. Someday he will publish them.

Bob: God is spoken here

Bob was a successful electrical contractor who I was working with, and as it turned out, one perfect example of how what seemed primarily a business relationship actually was a very deep spiritual connection. While I enjoyed his company and humor our conversations seldom extended beyond business.

That all changed, once Maharaj ji came. It turned out that Bob was incredibly tuned in to the spiritual world and while a committed Catholic, he would take Jaap Sahib to church and read it while waiting for Mass to begin.

He has stayed with me every step of the way. During meditation classes at the YMCA, a brief experiment that had its own place, deep in plaster dust, remodeling the farmhouse to create a nicer space for Maharaj ji, at our weekly IHOP breakfasts, Bob was and still is one of my closest and strongest pillars of support – a friend not just to me, but for those he cares about.

But one day as we sat in the parking lot after breakfast, Maharaj ji said clearly, "Link him directly to me." I understood, now to find the right words. "Bob, we are great friends but I have weaknesses. You are linked directly to Babaji and don't ever forget it." He understood and as a result, our relationship has only grown stronger.

It was Bob's phrase, "God is spoken here," that defined Gobind Sadan. He stays out of the limelight, away from programs unless forced. And feels deeply that the spiritual experience is ENOUGH of a contribution for Gobind Sadan to make. And he is probably right.

Baba Siri Chand ji and the Grotto of Lourdes

Bob is one to search out places of pilgrimage wherever he travels. Rather he is always drawn to them.

On a trip to Gobind Sadan with his mother Edith, and sister Roe, both of whom are also extremely spiritual, he had planned to return through France to stop at Lourdes.

While sitting at Baba Siri Chand ji's shrine, he looked up and saw the Holy Mother standing there. "So you're coming to see me," she said simply. Bob was more pleased than amazed as he shared the story with me.

But the more amazing part came at Lourdes itself. As he entered the grotto and looked up at the wall above the pool, there was Baba Siri Chand ji sitting, blessing the place. Such are the beautiful ways God reveals his truth to Bob.

Jean and the buzzing book and other 'Babaji moments'

I had never met Jean before. But after the first adult ed class at MPH she came up to me,

"Do you have a website?" she asked. Though Sarvjit Grewal had laid out the early framework we still didn't have our own domain. She continued, "Because I heard a voice a few days ago tell me, 'Bring my people to the internet', and this sounded like the fit."

Known as 'Netmom' to millions around the world, Jean is legend in internet history. A librarian by trade, she is the person credited with the phrase, 'Surfing the internet,' and memorialized on a Trivial Pursuit game card. She and her mother Marylee, an amazing spiritual being in her own right, were two of the gifts that Maharaj ji brought through the class.

When the class came to Gobind Sadan, Babaji blessed a copy of Jaap Sahib for her and they left happily. Shortly thereafter she was sitting at home and decided to pick up the book. It started vibrating in her hands. She couldn't believe it and handed it to Steven, her son. "Do you feel something strange?" she asked. "Yeah," he replied, "the book is vibrating." She called me, "Ralph, the book is buzzing." I tried to figure out what she was talking about. "The Jaap Sahib buzzes," she blurted out.

"Of course it buzzes," I replied. "It's blessed." That was her first Babaji moment. Just like surfing the internet she coined the phrase 'Babaji moments' and whenever something of grace happens in her life, "Oh it's another Babaji moment."

Maharaj ji continues to lift her to higher and higher positions and when she was awarded 'Woman of the Year' in Syracuse, she wanted her picture taken at Baba Siri Chand ji's shrine.

Larry – the technology monk

Jean's husband Larry always reminded me of a monk. From his long sandy blonde hair tied back in a pony tail to his imposing profile I could almost see his habit. But now the icons in his cells both at office and home were on the computer monitors which literally enclosed the rooms. Except of course for Maharaj ji's and Baba Siri Chand ji's pictures which were prominently displayed. By day, Larry runs the website for a major medical school and hospital in Syracuse. By night, and in almost every spare waking minute, he runs Gobind Sadan's website.

Larry's vision:

Maharaj ji said to him, "Build me a temple without walls." And so the website became that place which Larry has dedicated, every spare waking minute, to bring a true reflection of Maharaj ji's message and the beauty of his mission.

Sara – Jesus is alive at Gobind Sadan

Sara Farchione is a local pediatrician from a well-known medical family. She also turned up in the MPH adult education class with her sister Sue.

From healing patients she began to focus more on spiritual healing and spending more time with *Nam* and Jaap Sahib.

When she came before Maharaj ji in Gobind Sadan, she had some concerns about herself and her family. Maharaj ji told her, "Sit before Jesus and He will answer your questions." She was a little reluctant, having wanted Maharaj ji to tell her directly. But following instructions, she went and sat before Jesus and began to pray. Within minutes all her questions were answered and she was beaming. She went back to Syracuse and wrote an

238

article for the Catholic Sun – the regional catholic paper, "Jesus is alive at Gobind Sadan."

Sue – starting the circle
Sue loved reading Jaap Sahib and arrived one evening with the idea to go around the room verse by verse.

She would keep Maharaj ji's photo on her desk and when her children were really stressed out she would look at the picture and they would calm down. Reflecting on what Babaji means to her, she wrote:

"Babaji is the most Enlightened being I know and have had the Blessing to be in his presence. Visiting Babaji has been, IS, and will always be my experience of a lifetime. I connected with Holy Spirit.

When I was at Gobind Sadan and, for the first time, I was in front of Baba Siri Chand ji, I spontaneously thanked Him for being Babaji's teacher. The Love I felt coming into me was overwhelming. At that time, I Knew that Baba Siri Chand ji was with me always and a spiritual teacher of mine, also. He gives me Peace.

Nam is part of my life all the time. Often I am reciting Nam subconsciously before I am even consciously aware that I am.

Babaji is always in my classroom. His picture hung in the class opens chances to share God's Love with my students. They want to know about him. He helps me teach about the importance of Love and a personal relationship with God."

Marylee – I pray with the cardinals
Marylee was spiritually attuned from way back. Whenever we'd ever talk about church she'd just laugh and say, "I pray with the Cardinals." Well that was quite an image. A little old lady came in with a bunch of Cardinals at Mass. But she would heartily protest, "No, I mean the birds in my backyard." A Christian scientist, wonderful poet and story teller, she would make sure the group was full not just of her home baked cookies but of her home spun humor and wisdom.

Bud and Donna – Christmas at GS

Donna was one of 2 white teachers at the Native American school. She spent 20 years working with native children helping them walk the line between maintaining native culture and learning the tools of the world outside the reservation.

Donna was so impacted by her first visit to GS that she had asked Gyani ji when she would return. He told her that she would fly back and it would take Bud some time to get back. And that's how it happened. She was back with Joginder for the Christmas dedication of Jesus and Maharaj ji had her wade through the crowd distributing apples and bread to people as parshad. That was a communion service she will never forget.

She loves to tell the story that they were on the hill preparing for the celebration when out of nowhere camels appeared to add to the authenticity of the nativity.

Never count the candles

Ernest 'Bud' Young had been one of my early mentors at MassMutual, and a finer man would be hard to find. He often quipped after being elected President of the New York State Life Underwriter's Association, the powerful insurance trade organization, that they needed to find someone young and earnest and he fit the job perfectly.

He was warm and genuine from old farming stock with a beautiful professional tenor voice, but we never talked spirituality until one day I received a call that he wanted me to help him as a sounding board for his spiritual journey. I was more than flattered.

Bud joined us on a trip to Gobind Sadan and when he came before Maharaj ji he was just caught up in the glow. Maharaj ji ended his talk, with his now patented statement about aging:

"Birthdays are something to be celebrated, but don't count the candles. Just enjoy the day. Age is nothing for someone who loves God."

The whole room erupted in laughter that even I, while translating, got caught up in. As we exited, Bud turned to me, and said, "Did you tell him?"

"Tell him what."

top: author in meditation class at Baba Siri Chand ji's feet

inlay: Baba Siri Chand ji

bottom: Baba Siri Chand ji's shrine in Elbridge

RALPH SINGH, co-founder of the Gobind Sadan USA temple in Palermo.

Gary Vorla/Staff photographer, Jan. 17

2002: Many Quotes to Note

Marty Webster

top: Gobind Sadan USA.
middle: GS USA on fire –
flames shooting out of room
where Guru Granth Sahib and
Dasam Granth are held –
miraculously they survive
untouched – 18 Nov, 2001

bottom: author quoted in
local paper, *Post Standard*

The healing purple light – Joginder in prayer on the site of Guru Granth Sahib while new Gurdwara was under construction. Purple light descended and enveloped her and healed her breast cancer

MARY PAT FISHER, left, of Connecticut, talks with Bakaha Singh prior to the arrival Saturday of a Sikh spiritual leader on a farm in Palermo. The farm, called Gobind Sadan USA, will help the homeless become self-sufficient.

GARY WALTS/Staff photographer

Spiritual leader dedicates Palermo farm

Mary Pat Fisher before the dedication of Gobind Sadan, USA, 21 Nov. 1992

top: Maharaj ji in 'Green Room' with Dr. G.S. Anand and Surendra Nath discussing translation of Jaap Sahib

inlay: Author with Swaranjit Singh at his home

bottom: Author singing God's praises on veranda

"It's my 70th birthday and I was really concerned whether I would live long enough to fulfill some of my life long dreams."

"Bud, honestly, I didn't even know, so how could I have told Maharaj ji."

Judy – entering through a smoke filled room

Judy was a Methodist minister who coincidentally had taken over Deborah's church in Fulton. A good friend of Donna's she was curious enough to let Donna drag her along to one of our gatherings. This particular night we were in the basement, and had lit a fire for *havan* in the fireplace. Now it might have been the humidity or the temperature or a combination of both, but we couldn't get the chimney to draft properly so the room promptly filled with smoke. For Joginder and me smoke-filled rooms had been the norm at Gobind Sadan but the others naturally found it extremely uncomfortable. To make matters worse for a first timer, Jean had asked that we do Jaap Sahib in Punjabi so they could follow along. Well here's this Methodist minister, who was told about these uplifting sessions of spiritual sharing, finding people chanting in a foreign language while others gagged on the smoke. But much to her credit Judy saw some light through the smoke and continued to come back and joined us on a trip to India.

Whenever she kept Jaap Sahib and Loving God in her church, people would just automatically stop and pick them up and be touched. She told of her friend who was going through a crisis, who she had not communicated anything to about Jaap Sahib, walking by her bookcase and being drawn to Jaap Sahib. As Judy tells the story, "She just picked it up and left. A while later I received a phone call from her, saying she was much more at ease. She had taken that book, as she called it (Jaap Sahib), and gone for a drive, parked on the side of the road and just read it and her mind cleared." It was amazing.

Dick – experiencing it through both lenses

Richard Breyer was known world over as a consummate filmmaker and teacher. He was also known for his love of India. I had heard his name among the Syracuse Indian community as someone I should connect with but I felt all in good time. That good time came when we were at a PARC dinner together following the presentation of a wonderful documentary and Dick and I really connected. We began after 9-11 to think seriously of ways to use film as a means of bridging the gap between kids from different backgrounds when the arson hit. That was it. Dick wanted to do a film highlighting the arson and start some kind of exchange program between kids from rural districts and India. We approached local school boards through an old friend Lou at BOCES, who had worked with Roy and me on the Greenhouse project. He was enthusiastic and carried the offer to his group. We were then invited to meet with the superintendent of Mexico, the district where the kids who torched the place had gone to school. It was their desire to participate and when we offered the opportunity of going to India with us, the President of their board, Mark, jumped right in and was in India with us within 2 weeks. Thus 'North of 49' was born. Making the film helped in the process of bringing segments of the community together, and when we showed it, it spontaneously drew crowds interested not only in the story but becoming part of the healing process.

PATH VII

Translating the Sacred

22

Translating for Maharaj ji

Some of the most wonderful lessons I've learned at Maharaj ji's feet occur when He has called me to translate for Him in major gatherings or more intimate dialogues with those who don't understand Punjabi. While Maharaj ji's subjects include all religions and references to all of God's messengers, I wasn't required to translate for the many Hindu, Sikh and Muslim leaders or Indian audiences who could understand Him.

One professor once said to me, "What's so hard about translating for someone who's uneducated? We train translators all the time for even the most technical subjects. Everyone has a maximum vocabulary of x number of words. Learn those and you're all set." I just laughed. If even the brightest person's vocabulary maxes out at x, Maharaj ji's is x to the nth degree.

Not only is His vocabulary as endless as His vision, He will constantly surprise and delight me, and the gathering, with brand new stories from different traditions. Or just when I think I know what He will say next, He adds a wonderful new twist or uses words that I have never in my 36 years heard. When we say we can never know the mind of God, I can certainly attest to that.

The first time he told one of my favorite stories of Jesus in the boat, the word He used for boat was almost identical to the word for a common type of tree. So without missing a beat, I translated, "One day Jesus was sitting under a tree." Then Maharaj ji continued, "And the 'tree' began to rock in the water." I knew I was in trouble and had to backtrack and correct myself.

Translating a talk from a tape, when one has time to reflect, is a totally different experience. And I have had plenty of experience with that as well. I close my eyes and try to listen to what He is saying. But translating live for Maharaj ji is an entirely different process. Someone once asked me how I interpret for Babaji. I laughed again. "I can't even think when I translate let alone interpret," I replied. And that's the truth.

The only way I can describe it is that I become like a speaker in your sound system. I'm hollow. Until the wire (or wireless receiver) is attached to me and a current transmitted, I sit silently. But, as the current passes through me the sound begins to reverberate and people can hear my voice. Before I speak, I touch Maharaj ji's feet and ask for His blessings. He then turns on the current, starts transmitting the messages, and I start speaking.

Once we were to meet an official in New York on one of Maharaj ji's visits, and Maharaj ji wanted me to be very precise in my translation. As we got in the car, He turned to me and said "Give a lot of thought to your translation." I touched His feet and begged forgiveness. "Please Maharaj ji, if You think I will make many mistakes, then You please bless me so that Your words come out the way You want them." He laughed and blessed me and the meeting went very smoothly.

Mixing languages
Just when we get used to Maharaj ji's Punjabi, He will throw in some English words.

Suffer or Travel
Safir in Punjabi means to travel. So when Maharaj ji told a story from the life of Jesus and used the word suffer, I was stuck the first time trying to pick up whether he was speaking of Jesus suffering for the sins of humanity.

Simple or Sample

Maharaj ji uses both simple and sample. We must make ourselves 'samples,' living examples of the God's simple teachings. In essence, practice what you preach.

Which Jesus?
We were invited to meet a Franciscan friend of mine in His study. While in India, Maharaj ji rarely went to meet anyone saying, "The Raja comes to the darvish, the darvish never goes to the raja." But

246

Maharaj ji as gracious as He is, was willing at first to go to see people in the U.S.

We were ushered into a comfortable ground floor room in Greenwich Village and sat in overstuffed chairs. While the study was simply furnished, the wall before us was dominated by a huge German life-size wooden crucifix. When Elias joined us, Maharaj ji didn't waste much time in pleasantries. He gestured toward to the crucifix and asked: "Tell me which Jesus do you believe in? The one who is nailed on this cross or the One who is born of the Light?"

After Elias gulped, He continued, "Because if you see Jesus as nailed on the cross we don't have much to talk about but if you see Jesus as the Light, let us share our love of Him, for He is the One I love."

Don't they all love Jesus? James Hamilton, Esq. and the lost tape

When Maharaj ji first met with a group of friends at our home, He had asked them what their religion was. They went around the room listing their denominations. At the end Maharaj ji asked, "Yes, but aren't you all Christian?"

So when we met with the then General Secretary of the National Council of Churches, James Hamilton, Maharaj ji asked him point blank, "Don't they all love Jesus?" He laughed politely, "I wish I could put you in front of them," he replied.

I had borrowed what I thought was a better tape recorder from Churchill, but wasn't totally familiar with it. And while I had turned it on during the dialogue apparently I had not released a pause button. The whole historic meeting was lost. Maharaj ji was quite upset, but on the way out, we made sure that we captured the historic photo of Maharaj ji standing before the inscription on the green marble walls:

"There is One Lord, One Faith, One Baptism
One God and Father of us All
Who is Above all and Through all and in All."

Jesus is not a Christian – Church of Unity, Greenwich Village
Pam, an interfaith minister who again was one of our fellow NAIN travelers, invited Babaji to address her church gathering on a Sunday morning in the Village. This was not an ordinary church. The Church of Unity was founded by a Rabbi. It was known as an interfaith church and was the base of a new movement in which people were actually ordained as 'interfaith ministers'.

Sunday morning the Village is dead. People have been up partying the night before and even at 11 a.m. the streets were still empty. We followed the signs to a small building with stairs leading down to the basement. Pam was excitedly waiting at the door. She greeted Maharaj ji and just stood for a minute bathing in His Light before ushering us along the rows of neatly placed seats to where four more comfortable chairs had been aligned next to a small lectern. The altar behind held a large candle and symbols from different faiths. The man who served as 'Minister' opened the service with a prayer and then asked Pam to introduce Maharaj ji. She glowingly described what she knew of Maharaj ji and then turned the program over to me. Maharaj ji had asked me to speak briefly about his mission of working to overcome poverty and religious conflicts and of course healing the mind.

Maharaj ji began, "I want you all to know that Jesus is not a Christian." There was absolute silence. People no doubt might still be sleepy but they just stared trying to process what they had just heard. I knew I had heard the words correctly. It is a very simple sentence that even one not familiar with Punjabi can pick up. "Jesus Christian *nahi hai*" (*nahi hai* meaning 'is not') No room for error. Then Maharaj ji continued, "Moses is not a Jew." Now the crowd caught on. They started to laugh, nervously at first. "The Prophet Mohammed is not a Muslim," then they settled back comfortably and the flow was established. So this theme became etched in all our work. Rise above your borders and boundaries. They are manmade. Approach God with Love.

The Healers
After the service, they couldn't leave Maharaj ji alone. They wanted to know about healing, and told Maharaj ji that many of them were

healers, placing their hands on the affected areas and then they prayed for relief. Dati and Harvinder wanted to test them, but Maharaj ji cautioned them and the healers. "When you heal someone you take on all their bad karma. Are you prepared to do that? Have you cleaned yourselves?"

Then turning to our group, Maharaj ji cautioned, "Be careful, they will pass on all their bad karma to you in the process." The men quickly left their seats and the church.

Serving the Church or the Master

Many clergy friends are locked in a tug of war between serving Jesus or serving the church. It is not comfortable. And Maharaj ji's dialogue with some British Anglican Priests on the subject was one of the most powerful evenings I've had the privilege of translating. We ended up entitling it 'My Jesus':

The Messiah or prophet is not a matter of difficult philosophy. Those who bring God's message have the nature of a child. Therefore to gain their love, you should become children before them. There may be a slight difference between the way I approach things and the way you do, because you have grown up with a particular style of management and have learned things from books, whereas my book is whatever God tells me, I say.

Where that statue of Jesus is standing [Jesus's Place in Gobind Sadan], He came to me. I was just sitting, and all of a sudden He was standing before me. He was standing as you see Him today. He kept speaking with me for a full 45 minutes. He spoke with such force that when He said, "Bless!" it felt that there was no place in the entire universe that His voice did not reach. It felt to me that not only was there no country outside the range of His blessing and His healing, but also no planet, no star, no universe that was out of His range.

It felt that His words had reached the outermost limits of creation, touching each and every part of it. That is when I understood that Jesus is not under any one particular person's or group's influence. He has His own field. If He chose He would turn His healing to the animals, or to the earth, or to the sky. Wherever he chose to do so, He would just turn His gaze and heal all of creation. He had no particular court from which He healed people. Wherever He sat, that healing would occur automatically. That is why I say I didn't perceive that Jesus has any one particular place, or one particular way of blessing things. Wherever He was, wherever He stood, or wherever He sat, those things and that place would automatically be blessed and healed.

Holy words lead to Russia

In 1989, Swaranjit Singh took Maharaj ji to Russia with the help of Stepan who at that time was well-placed in the Government run media. One might well ask how would an Indian Holy man be invited to visit a Communist country? That might take a miracle.

The Miracle Cure

Given Swaranjit's position as Managing Director of one of India's largest manufacturers of tractors, Escorts Ltd., he was constantly receiving trade delegations from all parts of the world including the countries of the former Soviet Union. On one such visit, the talk had turned to spirituality and he ended up bringing the delegates to Gobind Sadan. When the discussion was over, one member asked Maharaj ji whether it was true that God could heal people. Maharaj ji laughed, "Of course!" And so Stepan related the story that his elderly mother had what doctors called an inoperable brain tumor and was not expected to live. Could Maharaj ji heal her? Maharaj ji gave him a small kirpan and Jaap Sahib and told him to put it under his mother's pillow and to go ahead with the operation. The surgery was successful and when his mother woke up, she was beaming. She then said, "All through the operation, there was this handsome man with a beard on a horse, beaming light on me. He saved my life. Who is he? I want to meet him." This of course was Guru Gobind Singh. Stepan was so excited he insisted on inviting Maharaj ji to the Soviet Union. And given some connections he was able to secure an invitation for Swaranjit and Maharaj ji's visit in 1989.

Maharaj ji on Russian Television

One of the highlights of the trip was Maharaj ji's invitation to speak on Soviet Television. As He Himself tells the story, "They began by introducing me and said, 'Babaji there are several million people watching you. What message would you like to give them?' I began speaking very briefly, and the host interrupted me and said please Babaji take your time we are very interested in your answers.

250

"I explained that religion didn't mean sitting idle. That everyone had to work. Jesus and all God's messengers worked themselves. And that the real communism was that of Guru Nanak who worked and shared with everyone. I told them that their symbols were a sickle and a hammer, but Marx never farmed and Lenin never stepped foot in a factory. It was just a theory.

"Then he asked me what I saw for the future of their country. With Perestroyka there was much hope of a new freedom. I looked straight at them and replied, "You may talk of peace, but according to my vision your country will be broken into pieces unless you change your current policies. You don't understand that with freedom comes many responsibilities."

Interestingly enough, my friend and Maharaj ji's devotee Bob Serafini was visiting Poland on business that week. He had turned on television and was amazed to see Maharaj ji being broadcast across the Eastern block.

He toured many historic churches and met with church leaders. As he surveyed the gold relics of the church, Babaji remarked, "Marx never studied the life of Jesus, he just looked at the conduct of the church." He then shared his visions with groups of scientists and intellectuals. From Moscow, Maharaj ji traveled to Tashkent and Samarkand and was hosted royally by the people there.

It loses something in translation

After Maharaj ji returned from Russia, he invited the producer of the show, Father Mark, the interfaith officer of the Russian Orthodox Church, to visit India along with his crew to see for himself what Babaji had been able to create here in Gobind Sadan. Maharaj ji asked me to come from America to help host him and to assist with translation. While translating for Maharaj ji with Americans was one thing, I had never translated certain spiritual concepts held sacred to clergy, let alone deal with terms specific to Russian Orthodoxy. While his translator was excellent, she was not totally versed in the subject either.

My introduction to Fr. Mark was quite cordial and the original historic meeting took place in Maharaj ji's garden. Over tea, with Swaranjit and Prem, Joginder and me as witnesses, his translator and film crew poised, he addressed Maharaj ji on camera, "I have been deputed by a group of leading Russians to visit you and understand what the future of our country will be." The answer was again not what he had hoped for.

"I see difficult times ahead for your country. It could be broken into many pieces."

Despite Fr. Mark's eloquence and the serious nature of his mission, he had developed a nagging sore throat and we did all we could to ply him with warm drinks and home and druggist medicines to ease it. But given the cold of the Indian winter it lingered on. I had the next day to translate his talk at the seminar on Jaap Sahib to a distinguished audience and the man's voice was clearly strained.

We were touring Shiv Sadan, driving through seemingly endless fields of wheat up to the windows of the jeep. Fr. Mark was bundled in a leather jacket and a scarf still nursing his sore throat. We stopped at a thatched hut on the banks of the Ganges which held a small *havan*. Maharaj ji got out and did ardas and parshad was distributed. Now parshad is as warm and soothingly oily to the throat as it is soothing to the spirit. So I offered some to Fr. Mark. He looked a bit suspicious and asked what it was. I replied, innocently "Sacrament," and gestured that it would be good for his throat. He took it and we went on with our trip. The rest of the day, he was somewhat aloof. We rode in separate cars on the way home.

The next day he was visibly upset with me. I asked him whether I had said or did anything to offend him and I begged his forgiveness. He said, "You know I am a Christian priest, yet you forced your sacrament on me. I am going to complain to Maharaj ji about this." I wanted to laugh but for him it was a very serious offense. So I literally got on my knees before him and asked forgiveness and explained that I had used the wrong term. That the only reason I had recommended the parshad was because it was hot and would soothe his sore throat. That broke the ice and from then on our relationship warmed up again. But it taught me a critical lesson in translation: not to assume a word which I may feel comfortable assigning to a situation or thing, will have the same meaning to the one I'm speaking to. From that point on I trod more

252

carefully on the often thin ice of cross-cultural and inter-religious dialogue.

Father Gregorios: Give me the hammer and I'll break down the walls

Whenever I was called to Delhi, one of my enjoyable past times was keeping up with the international press community many of whom I'd been close to during the 70's. On one such trip, I invited Earleen Fisher, then the AP Bureau Chief, for lunch, and then subsequently to Gobind Sadan to meet Maharaj ji.

As Maharaj ji would have it, that day Harvinder Singh brought Father Paulos Mar Gregorios, Orthodox Bishop of India and one of the Presidents of the World Council of Churches, to see Maharaj ji. This great theologian had met Maharaj ji some time earlier. At that time, he had a severe back ache. As a matter of course, Maharaj ji lovingly patted him on his back. The next thing you know, his back pain had gone away.

Fr. Gregorios came through the door laughing joyously, "You have broken down the walls of my mind, now give me the hammer and let me break down the walls we have created between our religions." By the time Earleen arrived, they were deep in dialogue which I had the privilege of translating.

In the middle of the conversation, Babaji turned to Earleen. "I'm not speaking about Jesus because Gregorios is here, I speak about Jesus because I love him." He was sitting all in white on a thick Kashmiri woven cushion, and sensed Earleen's query. "I suppose you would prefer to meet me in the fields. There, I am standing day and night with my followers and my boots are muddy. Here you just see me sitting on this."

Gregorios became so close to Babaji that any function, including Christmas would find him at Gobind Sadan. He had gone so far as to say: Babaji is the image of God today. He often would open his talks with lines from Jaap Sahib. And it was Fr. Gregorious who directed the Russians to seek spiritual guidance from Babaji.

Daniel and the Parliament of World's Religions

While in Berkeley, at the NAINConnect, I had met Daniel Ibanez-Gomez who was formulating the ideas for the first Parliament of the World's Religions in Chicago. When I found he was to visit India, I offered to let Gobind Sadan be his host community and he gladly accepted. I called Maharaj ji and received his blessings and with Mary Pat coordinating on the Indian side, Daniel arrived and was comfortably settled in by the time I arrived. He had become such a part of the family that comically Mary Pat introduced him to me, totally forgetting for the moment that I had arranged his visit.

Maharaj ji was very pleased to receive Daniel, in his drawing room, but I'm not sure Daniel was ready to hear Maharaj ji's message. "Your meeting will fail. Rather than bringing the leaders together, each leader will try to make their own points." But Daniel was too far along in his vision and when he returned from Dharmsala with a commitment of the Dalai Lama, there was no turning back. We sat together on the veranda of what is now Maharaj ji's house on the hill, looking over the program determining which slots Maharaj ji and the rest of us would fit into.

Daniel had determined that Maharaj ji should be featured on the main dais with Mother Theresa as the two most prominent spiritual leaders who brought God into action.

Shortly after my return from this trip, I received a call from Jim Kenney, one of the key organizers. "Ralph, we need a video short as a background introduction for Babaji's talk. You know, the lights will dim, the film will roll, then we'll bring up the lights and introduce Babaji to the audience." Sounded great. So began our first attempt at film-making and the short 'There Should be No Poverty, was born.

On conversion

While Maharaj ji's love for Jesus and all the Prophets is indisputable, His stance on conversion is equally clear:

"When Dharam is One, and all Prophets come from the same place, what is there to convert?" In His message to the Parliament of the World's Religions in Chicago, He likened it to bribery, whereby the poor are offered free education, housing, healthcare in return for converting to Christianity.

A young man came to him seeking spiritual truth. After listening to Maharaj ji's discourse, he excitedly said, "Babaji I want to become a Sikh. You have truly inspired me."

Rather than welcoming the man, Babaji responded, "Tell me what Prophet do you follow now?"

"I am a Christian, having been a Jew before, and I would like to follow your teachings."

Maharaj ji grew sterner. "Tell me, what was wrong with Jesus that you had to become a Jew? And what is wrong with Moses that you feel that you need to become a Sikh?" The man was startled and had no reply. Maharaj ji closed the discussion with his now classic line:

"Changing cars won't improve the driver. You have to improve yourself."

At Princeton University (July 26, 1990)

Maharaj ji over the years has received many invitations to address major international gatherings but seldom goes himself. Preferring to send one of us on his behalf. However something about the joint UNICEF-WCRP conference at Princeton, entitled 'World's Religions for the World's Children' pleased him and he accepted the invitation to join General S.S. Ubban, an old devotee and one of the organizers, on this trip.

It was quite an amazing procession across the walkways. There were Cardinals and Rabbis, Priests and community leaders from all over the world. Shinto priests from Japan, Buddhist monks of varying backgrounds, Muslim leaders, Zoroastrians, and despite the variety of their traditional raiment, Maharaj ji stood out. When the newspaper articles appeared the next day, it was Maharaj ji in his sparkling white dress that captured the front page.

The newspapers weren't the only ones to take notice. The organizers were very proud to announce that they were expecting participation from the Russian Orthodox Church for the first time, and that the priest would be joining us soon as he was coming directly from the airport. Soon a bearded young man entered the room in traditional black robes and was surveying the scene when he nearly stopped dead in his tracks. While the Priest was obviously jetlagged, he had come face to face with Maharaj ji who was sitting in the front row. Later when I asked him what had affected him. He said, "The light of God on the Saint's face was so powerful, I couldn't take another step."

During the break some prominent people, including Hermes, came up to him asking for his '*kalam*,' or prayer. Maharaj ji blessed him with *Nam*. Hermes stood in His aura as long as he could, then went back to the group.

The Prayer Service showcases Maharaj ji

Meanwhile the next day's main event was an interfaith service at the main chapel to showcase the key religious leaders from each tradition. General Ubban began coaching Maharaj ji that all he had to do was stand there with folded hands, say a few words in Punjabi and Ubban would translate them in English. More importantly, Ubban would explain in English the meanings of the prayers for the audience. I could see Maharaj ji smile as he listened. He had not come all the way to be set up on a dais like a figurehead. He had a message to deliver and whether the good General knew it or not, this was his show. The audience was his.

Standing near the lectern, his white clothes glistening, Maharaj ji began a classic 20-minute oration that held the church spellbound. There was pin-drop silence as he in his inimical way praised and narrated the life and teachings of Jesus, the Prophet Muhammed, Lord Krishna, Lord Buddha, Abraham and Moses and of course Guru Nanak and Guru Gobind Singh.

After the service, the Bishop from Chile embraced him, "Thank you for venerating Jesus," he said with tears in his eyes. Maharaj ji just smiled and replied, "Jesus is worthy of nothing less than our praise." The Rabbi from Brazil thanked him for his respect for Moses, as did the Buddhists and the Muslims and Zoroastrians. They asked me for copies of Jaap Sahib and whatever other literature we had brought.

One of the UNICEF officers came to Maharaj ji for guidance. "How can we gain peace in the middle East?" he asked. "Forgive your enemies," Babaji replied.

"But they killed my parents. It's so hard."

"But isn't this Jesus's order?" The man looked long at Babaji, asked for his blessings, then turned away to ponder how to proceed on the path of forgiveness.

Only the Bishop from India was a little miffed. Especially, when next day the front page of the Princetonian spotlighted Maharaj ji, he approached us quite tartly and said, "Why doesn't Babaji first settle the problems of Punjab instead of coming here to preach us?" Sunny (Hardeep), never one to miss an opportunity, retorted: "Jesus was never accepted by his own people either." After that the Bishop tended to avoid us.

Pardon my ignorance, but who is Guru Nanak?

One of the people who had noticed Maharaj ji's presence was a religion editor of the Associated Press.

Chuck White had referred us to him and he gladly invited Maharaj ji to visit him at his Rockefeller Ctr. Office. He led us down a narrow corridor past the International desk from where Sikhs at that time were being portrayed in less than kind terms. The AP by-line often followed the sensational headlines, "Sikh Terrorists..." Then ushered us into a simple conference room with a long rectangular table surrounded by 8 chairs. There were just the three of us (David, Babaji and myself as translator) so he courteously put Babaji at the head, sat to his left and I sat directly opposite him. He smiled from behind his glasses as he opened his spiral pad for the first question: "What brings you to New York? And how have you found your visit so far?"

Babaji shared his invitation to Princeton and the warm response he had received from everyone there as well as his delighted devotees.

Next question: "Tell me something about your mission?"

Babaji began in his inimical way, "God is one, Truth is one, but we humans have divided the message. Jesus taught love, the Prophet Mohammed taught love, Moses taught love of that One God, and similarly Guru Nanak taught the same thing."

Up until that point the journalist had been listening intently and taking copious notes. He suddenly put down his pencil and looked up at Babaji quizzically.

He asked, "Pardon my ignorance but who is Guru Nanak?".

I had to conceal my shock and could barely translate for Maharaj ji. Here was a senior religion editor for one of the world's leading media outlets, who had a great influence on public opinion and yet he had never heard of Guru Nanak. By association one could only assume that his understanding about the teachings of Sikhism were equally sketchy. What's more, he had a Masters degree in comparative religion from Yale.

Maharaj ji did not show his surprise, and patiently continued, asking me to give a bit of a background on Guru Nanak and his teachings. But later he commented that with all the time Sikhs have been in the U.S. and certain with all the publicity given in India to those Americans who have converted to Sikhism, it was appalling that the mainstream media still didn't have any idea about Guru Nanak.

Maharaj ji often tells the story of the group who had come to see him at Gobind Sadan during the days of unrest in Punjab. After he had spoken about the love and peace of Guru Granth Sahib, they remarked with some surprise, "Your religion is full of peace." Maharaj ji laughed and replied, "Guru Granth Sahib is an ocean of peace." To which the response came, "But Babaji, we don't read your Holy book we read the newspapers."

Preserve your identity, share your love

One criticism leveled at dialogue of any sort, and interfaith in particular, is that by entering into dialogue with others, we end up weakening our particular position. A Rabbi, deeply committed to interfaith understanding put this question to Maharaj ji:

"You tell us to break down the barriers that separate us. But if we break down our walls how do we maintain our identity?"

Maharaj ji's response:

"Share your love of God. I'm not suggesting that you stop your worship. Continue to worship in your own way, maintain your language and customs, and celebrate your holidays, but feel free to share love with others as well. You all speak of One God. Love Him."

The Rabbi nodded, visibly moved. It was a simple but elegant solution to the problem. We are not sinking to the lowest common denominator, delving into what has been called syncretism, which requires each group to give something up. Neither are we sacrificing what is visibly 'ours' or our right to practice our traditions. Rather it is adding love from your tradition to the human mix. The only thing we give up is hatred.

The Miracle Koran – Bringing Peace to a Divided Middle Eastern Family

The United States was on the brink of the Gulf War. The headlines almost urged the troops on. And in New York's highly polarized international community, the Jews and Muslims were squaring off and the Christians were either taking sides or determining how to mediate. Dati's living room on Barry Drive became a model of Maharaj ji's peace process.

A Lebanese family had come for Maharaj ji's blessings. A cousin of their family was in the ICU with an inoperable brain tumor and tubes were branching out of her to maintain her bodily functions. The doctors offered little if any hope.

Now this was not an ordinary Lebanese family. The father and son were Muslim. Their daughter, Dati's friend, who had brought them, had converted to Judaism. But not just to any branch of Judaism, she had become part of the Chasidim, the spiritual Orthodox order, maintained as a quasi-closed community under the leadership of the Lebuvicher Rabbi, considered a Messiah to his followers. And to round out the cast of characters, the cousin in the hospital was Christian.

The Jewish girl appealed to Maharaj ji to bless and heal her cousin. Maharaj ji closed his eyes for a brief moment and then without blinking or changing expression shared his vision.

"Place a copy of the Koran on her forehead, and sprinkle her with holy water, and she'll be fine."

The father and son were visibly upset.

259

"She is Christian, kafir, how can we place the Pak, the Pure, Holy Koran on her?"

The Jewish daughter screwed up her courage, "If it will save her life, I'll do it." To which the father and son both sneered, "You. You are kafir too. You can't even touch the Holy Koran. Who would ever give you a copy?"

Maharaj ji, more amused than upset, began to calmly counsel them: "Tell me what are you fighting about? Aren't you all children of Abraham? And doesn't the Holy Koran talk of Moses as the Great Prophet and Jesus as the Messiah?"

"Yes, no doubt, but Islamic law prohibits any *kafir* to even touch the Holy Koran. I myself am not a pure man and fear to touch its sacred pages," the son replied, his face falling as he held out his hands.

"Not to show disrespect to Islamic law," Maharaj ji continued, "but is not the purpose of the Pure words of Allah to clean those who are impure. If the Pure cannot reach those who are not clean then how will people ever improve?"

This prompted more active and even heated discussion among the family. And they took their divisions with them out the door.

Not more than an hour passed and the Jewish daughter returned. "Maharaj ji I'll do it. I have a copy of the Holy Koran at home. Please give me the holy water and let me proceed." She was risking the wrath of both her Chasidic Community as well as her parents. But undeterred she left for the hospital spirits buoyed.

By the end of the week the cousin had recovered and went home from the hospital. Unfortunately, despite the obvious miracle, which the Doctors were able to attest to, she was not willing to go public with the story. That far she couldn't go. She had saved her cousins life. But for us a feature story was in the making which would not only have highlighted Maharaj ji's power and presence, but might have changed the course of American policy and certainly given rise to more dialogue and hopefully better relations among the religious communities.

You are My Holy man
Maharaj ji was invited to meet with a group area leaders at City College of New York. This was the first time most of them had

been in Maharaj ji's presence and as they sat around the conference table listening to His words, the Light began to dance all over their faces. After delivering one of His best masterpieces, Maharaj ji ended by saying in His inimical way, "People hear that a "holy man" is coming and run away. Those who call themselves holy take money from everyone. I am not that kind of holy man. I am a hard working farmer who loves God. And I have just come to share my love with you."

By the end of the short talk, the group was poised with questions, and Mohammed Mehdi, then one of the most prominent Muslim leaders in the United States raised his hand to start off.

"Tell Him he is my Holy man." Now Mohammed is not one to be wowed by anyone. And this was the first time He had met Maharaj ji. When I hesitated, waiting for the next sentence, he slammed his fist on the table, "Why aren't you translating? Tell Him He is my Holy man for I see the Light of Allah on His face."

Mary Pat arrives

One evening, after a full day of programs, Maharaj ji turned to me, "Tomorrow a friend of yours will come, who will leave her family and follow me." This was wonderful news. A few candidates popped into my mind and I couldn't wait to see who the lucky person turned out to be.

I had met Mary Pat at NAIN and knew she had a radio program. I wanted to get Maharaj ji's message out, so even though she lived several hours away in Storrs, CT., I thought I'd give her a call.

"Mary Pat, I'd like to invite you to interview a great spiritual Master who is visiting from India."

"Okay, but, where are you?"

When I described our location, I could feel the enthusiasm wane a bit. But not being one to be daunted by small challenges she agreed. I didn't realize until later that she hated driving across bridges.

When she arrived, Maharaj ji was sitting in his chair in front of the picture window and we were on the floor at his feet. From Mary Pat's angle, it was harder to tell which was brighter, the sun streaming in the window or the glow on Maharaj ji's face. Either way, at times, she had to almost shield her face as she looked up. But she just soaked in His radiance. She was getting fuller and fuller with each moment and by the end of the interview she was his.

She would later share with the world that He was indeed her "beloved," who had appeared to her when she was dying post childbirth and saved her life. In that hospital room, she had pledged her life to him but begged to be allowed to raise her children. This was the moment when she had been called to fulfill her promise. And a beautiful moment it was at that. At the end of the meeting, Maharaj ji had me invite her to India to the seminar and the rest is history. And she keeps writing it with her wonderful dedication.

Don't call Lord Ram or Lord Krishna Myth

While Babaji didn't need me to translate for the many Hindus or Sikhs who came to him He called me to him to translate a statement He wanted to make in defense of Lord Krishna and Lord Ram. A prominent historian had written that they were myths in a high school text book. There was little that could arouse Babaji's ire more than someone challenging or besmirching the good name of God or one of His messengers. He started: "Don't call Lord Ram or Lord Krishna myth in the name of education. We must teach our children to respect all scriptures and all of God's prophets. This is not a political issue. India's ethical and cultural heritage is built on Dharma.

People may wonder why I as a Sikh would speak out when this seems to be a Hindu issue. It is our teaching to speak out whenever and wherever anyone's dharma is attacked. When the good names of Jesus and the Prophet Mohammed were attacked I was equally outspoken in their defense as well. This is the tradition of our Gurus. Guru Granth Sahib also teaches us to revere the Bible, the Holy Koran, the Torah, the Zinda Vesta, as well as the Vedas, as true.

Those who have any doubts about Lord Ram, Lord Krishna or any other of God's messengers should come to me. To create doubts in our children's minds is one of the worst things a human being can do to another. Especially with our children we should concentrate on breeding good thoughts.

No doubt by looking at the conduct of the clergy and the management of our religious institutions today it's hard to believe that a Lord Ram, Lord Krishna, a Lord Jesus, a Prophet Mohammed, a Guru Nanak or Guru Gobind Singh could have existed. But don't discard God because of the actions of people. To me there is no such thing as an atheist, just people who've been disillusioned by those who claim to represent God.

I am more concerned with those who have published the books. I understand that there are those who are allergic to dharma. But we shouldn't publish their ideology as historical fact for the purpose of teaching our children. We know some people believe that God is just a theory. Look what happened to Russia when they tried to say 'there is no God'. At one point Russia was the most powerful country. Now they are trying to return to their previous position in the world and are saying that God exists."

23

Dialogues on My Own

Wherever I traveled I always aroused interest at least, and sometimes suspicion. But mostly people just wanted to understand what I was about. Sometimes they were anxious to tell me about their beliefs and sometimes they were bent on convincing me that their way was not just the right way, but the only way. Regardless of how the conversation started, Maharaj ji always was able to draw the other person out of their entrenched position and provide a wonderful new spiritual understanding. Whether it was later sustained or whether they once again retreated behind their comfortable wall remained to be seen.

The same God?
It was not unusual for someone, even over a friendly lunch, to ask: "Do you believe in the same God (as we do)?" My reply was always, "Isn't there only One?" and smile. People have been taught that those who look different must worship a different God. This obviously creates a different starting point for dialogue. You are assuming your God and your beliefs are different. Whereas, in almost all cases, the values and beliefs are common, it's just the rituals, laws, and practices which divide us. Based on Maharaj ji's example, my approach was to allow the other person to understand that I loved the same One they worshipped, as much, and in some cases more, than they did.

Does anyone here believe in God?
Sometimes when people of faith sit around the table, they forget that they are supposed to make God's presence felt, not their own. But often the discussion descends into a debate rather than a dialogue.

At those times, Maharaj ji has urged me to ask, "Does anyone actually believe in God, or are we just debating our particular belief systems?"

A friend who served on the Bishop's council of his parish shared with me, that when he thought the Bishop was off base, he would simply sit back in his chair and ask, "That's interesting. I wonder what Jesus would do in such a situation?"

Christian or Christ-like

All cultures and religions are beset by fundamentalism these days, and fundamentalist Christians are well-known for their position that Jesus is the ONLY son of and ONLY way to reach God. I used to say to Christians, "My only problem with your brand of Christianity is 'only'." They'd look at me and ask what I meant. I'd repeat the phrase slowly and finally it would sink in.

I was having lunch with a friend who was a good Christian in a religious sense, he tithed, committed himself to church life and helped those in need. He was a true role model for many youth. To me, more important than just being considered a good Christian, he was a wonderful human being. In the middle of our luncheon conversation about how to overcome some of the social problems in our world, he looked at me and said, "Ralph, you know I agree with you, but from my perspective, until the world accepts Jesus as their Lord and savior nothing is going to change."

Now here's where Maharaj ji jumped right into the fray. I put my fork down and looked him straight in the eyes, "Do you mean that you want everyone to be Christian or you want everyone to be Christ-like? (I had never thought of those words let alone said them before in my life)". He literally dropped his fork and looked hard at me.

Then he erupted. He slammed his fist on the table. "That's the whole problem with Christianity, nobody tries to be Christ-like," he retorted.

I said, "OK, let's try to understand what it means to be Christ-like." I turned the placemat over and began to write:

Complete Faith in One God, our Father
Unconditional love
All forgiving,

265

Compassionate
Helping the poor
Healing the sick
Feeding the hungry
And several more traits that we could attribute to Jesus.

When I had finished, I looked at him and said, "Now I can go anywhere in the world, and sit among any group of people. If they ask me what I believe, or what my core values are, I'd show them this list. I guarantee you that they would all embrace me and say these are what we believe in also. But, if I put the word 'Christian' at the top, they would quickly push away from the table and leave."

Then Maharaj ji came up with the final clincher: "To me the final question which everyone has to answer, 'if we all believe in the same things, do we have to be Christian to be Christ-like.'" He had no answer.

To this day whenever I meet a fundamentalist, I share this story and it leaves them speechless as well.

Jesus hasn't gone anywhere
One other point I've raised with fundamentalists. After sharing how much I love Jesus, and how we pray before Jesus every night, the response often ranges from surprise to indignation "How can you love Jesus, you're not Christian? Or Sikhs don't love Jesus." I restate that I love Jesus and He has appeared to me many times (which naturally gets their attention). And then I say, "But I have a problem with Christianity." Maharaj ji gives me the courage and gives them the tolerance not to run me out. "You say Jesus has gone and will come again. I say Jesus has never gone anywhere, we just don't have the eyes to see Him." I've met many a good Christian who will take that to heart and some who've even said, I believe that too.

I've found when you show that you sincerely love the One who people worship, they can't help but accept and listen to you as a brother or fellow in faith. This is Maharaj ji's training and His blessing. Connecting with people from the heart who may be from a totally different faith or culture is the highest point of dialogue.

The Muslim Version – Complete or Final

To many Muslims, the Holy Koran is not only the words of Allah, it is the final revelation of God. However, Maharaj ji sees things differently and in a public forum had me suggest a reasonable alternative. We were in California. The University of the Pacific in Berkeley was hosting our NAINConnect and had invited a distinguished Muslim scholar to speak. During his talk he kept stressing the power of the revelation of the Holy Koran as the final revelation of God and Mohammed as his final Prophet through whom all will receive salvation.

Maharaj ji nearly ejected me from my seat. I rose and moved to the back of the room waiting for my opportunity to ask and kept rolling the question over in my mind.

When I was finally recognized, I started: "With all due respect and love for the Prophet, peace be upon him, I would like to comment on your suggestion that the word 'sealed' means final. The words of the Koran are sealed. This is true. But does this mean that Allah will never speak again. Can there never be another Prophet or revelation? And does this mean that it invalidates all previous revelation? How can you who on one hand declare Allah infinite and all Powerful determine that Allah will never reveal Himself again, and if Allah is the One God then doesn't it stand to reason that Allah's revelation would simply reinforce whatever was revealed before. I would be more comfortable translating the word sealed – as complete. There is no doubt that the Holy Koran is a complete revelation, but to suggest that it is Final turns Allah the Infinite into Allah the finite."

Once more Maharaj ji had placed the question of exclusiveness before the whole gathering. The man struggled to maintain his position. After all he was the guest speaker, an expert being questioned from the floor by an unknown Sikh no less. But in the end he had to at least give credence to this new possibility.

Many in the audience came up to me saying that these are the key moments of dialogue that open the doors to greater understanding. This of course is what Maharaj ji constantly works towards.

The Syracuse Mosque – Maharaj ji relieves the tension

When the sizeable Syracuse area Muslim community opened a beautiful Mosque in a prominent location on a main street near the University, there was a variety of reactions from the community, but more concern than appreciation.

In order to allay people's fear the Syracuse Area Interreligious Council, in conjunction with the Mosque's Imam and leadership, invited the clergy of Syracuse for an 'orientation visit,' billed as a polite get to know your new neighbor session.

After some simple refreshments of drinks and pastries, we were seated around conference tables. The group was comprised of 95% Christian clergy, with the addition of 1 Rabbi who was a board member of the Inter-religious Council, and one Sikh, me. The Imam, a soft spoken Saudi, graciously welcomed everyone and shared that we would always be welcome at the Mosque. Knowingly or unknowingly, he stayed away from any theological lecture and simply made us feel comfortable, and then turned the meeting over to the President of the Islamic Society. As the President, a strong-spoken young professional, launched into his prepared talk, the carefully laid groundwork soon evaporated.

"You all should know that the revelation of the Holy Koran supersedes all other scriptures and ultimately all will come to Allah, though you may not realize this now."

The clergy were stunned. They literally didn't know how to react. I was sitting at the back facing the head table and from my vantage point I could not see a single person ready or willing to respond. I raised my hand respectfully, "Dear Brother, I understand your perspective, but perhaps for those who haven't read the Holy Koran you might share that Abraham and Moses are given great respect, and Jesus is referred to as the Messiah and it states that Mary is greatly blessed."

He quickly seized the cue and went on to embellish how much the Holy Koran honors all the Prophets. I could literally feel the tension come out of room. The sighs of relief were audible, as if a large balloon, about to burst, was suddenly deflated.

268

Violence versus Physical Force

I was quietly sitting at breakfast at the University of Washington during our NAIN meeting, when a Catholic Priest from Ireland plopped himself down next to me and began, "You Sikhs are a violent bunch aren't you?" Given that he came from a country torn apart by years of violence between Protestants and Catholics, I could barely contain my amazement and amusement, but responded, "What do you mean?"

"Well Sikhs are known all over the world for their military prowess and they carry swords and knives as part of their religious symbols."

Having used this interlude to swallow my food and take a quick sip of tea, I was now ready for the full discussion. "Tell me, does that make us violent? And speaking of violence, ask your mother was your birth a peaceful event? Or the birth of a star for that matter. If we are defending the rights of others who can't defend themselves does that make us violent?

I personally am quite a pacifist. I've never been to war and abhor it. But if I'm confronted by a situation where I could save another from harm should I sit idle? For example: What if you witnessed someone assaulting a weaker person, a man trying to rape a woman or hurt a child what would you do?"

"I'd yell," said the Catholic Priest.

"And then if they didn't stop?"

"I'd call the police."

"And in the meantime if you saw the person in trouble or screaming for help. Would you intervene?"

"Yes."

"And if you had to fight with the person in the process or even hurt them would that be violence?"

By now he was really stuck.

I think he walked away with a different sense of what qualified as 'violence'.

But these are difficult questions. Naturally we would like everyone to be enlightened beings who do no harm to others. These are the basic commandments of all religions. But we are surrounded with inhumane acts all the time. Guru Gobind Singh ji was very pragmatic

269

about it. Try every means possible to avoid physical force, but when all the pleading and social pressure and threat of action fail to stop someone from harming another then "it is righteous and just to take the sword."

So perhaps, 'if we are intentionally trying to harm another out of malice then that qualifies as violence.'

And Maharaj ji always goes far beyond this, quoting the Gurus: "Just thinking evil about another is violence." By this definition, I would venture to say there is probably not a single nonviolent person in the world.

Youthing

Once when we were at Shiv Sadan, a mother and daughter came to Maharaj ji for blessings. I don't remember the problem but I clearly remember that the daughter looked older than the mother. Then I realized that the mother spent much time in prayer while her daughter was weighed down with problems. The mother was actually more youthful than her daughter.

I began to note that as people stayed in Gobind Sadan, their faces changed. The signs of stress vanished and their faces developed a natural glow. They were actually youthing. It was also quite obvious when people sat in Maharaj ji's presence for any length of time. Their defenses dropped and suddenly they were children again. I continued to observe and confirm this process in almost every case.

I was at a conference on Spirituality and Aging at Duke University, which featured some luminaries in their 80's on a panel telling what kept them young. When their presentations finished, I rose to present my findings: "I don't see any old people on the dais. Everyone of you has youthed. As the soul grows closer to God we are actually youthing not aging. We only age when we don't approach God." There was a general round of applause and appreciation.

Transfer the icon - Breaking down the exclusive view of God

I was discussing shared worship with a Catholic Priest at Elizabeth's Christmas party. He was telling me that it was hard for him to conceive of worshipping at any other religious place, as Jesus had to be present in order for him to really consider it worship. First, I thought I should say, "Tell me where Jesus is not present." But that seemed beyond his grasp. So I asked, "Have you ever tried transferring the icon?" He looked quite bewildered. So I continued. "God has no one face. Jesus to you is the face of God. But to a Hindu it might be Lord Krishna, to the Muslim (though they are forbidden from making images of the Prophet) it could be the Light of Allah, to the Sikh it could be Guru Gobind Singh. Let's say you tried to see Jesus wherever you looked. If you see Lord Krishna see Jesus in him. Similarly a devotee of Lord Krishna would see Lord Krishna in Jesus."

There is a phrase in the Bhagvad Gita:

"You are the supreme primal objective. You are the ultimate resting place of all this universe. You are inexhaustible, and You are the oldest. You are the maintainer of the eternal religion, the Personality of Godhead." 11.18

"There is no truth superior to Me. Everything rests upon Me, as pearls are strung on a thread ..."

That sounds remarkably similar to Jesus's words in the New Testament:

"I am the Alpha and the Omega
No one comes to the Father except through me."

If these statements are true, as I accept, the question to ponder remains: "Is Lord Krishna the form of Jesus when He said this, or is Jesus the form of Lord Krishna?" It depends on your point of view. But these are the points of view that are shaping the world: theocentrism, the exclusive view of God.

I was at a conference at an Episcopal Church, in New York and shared this formula with a world famous Irish Theologian and asked "Can you 'see' the same God through different 'icons'?" He looked at me quite quizzically and replied, "Then I would expect that you would arrive at two very different places." I shook my head and told him, "Quite the opposite." But seeing his blank gaze I quietly walked away.

The Tibetan who loved Guru Nanak – Walling up the Light

I was attending a conference at Fordham University of formidable scholars and theologians on what they chose to title, 'New Directions in Spirituality'. The meeting included the likes of Renaldo Pandekar, Huston Smith, and Ewart Cousins. I enjoyed engaging them in dialogue on what I called their unhappy marriage of religion as a social science and the power of God. It seemed to me quite obvious that it was precisely the separation of the mystical experience from religion which has lead to its downfall. Further, I found it hard to reconcile that this eminent group of intellectuals comprised a major contingent of the gatekeepers who determined not to expand their definition of "world religions" beyond the traditional "big five," Judaism, Christianity, Islam, Hinduism, and Buddhism, to allow Sikhism membership in their club. One, who shall remain nameless, went so far as to say, "If we admit Sikhism then how will we be able to draw the line?"

Later that evening, after the sessions, I was walking alone in the hallway. Through the doorway on the opposite end of the corridor, an entourage of Tibetans, some in business suits and others in robes, emerged encasing a high-ranking Buddhist monk who had been a speaker at the conference.

I expected the group to pass by and was as surprised as they were when the monk stopped, folded his hands and greeted me with 'Sat Siri Akal Sardar ji' (the traditional Sikh greeting), and followed with "Don't you know that Tibetans love Guru Nanak." He must have seen the astonished, but pleased expression on my face. He then proceeded to tell me a story I'll never forget.

"I come from a region in Ladakh where Guru Nanak is greatly revered. His Light was enshrined in a large rock near my village and each time we passed that stone we all would worship there, placing butter sculpture and incense on the rock.

"Over time, the Indian government decided to build a road through the region and deputed a Sikh Engineer to supervise the project. He dismissed the sanctity of the rock as local superstition and proceeded with the order to clear the path with his heavy equipment. But when he came to the rock, a great light issued forth and the equipment broke.

"Stunned by this event he delved further into the history. When he found that this was a place touched by Guru Nanak, he quickly rallied the Sikh transporters, raised money, and built a Gurdwara around the rock.

"Some time later, I was traveling to my village and was passing the rock, now enclosed in the Temple.

"My driver proceeded to pass the site and I stopped him. 'Aren't we going to pay our respects?'"

His answer should be a lesson to all of us. "They have built walls around the light. Now we have to take off our shoes and cover our heads and no one goes there anymore." The monk then smiled and he and his entourage passed.

Amazing! Later that year I had to fill in for Maharaj ji as the keynote speaker in Seattle at the NAINConnect when He couldn't come at the last minute. The title of my talk was 'Keepers of the Light,' and this was the story that I used to underscore that we in organized religions have walled up the light from the people.

The Millennium Peace Summit

Maharaj ji had sent me to the Millennium Peace Summit at the United Nations in the summer of 2000 with his message for the religious leaders: "We are responsible for the conflict in the world if we don't teach our people peace." Maharaj ji went on to challenge them to first make peace within ourselves and then among our religions, by celebrating each other's holidays. "When we break down the barriers between our religions the conflicts on our borders will stop." I distributed this message to everyone I met and subsequently engaged them in dialogue. I was promised a spot on the closing program to deliver the message directly, but with all the maneuvering that goes during such a spectacle, that time never came. I don't think they wanted anyone to upset their show by suggesting they themselves were standing in the way of peace.

God doesn't need to be legitimized

After two days of watching the posturing of those gathered, both at the U.N. itself and in the breakout sessions, I was standing in the hallway outside the Waldorf ballroom in between meetings. Light was streaming in through a skylight and Maharaj ji suddenly shared: "God's light is all around. It reaches through the smallest crevices to

273

touch everyone. Who are we gathered here in God's name. God doesn't need to be legitimized, we are just trying to legitimize our own positions."

Just then, a nice young woman walked up to me and asked me what I thought of the gathering. So I told her my thoughts. Suddenly she pulled out a microphone and asked if I'd mind stating it for the record. It turned out she was a religion correspondent for a major news outlet.

Visible identities

After the meeting I was sitting with two Orthodox Jews, both recognized leaders in their community. One had been among the delegation invited to meet the Dalai Lama in Dharmsala to dialogue about the issues of maintaining religious identity within a community that had been identified as a 'persecuted religious minority.'

I had literally fought with Sikhs about portraying themselves as a persecuted minority. I'd found that moniker simply plays into the hands of those political groups both within and outside the community who want to use it for their own agendas. It tends to polarize the community and leaves the question of faith behind. As we were discussing these issues, Maharaj ji had me stress a point that rang true to them:

"Until those of us who are observant are able to communicate that our symbols of faith and practices are simply expressions of the same universal truth we will continue to be marginalized by modern society and political movements. Our children and the public will be unable to relate to us and we will lose our relevancy."

They thanked me, but recognized that for them the die had been cast and they were caught up in the game of maintaining an identity forced upon them almost beyond their control. I could also say that my identity was beyond my control, but the ideal and identity of *Khalsa* was hardly forced, it was to be aspired to.

Khalsa – your name is character

The Return of the Templar Knights – the Defenders of Faith
While one can praise God, and find praises of God's attributes in Jaap Sahib, Guru Gobind Singh also sings the praises of one whose character is pure – the *Khalsa*.

Khalsa is one who is without anger, who helps the poor, who does not even look with lust at another woman. Maharaj ji often says, "Khalsa is another word for character."

Khalsa is the keeper of the Light. The defender of all that is sacred. He is the body of the Guru and the corporate body of God in whom God's Light dwells. The concept is put forth as an Order – as in the times of the knights – an Order of the Pure. Those who are pure in spirit – whose actions and deeds mirror the teachings of all traditions as they reflect the Light and Power of the Prophets. There is no greater rank in any armed forces, no greater title, no higher position than Khalsa. And it is Khalsa that those of faith aspire to be. Those who bore the insignia were few and seldom could they be counted on more than one hand.

Then Guru Gobind Singh decided to expand the circle – so that it would spiral upward and spread light in the darkness casting off the yoke of oppression and driving out both the inner forces of evil and those who would invade and torment a country subverting its society.

In the time of Guru Gobind Singh, he chose the dregs of society, those by his own account had never even a glimmer of hope that they could ever see the light of day –

To those who by virtue of caste or lineage could never be considered leaders
On them I bestow the mantle of greatness
By this act they will recall Gobind Singh.

Khalsa was and perhaps is the most powerful force for Justice ever forged in human history.

Humanism without authority fails. There is no greater form of humanism than embodied in Khalsa.

Maharaj ji says it is another word for character – another word for a truly good human being.

Khalsa is one who transcends, let's go of, and overcomes his anger.

275

Looks with dispassion,
Is the protector of the poor,
Does not criticize another and rather looks to burn away his own weaknesses.

But here humaneness is empowered to protect all.

Baba Virsa Singh is restoring *Khalsa*. His beacon summons them from across the globe, from all faiths and backgrounds to reunite and work to overcome the difficulties that plague the world.

Whether recognized by their turban or by the nobility of their words and deeds, this new breed of women and men will change the course of civilization.

The Indigenous Spiritual Experience

As you approach Syracuse from the South on Route 81 you pass a sign "Entering Onondaga Nation Territory." The *Haudenosaunee*, the People of the Long House, the civilization that existed long before the British and the French stepped foot on this soil. I say civilization because these people were indeed civilized. It was the Iroquois Confederacy that offered Benjamin Franklin the model from which the U.S. Constitution was established. Aside from politics they were certainly more attuned to the Creator than those who while professing a desire for religious freedom ended up not only making their religion more restrictive but made their civilization less inclusive and began to drive the Native people from their own lands and grant them "reservations." Comparatively small tracts of land (though they may comprise thousands of acres or even hundreds of miles in some areas) where they allowed the Native Americans to live under their own laws. And so the Onondaga, to make it clear that they were a sovereign people, set up the sign and travel on their own passport. The land in most of the county and the city in particular functions under a 99 year lease from the Nation. They are usually kind enough to renew the lease.

I can't remember exactly how I first met Oren Lyons, but being in Syracuse one is bound to run into him. Great artist, legendary athlete, and, most important of all, constant voice for the rights of the world's indigenous peoples. When Maharaj ji first came, I called

Oren to host His visit and Donna Young, being one of only 2 nonnative teachers, helped facilitate His visit to the school. Maharaj ji was welcomed at the school, a beautiful modern building, by Audrey Shenandoah, who was one of the Matriarchs and in charge of language and cultural education. Maharaj ji has always said that it was so important to keep one's language and culture otherwise the ways of the people will disappear.

Oren shared with Maharaj ji how he knew of the 'Lions of the Golden Temple' from an incident in England. He was traveling on his native passport and was stopped by customs. It was a Sikh who came to his rescue and convinced his colleagues to honor the document, and then confided that he too was part of a proud and once sovereign nation.

Later it was through the Haswells that I met Tadadaho, Chief of Chiefs Leon Shenandoah, and became a friend to him and his sister Alice Papineau. Leon as the Faithkeeper of the Iroquois was caught in the middle between maintaining traditional ways and laws and the movement towards modernization. Many people married off or moved off the reservation but still wanted to maintain their ties. Many people on the reservations wanted to have the best of both worlds, which is understandable, but one must ultimately choose one's allegiance and uphold it.

And many wanted to use their tax exempt status to leverage business ventures even if it did not accrue to the nation. This crossed the line. And so fights broke out even among family members who maintained gas pumps or 'smoke-shops' on the fringes of the reservation where people could by goods at a bargain.

Many times Leon had to draw the line and take a tough stand which created bad blood among the groups. Despite the challenges, he lived into his 80's and always had a cheerful welcome for me whenever we met.

I got word of his death and drove the 20 miles down to the Nation just as the sun was setting. He was lying in state in the little long house, a small white wooden building, resembling a colonial church. I was completely alone with him. As I sat watching his still body, dressed in his simple but elegant white Chief's attire, hands clutching his ceremonial eagle feather, a powerful vision appeared. His spirit spiraled upward extending into an eagle. The words it spoke touched me deeply and captured the struggle of this great man's life and his hope for the future of his people. I went home and quickly typed it out and shared it with those closest to him at the funeral the next day.

The Eagle Soars

A Tribute to Tadadaho

From a single feather
Clutched by the hand that no more
Holds out its greeting

The Soul spirals upwards and spreads its wings

The Eagle soars

"Tell my people that I carry the message of the Creator
to the spirits where I journey

Tell the ones who love me that I will always
Watch over them

Tell those who hated me
That I acted not out of malice toward them
But out of Love and obedience to the Creator
And the Ways of our People

As Father to one child, I could laugh at the
Mistakes which lead the child astray
And still hold them close

But as Father to our People
I must turn away from the child who goes
Their own way
So my people will know the difference

Yet my heart aches with love to be able to again
Embrace those who once played on the grass by my house

Tell this to my people"
And the Eagle Soared

7-24-96

Visions of the First Nations in Canada

We were at a NAIN retreat at a First Nations' (Indigenous People's) Training Center, maintained, interestingly enough, by the United Church of Canada. Unlike the early missionaries and governments who 'stole' children away to boarding schools and stripped them of their identity – their language and culture, the modern Church had recognized that it was not necessary to leave one's traditional ways to be part of the Church. And both cultures could benefit from the interaction. My friend and colleague Bruce was at the forefront of this movement to maintain traditional ways while adding traditional wisdom to the Church and Canadian Society. For aside from being a "Church" center, the staff were sought out by everyone from government agencies and corporations to help with conflict resolution.

As Melody, one of the center's staff expressed it, "We carry two bundles." Our love for our traditional ways and our love for Jesus. She had been duly ordained as a minister in the Church and was recognized as an 'elder' among her nation.

Interestingly enough our formal time started with the kindling of a sacred fire that would remain burning throughout the period. The 'firekeeper' was a spiritually attuned young man. As the fire was kindled as the plume of smoke drifted upward through the slit in the top of the tepee a beautiful cloud formation drifted overhead. Tinged with the pink of sunset and set against the turquoise sky, a bird spread out its wings above us. It was a fitting beginning and recognition to the presence of the Spirit of the place that this young man's totem was the 'Thunderbird.'

The Sacred and the Profane – Tobacco or Taboo

I welcomed the opportunity to keep the fire, and in fact took 'roles' there just as I would at the *havan*. There was only one difference. While we put *smagari* (loose incense made from over 20 different dried flowers, seeds and barks) in our sacred fire, the native people offer tobacco. Now in order to appreciate my position, you have to understand that I personally am violently allergic to tobacco smoke of any kind. If a smoker walks in the room, the stench from his clothes is enough to nauseate me. On top of that, for a Sikh, tobacco is taboo. As it is a powerful drug, Guru Gobind Singh had forbidden its use among Sikhs lest they become addicted. Even animals had recognized its potency. There is a wonderful story of Guru Gobind Singh ji's horse refusing to carry Him across a field of tobacco. The thought of anyone putting tobacco in the *havan* was horrendous. Clearly sacrilege, meant to profane a holy place.

But here I am in another environment where tobacco itself is sacred. I knew that God could make the profane sacred. According to Jaap Sahib, wasn't God present everywhere and from that perspective wasn't everything sacred. Perhaps it was how we used it that would make it profane. And that proved true. At first I offered it at arms length moving back into the recesses of the tepee to avoid contact with the smoke. But then as I realized the transformation I relaxed and fed the fire just as I would have the *havan*. Neither was I affected by the smoke nor did my clothes even carry a scent of tobacco.

Sacred Words – Sacred Bonds

In my conversations over meals I found these deeply spiritual people trying to reclaim their roots. They had lost their language, their culture was threatened and their religion was mocked. One of the key components was their recognition of the presence of the spirit of the Creator in everything. And a recognition that they were part of nature not its master. So the trees, the animals, the water, and most of all the earth were given great respect. Each had its names. Those names were not assigned by scientists to catalogue a particular genus, they were the actual name, the words given by the Creator that empowered and activated the being. So for example – 'Tree' would be calling to the spirit of the tree, actually invoking its presence. When they lost their language they lost their connection and their power.

As I pondered these wonders of God's order and the decimation of a culture by those who would call themselves civilized, Maharaj ji showed be great visions. I was awakened early in my hotel to meditate and watch the sunrise.

Slowly a slit of light began to emerge on the dark horizon. Radiating upward it quickly spread across the plains. When people speak of 'The Great Plains' it is really something to behold. Outside of telephone poles and buildings, there are no natural obstructions for as far as the eye can see, except for the occasional stand of trees. So dawn rises in layers across the clouds, like curtains billowing above a giant stage. And as the curtains rose and the stage was dimly lit, a White Buffalo (the Sacred Animal of the Native People) appeared. His voice was deafening and the lesson unmistakable.

The White Buffalo

The Buffalo appeared beneath the crimson curtain at sunrise stretching out across the plains.

"The voices of my people are silent. The sacred covenant broken by your treaties. Your laws break their spirit. My Law makes them strong.

You give them your land to connect to as a symbol. No reserve can contain My Spirit. How can it contain my people. You bargained and sold what is mine. How can you Value what is not yours.

Tell my people to regain their voice. No longer can they live as sovereign nations when they have no Law. They are bound together only through the Great Law and they will live as great warriors among all the peoples of the earth. Warriors of the Great Law, fighting the injustice - corruption - weakness that has conquered them.

They must become warriors against their own weaknesses. Now they look to fight with others. They fight with each other to show their power.

My Power lies in Peace. My Strength lies in silence. Teach them again to sit around the Sacred Fire.

Teach them ceremony that they might reconnect with My Law.

Then they will conquer their greatest enemy - the enemy within themselves which has destroyed their soul.

Only then will they hold their head tall and walk shoulder to shoulder.

What can our women do when the men don't listen? How long can they wail? The mothers and sisters who face the pain.

The pain of the anger - the pain of the fist - the pain of despair. The women can listen to me.

Speak to me - teach their children to speak to Me."
8-4-01

Language

We used the names given by the Creator. We called the tree by the name the Creator gave. These words linked us to the universe. Language did not set us apart it, but bound us together, not just as a people but as part of God's creation.

Now we are asked to teach our children 'our' language. But it has no meaning outside of ceremony.

Language revealed the Creator's power. Words honored the Creator and His Law.

Now words are used to bring honor to you (and disgrace to me and the Creator). Your words enforce your law and violate ours and that of our Creator.

Language is powerful medicine. It can heal all. But we are not the ones to speak. It is our time to be silent and first listen. Listen for the Voice of the Creator. Learn His Language. Listen to the Voice of the wind – the water – and see His face reflected in the Sacred Fire.

You will then see His Face in all.

Feel the embrace of Mother Earth caress your feet. Rising up to meet you in the morning.

And kissing you good night as You lay down to sleep.

Then your language will return. The Power in Your words.

Now your words have no power.

If language has no Power you may yell and scream and curse to no avail.

When your words are once again full, then even silence (no words) will suffice.

Even a whisper will move people.

8-3-01

Wind

When the wind rustles the leaves, they sing its song
The grass bows, the dust swirls
Because the wind carries the Message of (our ancestors)
The wind carries the words - The Voice of our Creator.

8-3-01

In the Present or Presence

Following 9-11 there was an informal gathering of local spiritual leaders to listen and share thoughts with the public. It was set in a park around a circle and as the sun dipped the questions began to rise. One student asked the local Buddhist master, "Why do we have to dwell on the present. When there is so much pain why can't we just move beyond it?"

She replied that in meditation Buddha wanted his disciples to experience each and every emotion fully so even though the present may be painful, we must experience it.

Maharaj ji immediately told me, "Tell them presence, not present." I formulated my response.

"Perhaps the Buddha meant to be in the presence. If Truth and God are all pervasive as is the Buddha Nature, if however we have to experience the pain of the world we do so in God's presence we will be able to gain strength and wisdom and move beyond." It was a wonderful moment in the gathering as the student and Buddhist master appreciated Maharaj ji's thought. It was as if the whole circle was lifted up.

Communion in Russia

Over lunch at the Millennium Peace Summit, I had met a senior Russian Orthodox Church official. He invited me to call on him whenever I was in Moscow. Quite fortuitously and equally accidentally, I ran into him while at *Dom Journalista,* the National Press Club of Russia. Church officials had gathered there for a major announcement and I was just visiting a friend to talk about plans for Maharaj ji's next visit. The Chaplain was quite surprised to see me and asked me to call when we both were free.

Though he had an incredibly busy schedule, he invited me to visit him during a major celebration at a local church on the outskirts of Moscow. As it turned out, it was the time of the historic visit of the delegation from the World Council of Churches and I visited briefly with them while the service continued inside.

As Chaplain had invited me to the service, I thought I might as well go in. So I told the group, "While you're waiting here I think I'll go and commune with Jesus."

I had no idea of the format of the service so I walked up the steps and pushed open the old heavy wooden door and was greeted with a church packed with worshippers all raising their voices in praise of God. While I received a fair number of strange looks, I didn't feel out of place. I presented my flowers that I'd bought as an offering to the first priest I met and observed two lines. One was processing forward towards the altar for confession, the other was moving away. As I knew I was not there to confess, I joined the line moving towards the back of the church. About half way down I saw some old women standing next to what seemed to be two octagonal wooden boxes filled with liquid. They were ladling out small cups for those in line. Suddenly I realized that I was in line for communion. I knew the strict rules of the church. After all, if the President of the World Council of Churches and his colleagues did not feel they could worship in an Orthodox Church, then how would I be treated. I left it in Maharaj ji's hands. As my turn approached, I kept smiling at everyone and praising God. But as the old woman looked up at me, her face suddenly knotted. Though I don't know Russian, I knew what she was saying. "Are you a Christian?" she practically shouted. I smiled and pointed my finger heavenward. The women around me encouraged her to go through with the offering so I happily drank the cup of warm white wine and took the small cracker-like wafer to eat, and moved quickly to a position in an open area near the back of the church. I had taken communion before, but that was only a sip out of a priest's goblet. But a small cup was more than I was used to. The heat of the wine was beginning to rise to my head. Fortunately, the services required standing and kneeling on the stone floor so I was able to move and begin to work the alcohol out of my system. I bought some candles to light before the beautiful icon of Saint George – slaying the dragon. As in most orthodox churches, every inch was covered with the most beautiful images of Jesus, the Holy Mother, and the Saints. High vaulted ceilings reflected both the sun light streaming in and the sounds of voices rising to the heavens. It was a beautiful scene and my soul was lifted up throughout.

However, after the service walking out in the sun, the wine began to take its full effect. I was hardly able to carry on a coherent conversation with the Chaplain, the stated purpose of my trip, but I trusted that we had resumed our friendship and we could build upon it on my next visit. His young colleague was another matter. Quite suspicious of potential threats to the church and its culture, he told me that it was the responsibility of the Interfaith Conference, of which he was an active member, to unite against the enemies in the form of 'foreign religions,' which try to subvert 'our culture'. I shared that while preserving one's culture was indeed a noble cause, we in the international interfaith movement also unite against the enemies of society. But more typically we come together to combat poverty, ignorance, prejudice, and hatred.

PATH VIII

Reflections – Beyond the Notes

"Please Control Your Minds – All Your Thoughts Effect Me."

Surviving Maya : The Hardest Thing About Life is Living It

Though the sounds of the world can be deafening at times and the enticing beauty, Maya, continually tries to wrap her arms around you, Maharaj ji's Voice keeps me focused.

It was only if I didn't listen or rushed ahead without taking time to ask: "Which office should I go to this morning?" that I would get into trouble.

That is the whole purpose of prayer to seek guidance and the strength to follow the directions. For life is not an easy course and it becomes a tough taskmaster when you try to follow God's path. Those not conscious of God's presence are simply flung from one end to the other and have to face their ups and downs sometimes without even realizing they are being tested but to those who He has admitted to His school, we must try our best to understand the rules and obey.

Far too often we miss a clue or ignore a warning and rush off headlong in the wrong direction only to be brought to a screeching halt or dead end. Then we have to retrace our steps sometimes with heads hung or tails between our legs.

24

Discernment – Follow Your Path

The problem is that the road we take always leads some place.
Whether it leads us to clarity or into more darkness is the key.
Faith dictates that God is always with us even when we make a
wrong turn.

But our prayer should be:

"Don't let us take the wrong turn. Give us the power to see the
right way."

Even better, "Don't even show us another way. Put us on the
right path and keep us there."

Living with mistakes

Maharaj ji always counsels:

"Don't look back. Let whatever has happened pass and move
ahead."

Don't let a mistake dim your confidence or diminish your
commitment. Just ask forgiveness and learn to look for His Light.
Forget your own thoughts.

Spend more time in meditation, surround yourself with the Guru
and good counsel. But listen to the Guru first and then follow the
orders.

Sat bachan

Sat bachan means to accept your word and whatever you say is right.

Maharaj ji teaches that this is the way to follow your Guru.
Forget yourself. Like a soldier asking his commanding officer, we
should pray: "What is your order for me for the day." Then follow
it. A Sikh stands in prayer twice a day before Guru Granth Sahib,
with hands folded and then receives the order. No doubt, God
speaks to us from His scripture, the question remains whether we
follow it or not.

Peeling off layers

Whenever Maharaj ji would call me back to Gobind Sadan, it was like entering a decontamination bath. All the grime from the world that I'd accumulated while I was away would slowly loose its grip. As I prayed, I would feel my self emerge again. Like peeling off layers, the different parts of my defenses and identities that were necessary for survival in the world all slipped away. Even the imprints from the organizational titles or designations that had been conferred on me, like plaques on an office wall, all disappeared and I was left standing naked before God; nothing to cover up my behavioral flaws and nothing to stand in the way of my love. It was really a great relief. For as strange as it may sound, the more the world puts on us the more we have to strip away to be in God's presence. Like refinishing old furniture, we find the beautiful natural wood grain covered up by several layers of paint.

Unfortunately, when it's time to leave, we slowly don the armor of the world and head out again.

Once, Mark, a friend deeply touched by his first visit to Gobind Sadan remarked, "How can you ever leave this place?" My answer came simply, "You can't. Unless you can carry it with you, you can't leave."

The Title Trap

When I think about my studies, the only real difficulties I've faced are when I've thought I must prove myself and take charge. When I've stood straight and tried to take the storm on by myself. When I've had positions or titles, other than His devotee. Titles too are traps. They brand us as special, and when we forget that the only thing special about us is not a worldly position, but His love, then we get stuck and fall. When I've learned to accept each stage and not to struggle too hard with the lessons, but learn from them, He has cleared away even the toughest obstacles.

That is not to say I haven't had to take on my share of responsibility. He has insisted on it. And there is much more yet to be done. It's just when we think that we are in charge, and we forget the One who is standing behind us, holding us up, that He steps back and we fall.

290

Some lessons have overwhelmed me. I've gotten caught up in them and allowed them to ensnare me, like the anxiety that builds over an especially tough math problem or a test question we're really not prepared for.

And instead of simply saying, "Maharaj ji I don't understand this, what should I do?" We plunge headlong into it and only when we've been thoroughly beaten do we cry out for help.

Are we not students and He the ultimate Teacher? When the teacher puts a problem on the board and asks the students to solve it, do we think He doesn't know the answer? So, if the Guru asks us our opinion or places a worldly problem before us why shouldn't we think that similarly He is testing us. And if we have not experienced the problem before or if we are still having difficulty with the concept – ask. Ask Him for He is always with us. And He knows everything about us. And cares more about us than we could ever care for ourselves. He knows the tests we will be given. He designed the curriculum. Can He change a question on our test? Surely. Can He give us credit even if we get the wrong answer? Definitely! But only if we are sincere in our Love and sincere in our attempt. It is for us to only try, try hard, give everything, our very soul to the pursuit of His Truth and He will see that we pass. Without Him we are all failures, and we will make the same mistakes over and over and over again until we look to Him for the correct answer. He sits inside us, watching and guiding our every move, our every thought. He is Guru.

The 'correct' answer

When the Guru asks you a question He already knows what answer you will give and why you will give it. He may be testing our knowledge or simply checking to see if we are paying attention. But in Maharaj ji's class, it is not so much what answer you give that make the response correct as much as it is how you answer the question and the emotions that surround the process.

When Maharaj ji asked me a direct question my first thought used to be, "What can I tell the Guru, the Guru knows everything and how can I tell the Guru anything?" And I'd shrink from answering the question. My reasoning was sound – the Guru does know everything, and even knows what is in my mind and the answer that I will give. I also thought that this showed my humility and reverence for Him, one quality He encouraged and the other He engendered. Unfortunately this was the 'Wrong' answer. This shows total lack of confidence.

The second type of response was even worse. When Maharaj ji asked my advice – I would think 'Oh the Guru is asking Me. I must know the correct answer.' It was hard to determine whether I was more sure of myself or full of my self.

Now I see that after years of lecturing, the Guru wants to see if we know the right answer or have understood the lesson.

So whenever the Guru asks our opinion or for advice, we should 'listen' to His Voice inside and ask that Voice – what does the Guru want. Then give Him the answer He Himself has told us.

This should not be such a difficult concept to understand. Many teachers provide the basis for their students' understanding and then test them on what they (the teachers) have taught the students.

Let's assume that the Master has told us in review class that February has 29 days this year. If he then asks us in class, "How many days are in February 2000?" He won't be happy if we say: "I don't know" or "I don't remember." He'll think that either the student has no confidence, or he has not paid any attention to His lectures.

When we think, "I know the answer," we are forgetting that the Master taught us everything we know, and before coming to His class we knew nothing. He will think that this student is blind, he can stumble at any moment. He thinks he knows everything.

But when the student answers for the question, recalling the words of the Teacher, the Master is truly happy. "Yes, this student has learned."

For giving the 'correct' answer is not what distinguishes us, it is understanding the answer and how to find the right solution.

Listening to the Voice of the Guru, following and asking the Guru will always provide the 'correct' answer.

The rules of class

Often I think that while we like to call ourselves – 'Sikhs' or Disciples, we forget the rules of the classroom. A good student rushes to class excited about the subject. The more challenging the assignment the happier he is. When the teacher puts a difficult question on the board or on a test, the student eagerly rises to the challenge – trying to figure out how the Master has tried to trick him.

But when we deal with life's lessons we are suddenly shaken. "Please don't make this test so difficult," we cry. And we constantly look for ways out. Why does this problem keep cropping up? Why are we always facing this situation?

We've forgotten that the good teacher will only put in front of us the material we have yet to learn. If we get an 80 on a test, we may never see the 80% we got correct but the 20% we get wrong will keep coming up again and again in all possible forms and through countless people and circumstances. Until we discover the secret – of what weakness within ourselves is not letting us see the problem clearly – which of our blind spots is causing us to misunderstand the simple solution time and time again. And when we finally see within ourselves what we are holding on to and refusing to let go – which of our vices rears its ugly head – then we can be free. Free to put it before the Guru's Light and allow it to be burned away. Then it won't bother us again. And if it does, then we should already know the solution and apply it until it no longer has any effect on us. Only then will the Teacher withdraw that problem from our test. Or if it appears again, it is automatically answered correctly.

So it has been for me to learn to be a good follower – a good student – helping other students with their lessons – but never considering myself a teacher. And constantly praying that I be given the strength both to understand the problem and to overcome it.

Patience

One more point: patience. Whenever we come into Maharaj ji's presence He blesses us. Often this happens without Him even hearing our concern, without Him even listening to our problem. Why should He? He knows what we're going through. Perhaps He knows our condition better than we do. He knows how and when it will end.

293

Maharaj ji has told us that even before a person arrives, his soul arrives and begins to share all its problems. "I see the two of you sitting before me. By the time your body arrives your soul has already told me everything."

Whatever the problem, Maharaj ji usually says, *"Subh tik hojaiga."* (Everything will be all right.) Then He raises His right hand in blessing and says, *"Mehar."* *Mehar,* loosely translated means anything from 'My blessings are with you' to 'You are blessed.' But it does not mean, "May God bless you." When Maharaj ji says, *Mehar,* it is a fait accompli. You have just been blessed. Whatever the problem is, it will be solved. Now when will it be solved is another matter. For like God, Maharaj ji's time framework is different from ours. He can see forever.

Children on a trip

We, on the other hand are like children on a trip:

"Daddy, when will we get there?"

"In a little while, my child," the father answers.

Five minutes later, "Mommy, how much longer?"

"Not much longer maybe twenty more minutes."

Three minutes later, "Daddy, are we there yet?"

So even though Maharaj ji has already given His blessings and told us in essence "It will happen."

"Your disease will be cured." "Your business will improve." "You will get the job." "You will overcome this difficulty." We are like children incessantly asking, "When?" Never satisfied to take our medicine and see the result. Never willing to make the sacrifices, He is expecting us to improve our selves.

Maybe we're not ready yet

Maybe we're not ready to appreciate the gift He's about to give us. Maybe we're not responsible enough to handle it. Maybe there are things we still have to learn about and overcome our shortcomings before we are ready for the next stage, whatever that may be. Perhaps we haven't learned the basic lessons well enough and we look at the others around us who are doing 'better' or at least doing something else. And suddenly we think, "I should be doing that too." We leave our course of studies and begin to follow the others or ask to have what they have.

Maharaj ji doesn't like this. We each have our own course and we may find that by taking on someone else's lessons we may actually fall behind in our own instead of moving ahead.

So it is best to be patient. Ask what we should be doing while we are waiting. Maybe it's more path, more *Nam*, more seva. And then when the 'gift' arrives – we are truly ready to serve Him and use it properly. So many times when I've stopped to ask – Maharaj ji has shown me that there is still a gap in my knowledge that needs to be filled. And if I were only pushing to get the result I would not have been properly prepared and failed in the entire venture.

That's not to say that we can't "check in" from time to time and ask if we're still on track – or if there's something that still needs improvement. But not with the idea of His fixing the problem for us. If we have a flat tire (puncture), we can get out and fix it ourselves.

Nam or Hukam

The chicken and the egg of Sikhism is "Which came first – *Nam* or Hukam?" Standing with Harvinder in front of the water tower, Maharaj ji gave us this answer: "It is through *Hukam* that you receive *Nam* and are able to recite it. But it is *Nam* that gives you the power to 'hear and follow' the *hukam*."

Understanding God's Order

Perhaps the most difficult lesson for everyone is understanding *hukam*. What is God's order for me? What does God want me to do?

Coming to Maharaj ji answers the big question of existence: "Why am I here? The answer: to serve God and recite His Holy Name."

But how specifically on a day to day basis are we to carry it out? How do I live according to God's will? What is God's plan for me? One simple answer is, "We just do it."

Understanding The Big Picture: God's view of the World

Maharaj ji will often encourage if not entreat us to 'look with gyan.'

Whether it is our own problems or the conflict in the world, gyan (God's enlightened vision) gives us perspective and shows us the really 'Big Picture,' so we have a better understanding and are better able to deal with our difficulties. So what does 'gyan' show us?

At one level everything is under God's order, and everything is proceeding according to that Divine Plan. Whether we understand it or not from that perspective, is irrelevant. All we have to know is that there is a plan and we are an infinitesimally small part of it.

But in this world, for whatever reason, and certainly from our perspective, what we do does count. Those are the rules. Whatever we do does count in our favor or against us according to the law of karma. Our actions, past or current, determine our future actions. Now those could be from yesterday when we got angry at someone or from a past life when we helped someone, but they definitely play out in our daily lives.

It's simple to see in the present. If we help someone, we feel good and we tend to perform better. If we hurt someone or did something else wrong, it's likely to trouble us and we would perform poorly or at least not as well. Now if we can understand that those negative things carry over to our next life, like failing an exam and having to make up the test, or being kept back a grade, then we can understand the concept of karma and the fact that the soul is in an eternal school until the Principal decides that we have passed. So if we know that *hukam* on one level is for us to follow Truth, Dharma, the universal values that create goodness within us and justice in the world, then we should try our best to do good.

But where do I fit in?

The Guru knows everything. He not only knows the *hukam* for us, but He can even change it if He pleases. Most people go through life without ever asking what is God's order for me? Perhaps they don't think they could get ever get an accurate answer. Or perhaps they prefer not to ask because they are afraid of the answer. But the science of astrology has been around for millenniums, and, in India at least, people flock to astrologers for advice on their day to day affairs.

I personally think it's wrong to use the Guru as an astrologer, to ask him every little detail of your life. Brig. Sahib once told me, "I can't bother Maharaj ji every minute for His *hukam*, so I simply pray before leaving the house 'Maharaj ji please be with me all day and make me do what you want me to do' and with that I shove off trusting that He will direct my actions."

But when there are certain important issues in our life which need clarification, the Guru will certainly hear our request.

So when do we go to the Guru and how should we ask?

First, how should we ask? Many people come to Maharaj ji as if they are presenting a business proposal to their banker for approval. "Maharaj ji, I'd like to … go to America, open a business … get married … take this course … have a boy and on and on the list goes.

Maharaj ji typically answers, "Go ahead". If you ask the Guru for what you want, He grants it. But is that his *hukam* for you? By granting your wish, He is not saying you'll be happy, you'll be successful, what will happen if you take that course or go down that road. You are asking to do it and in His Beneficence He is allowing you to do what you want.

The other approach is "Maharaj ji, what is the *hukam* for me?" Now this question could be asked outright with no thoughts or preconceived notion of what you want to do. In which case Maharaj ji will tell you at that moment what God expects of you. Or you could go to Him with a proposal such as the litany of lifetime options mentioned above, but instead of asking for it, you ask Him, "Maharaj ji, I was thinking of doing such and such, what is the *hukam* for me?" And now most important, when He tells you the answer, you must follow it. Otherwise, what is the use of asking. You may want to do something that sounds great, and may be great for a little while. It may solve one of your problems but Maharaj ji can see how it will effect you not just now and not just in this lifetime, but forever. And he can see how many additional problems this "solution" may create that you didn't even know you had.

We may ask which college our children should attend? What career path is best? Who will make a better match for my child?

We may ask about business trends and whether it is the right time to make a particular move. Once the Guru accepts you as His disciple, He is happy to guide you.

But, we must be careful. Maharaj ji often says that people are in the habit of asking for long lists from God without ever spending any time in service or prayer. We don't want to fall into that category.

Ask in Prayer

Leave aside the major questions that we want personal guidance on, we should ask Maharaj ji in prayer every day. After our prayers, we can rise, fold our hands with the deepest respect and supplication, and as humbly and sweetly as possible ask: "Maharaj ji what is your *hukam* for me?" Then just as Brig. Sahib stated, ask "Please don't let me do anything that you would object to, but rather make me do only the work that will please you. Please save me from my weaknesses and allow me to serve You as it pleases You." Bow reverently and get on with another day.

Beg forgiveness before we sleep

If in fact we fail somehow during the day, then at night before we go to sleep ask His forgiveness. Maharaj ji has often said, before we go to sleep we should check our minds, and ask, "Did we hurt anyone's feelings today? Did I lose my temper? Was I jealous, or lustful, or greedy?" And if so, which is usually the case in all of us, beg forgiveness there and then, and the next day try not to make those mistakes again. Like an athlete watching game films to review his weaknesses and improve the next game.

Spiritual practice – Jaap Sahib, *Havan*, Lighting Candles

This is where spiritual practice comes in. While we're waiting for our time to come, we should fix the tire ourselves. We should work on overcoming the weaknesses within us that may be blocking our progress. We must prepare ourselves.

As a doctor gives a prescription for a particular illness, Maharaj ji prescribes Jaap Sahib. It is indeed the cure for whatever ails you.

Some people keep their minds occupied by knitting, reading, playing games or watching TV. But that does not change their karma, or solve the problem. They are just distractions. That's not to say that any of these past times are bad. They are just not solutions to the problem. Jaap Sahib actually solves the problem.

Thought Monitor

We have monitors in classes to make sure students aren't cheating on tests; monitors in halls or dorms to make sure kids don't break the rules. We have radar to monitor the traffic flow for speeding on highways and air traffic controllers to make sure planes don't crash into each other taking off and landing and radar to keep our airspace safe from invasion. However, who monitors our thoughts to keep our anger, greed, lust, and pride from attacking us? No doubt, we have a conscience that until dulled by society keeps us alert to the pitfalls and potholes of life. But how do we monitor our minds so errant thoughts don't plague us, distract us, divert our attention, and ultimately defeat us or lead us astray? This is or should be the key question of life. The answer lies with God and in all scriptures. This is the true purpose and meaning of meditation and prayer – to build a defense against our thoughts. Against the negativity that surrounds us so we can always be positive, add positive energy to a conversation or relationship, and rise above the darkness of the world. Simple enough in theory but in practice learning to control or monitor our thoughts is by far the most difficult task any human being must face. While much spirituality is marketed as a feel good relaxation therapy the real challenge of spiritual progress is not just stress reduction so we can feel better but anger and greed reduction, lust reduction, and making us better human beings. There are tons of diets on the market to reduce our waistline and exercises to build our bodies but still the world is beset by worry and corruption at all levels. Drug use is rampant and we are on the verge of another world war. The solution lies in hard work within. More than the mental gymnastics we use to tune our minds for our business pursuits we need to spend time daily to develop the skill and power to ride herd on our wild thoughts. In Gobind Sadan, Babaji has people focus on a single prayer or recite *Jaap Sahib*. Spending time praising God, you begin to emulate and imbibe those good qualities. When we pray to God as the One beyond anger, our anger begins to subside. With *Nam*, we focus and occupy our minds with something more powerful than any worldly song and any worldly desire. Like a pacifier to a crying baby, *Nam* soothes our burning mind but beyond pacifying, it strengthens our minds so we are not as irritated next time and slowly we are able to actually overcome those "hot-buttons" which set us off. But we must be alert to see them coming. That Power of God within us is beyond our minds. It is always alert, never sleeps, and knows our every thought.

Involving God in our lives, is like turning on our internal alarm system, our rapid defense response team, or an anti-virus program on our computers. Then the virus of anger, greed, lust, and hate will not attack when they see such Power amassed against them. Naturally, as humans, we have our lapses and fall prey to bouts of anger but we can overcome it with constant practice and constant prayer and God's blessings. The day we understand that like weight loss or bodybuilding, this is a lifelong and even many lives-long practice and we develop a way to discipline our selves and our thoughts, peace will come to our minds and the world.

Deja vu

How many times have we felt we have met someone before or been in this place before. This is the spiritual realization that we have been together before. "Been there, Done that," carries over from many lives. We have in fact done this before. We have played these roles before.

Don't be afraid

When Maharaj ji first appeared to me in the vision in New York, He spoke twice. Each time 3 words:

"Don't be afraid" and "Meditate on this."

Fear was the problem, and meditation the solution.

As a child I was totally fearless. So much so that I would climb the tallest trees and swing from the uppermost branches of the mulberry tree in our neighbors vacant lot, ride big-boy bikes, wrestle and play football with kids twice my size. Fear never entered my mind. Rather there was so much sense and wonder of Your presence – the force around me that I knew I could not be harmed.

300

But when the Voice left me, as I had been forewarned, fear became so dominant that I became hesitant to even attempt sometimes the simplest of tasks. Life became a constant struggle, with my mind placing obstacles before me even before I could begin the work. The solution was just ignoring or overcoming the fear and working through the problem.

But fear can be and is meant to be debilitating. The most powerful weapon of our enemy – if we accept the notion of evil – gains power over us by instilling fear.

The Gurus simply saw the evil and laughed at the poor creatures who grew out of evil, challenged them to battle and handily defeated them. Durga Mata demolishing the Demon Kings, and Lord Ram defeating the demons bent on terrorizing the *rishis* to stop *havan* and the forces for good.

"If we fear evil, if we feel the negative is more powerful, then where is our faith?" Maharaj ji asks. And what can the future of the world be?

The second thing Maharaj ji said was: Meditate on this – This was the solution, like Jesus in the boat, powered by *Nam* – when we give more credence to our fears then we can't say we have faith.

Meditation is concentrating on developing the Power of truth within, empowering the good and vanquishing the evil. It allows us to recognize the game and not fear it. We are trained to be pros at the game of life. Let's play it like pros.

If we give our opponent more power, see him as more powerful than us, then how can we win. Yet we do this daily. Despite my lessons, from time to time I have suffered from attacks of fear and anxiety, especially when He takes me to the next level. But Maharaj ji has always brought me through.

Meditation is such a great power. And there is nothing more powerful than the Guru. These simple lessons mean that you remain strong, stand your ground. Don't react out of fear or anger but like the Gurus, fight simply to vanquish the obstacles which stand in our way. Doubt should not block our progress. Once the game plan is in place, once the order is given then doubt should not arise.

301

As Maharaj ji says, "The world is beset by the disease of worry or of fear." Guru Nanak says, "Conquer your minds and you'll conquer the world." It has taken me years even with the Guru often standing beside me to come back to my childhood state of fearlessness.

I'm not sure we are ever truly free. But by surrendering and letting go, by listening and following the orders, we are able to rise above it.

The Boxer

One day I was sitting at home in front of our living room fireplace *havan*, when an amazing vision enveloped me. It was an extremely trying time for me. I felt beset from many directions and attacked from others. Each day brought new challenges to add to the ones I hadn't yet overcome. I was close to drowning.

In the vision, I was a boxer bruised and bloodied standing in the middle of the ring, and standing was the operative word. Outside the ring, all those who I was or had been in conflict with were standing applauding me and bowing with hands folded. I was astonished. "We are your karma. We are just playing out the roles given to us by God. We have no enmity with you. You are a great warrior, a great champion. We are just your sparring partners." What a revelation. Everyone in our lives is simply an enactment of our karma. That's why Maharaj ji so often tells us to forgive or rise above a moment or even a period of stress. If it is just our karma playing out then what is there to be angry about. Recognize and learn the lesson and move on. Easier said than done. But you can't play the game unless you understand the rules.

When Jesus walked the earth

Maharaj ji has often said when people complain about the state of the world: "What has changed since Jesus walked the earth? It is the same earth, the same air, and the same water. What has changed is us. We humans have erred. Once we return to the path then all will be fine."

During an interfaith service

In Syracuse, we held an interfaith Thanksgiving service that included congregations from many different traditions. At the end everyone joined in singing praises to the One God and the Voice spoke loudly to me. God was so happy that all have put aside their differences, the Voice said, 'Tell all those who have cursed their fate that they were born at this time that they would live to thank God that they were born at this time."

25

Reflections on a True Master

While it may seem totally improper for a devotee to try to put into words what he finds unique about His Master, I must share a few of what I have found to be His special qualities.

Humor

Maharaj ji's laugh shakes the whole world.

Celia, a well-known Interfaith 'activist' from England, was among guests at a Gobind Sadan Institute International Seminar at the time Swaranjit's great documentary on Maharaj ji's life and mission, 'Spreading the Light of Truth' was being filmed. As with many of us, she unwittingly became one of the subjects.

Describing her experiences in meeting Maharaj ji she said: "I didn't quite know what to expect that by coming here I would come face to face with God, and I was quite glad to find that He had a great sense of humor."

Indeed the power of His laugh is something to behold. It is what some might call uncontrollable. Maharaj ji's whole body shakes and the waves ripple across the surrounding environment, breaking whatever state of dull or sad complacency the world had resolved itself to sink into at the moment. I'm sure it is also meant to break the karmas associated with the act that triggered it and with the perpetrator.

That is if you know enough to laugh along. It will clear all the blocks. It is understandable to feel a bit embarrassed (and somewhat repentant is acceptable) but if you feel even a little annoyed at having been made the brunt of a joke, then the karmas stay and may even become more recalcitrant.

He wants us to learn to laugh at ourselves. Laugh in the face of danger and laugh in the face of darkness and difficulties in our lives. While many have written on the therapeutic power of humor and some have gone so far as to make laughter part of their daily morning exercises, no one demonstrates it better than Maharaj ji. It is as spontaneous as his singing, and can be triggered by a simple comment from a devotee or just a truly funny incident in our collective lives. Finally when the world or the karmas are cleansed, He catches himself with a patented, "*Oh ho!*" and the quake is over. But the aftershocks of happiness can and do last for lifetimes.

The glow of love

In Japji Sahib, Guru Nanak referred to the glow of God's love on the faces of His beloveds.

All one has to do is walk into a room where Maharaj ji is present to understand this line. His face beams a radiance that the sun could only hope to maintain.

And while Pandits and Sadhus paint a line on their foreheads to symbolize the awakened third eye, Maharaj ji's 'channel' as I might call it, is so deep it actually glows when He is communing with God.

Humility

Be humble before God, but stand strong among men.

People often associate the term "meek" with its synonym "timid." Maharaj ji continually demonstrates that humbling oneself before God is hardly a weak position, but one as close to absolute power as you can come. And it is a non-corrupting power. For God directs us to do good and speak out against evil.

Maharaj ji is constantly challenging those with power to put aside their corrupt ways and to serve the people. He has often said, "If we can straighten out the politicians, the clerics, and the media, the world will find its way to peace."

Self-Sacrifice

24 hours a day, Maharaj ji has given himself to the mission and to his devotees.

When He is not holding audience, calls come in at all hours from all over the world. Even when he is not visibly sitting with people, while he is in private He is circling the globe and fighting battles on our behalf of epic proportion.

He literally takes the burdens of the world upon himself. And if His body suffers that is just a means of cleansing our sins.

Hands that hold the world

Anyone who has sat for even a minute with Him notices the divine dance of his hands. They bless and they punctuate from finger to full palm up. I understand the Buddhist concept of Mudra – the many armed and multi-faceted Bodhisattva, but no artist no matter how adept could ever capture the number and exact poses that Maharaj ji's hands have taken.

Concern for his devotees

Maharaj ji shows interest and concern for every detail of our life. Our cars, our homes, our physicians, our family's difficulties and successes, marriages and businesses, He is so concerned for our wellbeing, no earthly father could ever show so much love. And this is not just us. All His devotees.

When Joginder had cancer, Maharaj ji immediately called the most prominent Doctors to make sure she would have the best possible treatment. And when she was about to undergo surgery, He kindly took her call from America and blessed her so that any remaining anxiety was left in that room.

The Broken Mala

We were sitting in the lounge of our local newspaper waiting for the reporter, when suddenly the string on Maharaj ji's mala snapped sending beads skating across the floor.

He was visibly upset and sent us scurrying after them. The four of us were down on our hands and knees looking under every table and chair in the lounge. I've rarely seen Maharaj ji so concerned about anything. And then I suddenly realized, each bead on the string represented someone or something that Maharaj ji was taking care of. It would be like losing a piece of one's self. More importantly, His mala was the spiritual community being built and one bead lost meant a break in the link. This was the string that held the world, if not the cosmos in order. Finally we found the last bead and breathed a sigh of relief.

306

Toughest taskmaster

Maharaj ji has often said living in a Dharmastan is not easy.

Maha Kharari Sukh Sar
Hardest of all – but an ocean of joy

It is like the verse from Anand Sahib,

This path is thinner than a hair and sharper than a sword.
But it is filled with love.

The closer to the Sun, the hotter it becomes and the tests and forces are very unforgiving. But the Guru is all forgiving.

Care for those in need

Just when people feel they have lost everything and given everything, Maharaj ji will open Heaven's Chest and suddenly riches will descend beyond people's wildest dreams.

To the poor, He has presented the most beautiful of weddings for their daughters.

To those struggling, he has opened the flood gates.

And to those who know not what to ask for, He fulfills their innermost desires.

Concern for humanity

Today people have become so close-minded and full of fear. Maharaj ji often says: "Throw open the gates of your mind. How can you see when you keep the doors and windows of your house shut. Open the doors and make them so wide that an elephant can pass through. Now you are so narrow minded that these thoughts cannot penetrate. Become broad minded and the Love of God will envelop you."

Once when Maharaj ji was sitting in Chandigarh with Nirlep Kaur translating for me, I asked what he foresaw for the future of humanity. I want people to reach their wonderful potential of what it means to be human. Enjoy and celebrate life to the fullest. Whatever they undertake they should do with full commitment to a standard of excellence to show their 'God-given' talents. If they play golf let them excel. If they ride horseback let it be with great skill and grace. In their businesses and workplaces let them maintain the highest standards of excellence and integrity. In their personal life their character should be above reproach. And through all the trials and tests of life let them be happy.

That is why after He raises His hand in blessing, Maharaj ji always says:

Khush raho

Just be happy - Be happy and stay happy !!

And this is our wish for you.

Studio Pammi, Chandigarh

In Memorial

Before this book could be published, His Holiness Baba Virsa Singh ji, internationally renowned spiritual leader, beloved founder and preceptor of Gobind Sadan, had left this world on Monday morning the 24th December, 2007, to continue His battle for Goodness on another plane. Throughout His life on this earth, Babaji was an outspoken advocate for and champion of inter-communal harmony, he was a Healer and Spiritual teacher to countless individuals throughout the world. He was known for his prophetic statements about major world events such as the break up of the Soviet Union and the impact of the Iraq War on American life. Since His childhood, countless miracles which he had performed have been documented, like giving sight to the blind, healing leprosy, and allowing the cripples to walk. But, Babaji himself always felt the greatest miracle was changing the human mind towards good. He always said, "God is the only Doer, the One who gives you everything. Give all your love to God."

I had been in the United States on my semi-annual trip, catching up with family and business affairs. I had called Maharaj ji several times and could tell that He wasn't well. But He always pulled through and there seemed no cause to worry. My daughter-in-law asked whether I wanted to cut my trip short and return. I reassured her that everything was all right.

On the night after my return, I knelt beside Maharaj ji's bed. He was lying comfortably and was happy to see me. I related the story of the trip and especially brought him up to date on the family, His mission, and shared more portions of the book. "People will find it very interesting. You've revealed many new things. It is blessed.

Everyone will join you in this mission." As He relaxed, He said with great love, *"Chalo, Put ghar vapas agya"* (My son has returned home.) Tears filled my eyes. I bowed, kissed his hand, and took my leave.

The next night He was unwell. As I stood at the foot of the bed, He looked up and said, "How is Ralph Singh doing?" I almost missed it. "If my Guru is well, then I am happy," I finally responded. But, my Guru wasn't well. Maharaj ji lay quietly on his bed. Meanwhile, the world of His faithful prayed and expected that even now He would get up. After all, He had healed them of the incurable, solved their intractable personal and business problems, subdued terrorist outbreaks, brought bounty forth from wastelands, and blessed them with a life lasting peace to their troubled minds. There was nothing He couldn't do, even conquer death, if He willed it. As I tuned my mind to His words, He spoke clearly and sharply:

"I have nothing to prove. You may want to see a miracle for your faith. But, I need nothing. I have lived my faith. Any questions, the record stands and speaks for itself. If you want a miracle, you do it. I have done mine. I have transformed all of you into Warriors for Truth. I've made heroes out of cowards, and the story has not even begun. You will see such Light and happenings that you could never have believed. As I have said, again, and again I will work even greater deeds through you. All will join you in this mission.

Do not despair. I am always with you to bring joy. Let there be no sadness. The pain of separation is for those attached to a body. My spirit always has been and always will be with all of you. Recite *Nam*. Do Jaap Sahib. Love each other, and welcome all who come in my name."

Early the next morning, He had left. In passing as in life, Maharaj ji's connection with Jesus will be etched in history. He left on Christmas eve, was cremated on Christmas, and His memorial was held on the Day of Epiphany, January 6th, Russian Orthodox Christmas.

When people ask: "How did He die?" I say, "He didn't. Great souls take our sins on themselves and leave when it is their time." "How old was He?" I respond, "Ageless. He has been with us forever and will remain for eternity." We may ask 1000 'whys' but as Maharaj ji Himself stated, "I have nothing else to prove. I have lived my faith."

Maharaj ji had completed His earthly journey. Now, I have to complete mine.

Epilogue-I

Joginder's Story – the early history from 1967

My wonderful wife Joginder, one of Maharaj ji's greatest gifts to me, was one of the first people to step foot on Gobind Sadan's sacred soil and her early recollections follow. Her efforts along with those of our early classmates form not only the base of the story, but the foundation of what Gobind Sadan is today. I have included Joginder's story here. I'll leave it for the others to tell their own experiences.

The Lonely Road

I have always walked the lonely road – sometimes scared, tempted, punished by my parents, mocked by friends, and discouraged by fellow travelers. But my love was so great and His pull was so strong and Maharaj ji's Power so always present that nothing could take me off the path.

In the beginning, after I met Him, I had to see Him every day. I couldn't live without being in His presence. Then, the road to Gobind Sadan was completely deserted. Where now mansions line the road, there was nothing. I would walk three miles, sometimes in the dark, through this dangerous jungle, with wild dogs barking or trying to bite me, and lecherous men looking at me.

But in the end I was always led safely into His presence. The reward for walking the lonely road is that He is always with me. The harder and more dangerous it became, the more He would bless me, and the more I would feel His presence.

The Divine Meeting

One Saturday evening in 1967, my mother went with our neighbor named Sehgal to visit a holy person in Maharani Bagh. She stayed there overnight. When she came home the next morning, she was very happy and excited that she had seen a holy man and that they had prayed there all night long. She was awed by what a wonderful experience she had had.

My younger sister and I decided to go and see for ourselves, and behold – have darshan of – such a holy person. I was 20 years old at this time. We went with our mother on the bus. It was a long trip from our house and a long walk from the bus stop to our destination. We reached there at 9 a.m.

We took our shoes off and washed our hands and then went to the prayer room. It was a small room with white sheets spread all over the rug. The Sikh scripture, called Guru Granth Sahib, was reverently displayed. Baba Inder Singh was singing hymns, or as we say, "doing kirtan." We bowed to Guru Granth Sahib and sat down. In a few minutes, the holy person himself, Maharaj ji, came into the room. He was dressed all in white: a white robe, turban, and socks. He bowed down to Guru Granth Sahib and started fanning it with a special whisk, known as chaur sahib.

What an experience. He looked so beautiful and peaceful. It looked like the whole world was under His control and there was light all around Him. I felt that God just landed here to bless us all and bring peace to the whole world.

The blessing of His Mother

There was an older woman sitting next to me. My mother told me that the woman was Maharaj's mother. I thought how lucky she was to be the mother of such a holy person. I respectfully touched her feet and something happened to me and I started to cry. I couldn't stop crying. The tears of joy were flowing from my face into my *chunni* (scarf), and it got all wet. We stayed through the whole ceremony, which was very nice. Afterwards, Maharaj gave us all malas – prayer bead rosaries. He told us to recite the phrase 'Ek Onkar Satnam Siri Waheguru' all the time. It means 'There is one God whose name is truth, and praise to that wondrous God.' The

313

whole experience was out of this world. I had never before felt like this.

That day changed my life forever. Something had changed within me. I thought about Maharaj ji day and night. Everywhere I looked, I saw him.

At that time I had a job in the Delhi Development Agency as an architectural draftsperson. Before I used to go to work, I would go to see him every morning. I started to pray more often. I prayed before I went to work, at home, on the bus, while walking, and during my lunch hour.

One day my mother made curry for lunch. She always made very good curry. So I asked my mother to put some in a container so that I could take it to Maharaj ji. I hurried away with the food and didn't eat any lunch myself. I was just on time before He ate lunch. I gave the curry to Mrs. Majithia and told her that the curry was for Maharaj ji. She took it to Him and brought some back for me to take home. It was a long walk from their house to the bus stop. I had to change three buses to go home, but finally I reached home and I had my own lunch.

Sometimes I would go there during the weekend and pray and meet more people who would share their experiences with me. I felt so lucky to have met such a holy person in my lifetime.

9 Teen Murti Marg

After a few months, Maharaj ji moved to Mrs. Nirlep Kaur's house at 9 Teen Murti Marg. I decided to go there every morning before I went to work. I would get up at 1:30 a.m., take my shower, and meditate and say all my prayers. Then after breakfast, I would go see Maharaj ji. He never said a word to me. I would just go there, He would give me parshad (blessed food) and then I would leave for work. It felt so good and peaceful to see Him. I felt that He was with me all day long. If I couldn't see Him I felt that something was missing. I always kept his picture on my desk, and prayed during the breaks.

Teen Murti was very far from our house and I had to change buses twice to get there. It was still a very long walk from the

314

bus stop to their house, but I never minded at all. Even after I saw Maharaj ji, I would have to take another two buses to go to work. Sometimes I would arrive at work late, but it was worth it just to see Maharaj ji and get His blessings before I started my day.

Maharaj ji changed me so much. It is incredible. I used to get scared so easily. If I had to go from one room to another room, I would always look behind the doors and under the bed to make sure that no one was there. After I met Maharaj ji, all of that went away.

Sangat Gatherings

Randhawa Sahib (Gurbachan Singh who was in charge of Horticulture at the IIT campus) started holding *Akhand Path* in his house at I.I.T Gate. It takes 48 hours to read it all the way through, so we all took turns. I would to go there in the evening after work, read for two hours, and then go home. My parents used to worry about me.

Every Tuesday evening there was *kirtan* in Randhawa's house. I used to go and take part in the singing. Maharaj ji had blessed Randhawa Sahib to pray for sick people. So after Kirtan, he would pray for the different people and they would be healed and all their prayers would be answered.

Sometimes there would be *Havan* (sacred fire) in someone's house. Then I would go there to take my turn to pray for two hours and then go home. People used to talk about me and say that they didn't even know who this girl was but they were happy to see that I was so devoted that I would come on time, pray, and leave.

After a few months, Maharaj ji built a *havan* and prayer room for Guru Granth Sahib in Nirlep Kaur's garden. Then we took turns reading Guru Granth Sahib, while two others sat at the *Havan* reciting Naam and Chaupai Sahib (one of Guru Gobind Singh ji's hymn of praise). We needed three people at all times to pray. So, I used to go every morning before work and evening after work. Sometimes I would even stay overnight so that I could participate in the prayers.

Maharaj ji or my family

My parents didn't like me to stay away for two nights without coming home. My life changed so much that the only thing that I could think about was Maharaj ji and the importance of prayer. Nothing else mattered to me anymore. One morning while I was sitting in the small room waiting to see Maharaj ji, my father came in very upset. When Maharaj ji came out of His room, my father and I both went in to see Him. My father was very angry. He told Maharaj ji that he didn't like me staying there overnight. Maharaj ji closed His eyes and said, "Since she was up every morning at 2 a.m., I cant' say anything to her. Everything is in God's hands."

My father was still upset. But there was nothing he could do, so we both left for work. It was very difficult for me to see my parents so upset, but I was not doing anything wrong. I saw God's light in Maharaj ji, and my parents did not. It was very difficult for them to understand why I would go there every day. Even at work, girls used to tease me and ask why I would pray so much.

This was my routine. I would sleep for a few hours, pray, and then see Maharaj ji. After that, I would go to work. After work, the other girls would often go to see a movie. They used to ask me to go with them, but I wasn't interested at all. They couldn't understand why I would pray so much and would go to see Maharaj ji every day. Sometimes they would laugh at me, but nothing bothered me at all, because I saw the light and they did not.

My First Glimpse of Gobind Sadan

One evening in 1968, I went to see Maharaj ji at Teen Murti but He wasn't there. They told me that Maharaj ji had gone to some property that He had purchased near Mehrauli. When I asked how I could go there too, they told me that the drivers at the nearby taxi stand knew the way.

I went to the taxi stand and fortunately, one of the drivers on duty was willing to take me. It was already 6 p.m., with little light left, and it was a very long drive. After we passed Mehrauli the road became very lonely. I was a little scared because there were no buildings anywhere on either side of the road. There were weeds

316

and bushes everywhere. I kept praying, and after a long drive of almost an hour, we reached the farm.

All I could make out on this empty land was a small tent. As I approached, I saw Maharaj ji standing there and bowed down to Him. He blessed me, and I felt very satisfied. I had received what I came for. I turned around, got in the taxi and started home. It was starting to get dark, and I was still a little scared, but I was not worried at all. I knew God would take care of me and I would arrive home safely. And, I did.

Sometimes people would invite Maharaj ji to their homes in Delhi and He would go there and speak. One day Maharaj ji came to Sehgel's house in Sarojini Nagar. After that, He came to my parents' house, too. We sang kirtan and afterwards, Maharaj ji spoke. He told everyone to recite "Ek Onkar Satnam Siri Waheguru" all of the time. He then gave *parshad* to everyone. He visited my parents' house on two different occasions.

Building Gobind Sadan

Now that Maharaj ji had purchased this farm property, He started to build. At first, there was no kitchen, so we would bring our own food. People went there on weekends to work in the fields. The fields were full of weeds and we pulled them out with our bare hands. There were so many thorns that our hands bled, but we never felt any pain. Maharaj ji used to say that people working there would have all their sins washed away. We would then work extra hard and we never felt tired. We sang God's praises and time simply flew by.

In the evening, Maharaj ji would send a truck to take everyone to the nearby bus stand in Mehrauli. From there we would get on buses and go to our homes. We all looked forward to the weekend so that we could go there and work together again. By the time I reached home, it was very dark. I still had a one mile walk from the bus stand to my house. One day a big dog was following me and started to bark at me. At first I was scared. But then I shouted, "Ik Onkar Satnam Siri Waheguru!" and the dog ran away.

Vacations were always spent working on Maharaj ji's farm. Adults would take leave from their office would join the children off from school and work all day. As we built the area, men would dig, and women would carry big bowls of dirt on their heads. We women used to ask men to fill our bowls with more dirt so that we could work harder and earn more blessings. We used to move very fast so that we could work harder than the other person, and race to see who could make the most trips. We were all so happy. By evening, we were very dirty, but no one cared. We never felt tired or sore. Day after day we'd return to the fields, and always felt good and full of energy. Sometimes we carried bricks and others would carry mortar. Everyone had a job to do. No one would rest during the day. Everyone wanted to do more work. We had very little water and had to bring our water from the farm next door. Each of us would carry two buckets and make many trips. Our hands and feet were full of sores, but we never felt any pain or discomfort. We only felt happiness and blessings.

Sometimes we needed gravel. So we would break the big stones with hammers by hand. We used to sit on the stones in the hot sun and smash them. This was really hard work, and we got very sweaty, but we never felt hot or tired. This shows that there definitely was a power working through us. Maharaj ji was always around, but when we physically saw Him, we would work even harder. Time would go by very fast. We would even eat in the fields. In order to clean our dishes, we used dirt. The dishes shined and were completely clean, and we never got sick from doing this.

Weekends in the fields
On the weekends, Maharaj ji would serve us a special breakfast of *parantha*s (stuffed bread) or *misi roti* and made sure we ate well so that we could work harder. We would then go to work in the fields. We would work all day in the fields, have our lunch in the fields, and even have our evening tea served in the fields.

Sometimes Maharaj ji would give us a mixture of half a glass of butter oil (ghee) in a glass of hot milk. While this combination is very good for you, gives you lots of strength and energy, it was so heavy it was difficult for us to drink. But Maharaj ji had served us Himself and was watching us so we had to drink it.

Maharaj ji had many cows and buffalo. People collected the dung which was very good fertilizer. The longer it sat in one place, the better it was for the fields. It smelled very bad. We had to carry big bowls of dung on our heads, and then the men would spread it in the fields. It's amazing but the smell never bothered us at all. We would work all day laughing and singing.

No one ever sat idle

We needed three people all the time to pray. One person would read Guru Granth Sahib, one would meditate, and the other person would read Jaap Sahib or Chaupai Sahib. So those who could not work in the fields would stay back and take part in the prayers. This way everyone was involved: either working in the fields, or taking part in the prayers. No one ever sat idle.

One big family

Maharaj ji taught us to respect each other. He would tell us to call all the men, Bhai Sahib (brother) and all the women Bhenji (sister). All the older men would be called Bapuji (father). All of the older women would be called Mataji (mother). We were like a large family. Everyone loved everyone else.

There were many different kinds of people who came to work and live here. There were villagers who had never attended school, and there were very highly educated people from the city. We never felt that someone was better than us, or beneath us. In fact, it was quite interesting to watch the city children mature under the watchful eyes of the villagers who oversaw the field work.

Singing away our fatigue

Many times, we would work until dark. Sometimes Maharaj ji had to provide lights so that we could see in the dark and continue working. After a full day's work, Maharaj ji would sing. When He sang it was so beautiful that it seemed like all the trees, earth, and birds were joining him. If anyone felt tired, after hearing Him sing, all the tiredness would go away. We would then clean up and take showers. Maharaj ji would serve us dinner and instead of going to bed, we would go to *havan* to pray. Sometimes we would just sit and talk about Maharaj ji all night long. Everyone would share his or her experiences.

319

Standing guard at the bathrooms

We had no bathrooms. We would have to go in the fields. In order for us to bathe, they built three walls and we put up a curtain. One girl could bathe while another girl would stand watch outside. This way we would help each other. This is how it all was in the beginning.

The First Akhand Path

As Bibi Jaswant Kaur opened the pages for parkash and took the first hukam, gold flecks fell from heaven. She and Gurcharan gathered them up in their chunis, but when they showed them to Maharaj ji, he quietly took them away. Some things are best kept secret. God will reveal His power to the world in His own time. And now the miracles that continually happen here cannot be hidden.

1969 the complex was complete

At the end of 1969, after many months of hard work, the main complex finally was completed. We had some rooms where people could stay. We had a prayer room, a *Havan*, and Baba Siri Chand ji's room, where we could pray. Maharaj ji started Akhand Path at the farm. It was near the *Havan*, in a tent where Maharaj ji used to sit and listen to our reading.

People now could stay overnight, taking turns to pray. In the morning, they would go to work, and other people would come in the morning to pray. Every evening at the *Havan*, we would sing Baba Siri Chand ji's "Arta" and Chaupai Sahib.

Sometimes Maharaj ji would sit and we would all gather around Him. He would tell us the importance of prayer, and tell us stories of different saints, our Sikh gurus, and other religions.

Loving God

One day while Maharaj ji was sitting with us, He said we should all love God. I thought to myself, "How should I love God?" So I asked. Maharaj ji replied, "Whatever happens in your life, think God is doing that. That is God's love."

There was so much going on. You could pray, clean, cook, or work in the fields. Maharaj ji would be out all day long and He used to sing to us. This was very enjoyable.

320

I didn't want to be anywhere else. There was such a strong pull. If I went any place other than Gobind Sadan, I felt very uncomfortable. I would go to work from there and after work I would go back to Gobind Sadan. I would go home just once a week to do my laundry. It was getting very hard for my parents.

My parents again test me

One day in the afternoon while I was praying, my parents came to see me. They wanted me to go home with them. They stayed for a little while, but I did not return home with them. Afterwards, I was very upset. One of the elder members of the community, told me that I should obey my parents and go home and not stay at Gobind Sadan anymore. This made me so upset that I started to cry. When Maharaj ji came to pray, I was still crying.

Maharaj ji was doing Chaur Sahib (fanning) to Guru Granth Sahib. We were all sitting and listening to the prayers. But I had my face covered in my scarf, and couldn't stop crying. When the prayers ended, Maharaj ji sent Baba Inder Singh to tell me to go to the *havan* and do Jaap Sahib out loud. Then he called the elder and told her to go home for three days and then come back. After three days, Maharaj ji told me that my parents didn't want me to stay there any longer. He said I should come to pray and return home each day.

I had to see Maharaj ji every day

It was very difficult for me, but it was Maharaj ji's Hukam (order) for me to stay at home, so I did. I traveled every morning to pray at the *havan* and then went to work. In the evening, I would leave work and go straight home. This made my parents very happy.

In a few months, it was Maharaj ji's birthday, and I wanted to be in Gobind Sadan praying and doing seva (service) with the *Sangat* (congregation). As usual, I woke up at 1:30 a.m., took my shower, and said all my prayers. That day, the pull was so strong I decided to walk to Gobind Sadan (over ten miles), even though I knew it would be a long walk. I left the house anyway, and walked for a mile. Though I was very scared, I kept going. Once I reached the main road, a truck drove by slowly and the driver saw me walking by

321

myself. I got scared, and turned around and came home. I waited until breakfast, then went to the bus stop to catch the first bus at 6:30 a.m.

He knows my every thought

Once I reached the Gobind Sadan bus stop, I still had a mile to walk. I cried all the way, and kept talking to Maharaj ji in my mind. When I was almost there, I could see Maharaj ji on the hill and the *sangat* was working in the fields below. Maharaj ji started walking towards me. He met me half way and I bowed down to Him. He blessed me and then said exactly what I had been saying to Him in my mind. He repeated the exact same words back to me. He then told me to join the other *sangat* in the fields.

After lunch, He told Gurcharan, Inderjeet, and myself to work in His garden. We all were very happy. We felt that we had been promoted from the fields for the day. I worked all day there and then went home. It was very difficult for me. I kept feeling that something was pulling me and it was a pull of love toward Gobind Sadan.

Back at Gobind Sadan

After a few months I began to stay overnight at Gobind Sadan. In the evening, I would leave work and go directly to Gobind Sadan. But I would go home every morning to change and get ready for work. I had to change two to three buses to reach there.

Maharaj ji watches over me

There were only two buses on that route to take people back and forth from work. The last bus out of Mehrauli in the evening was 6 p.m., which I missed many times. I would have to walk the three miles to get to the farm. I had full faith that Maharaj ji was watching over me and no harm would come to me. Sometimes while I was walking, a man might ride by on a bicycle and he would see me walking by myself. I used to get very scared, and I would pray. Right away, someone I knew would come by on a scooter on his way to Gobind Sadan. They would stop and give me a ride. I knew that Maharaj ji had sent them for me.

After some time went by, I started to stay there and would go home only once a week to do laundry.

God tests your faith

God's path is very difficult, and He tests your faith all the time. My duty in Gobind Sadan was to stay up all night long, to wake the people up for their prayers and serve them tea. I would then go to bed at 5:30 a.m., sleep until 8:00 a.m., and then leave by 8:30 to catch the bus to work.

Maharaj ji never came out of His room until 9:00 a.m., so I could not see Him before I went to work. If I caught the bus on time on the way back, I would be able to see Maharaj ji in the evening. But many times, I would miss the last bus, and had to walk. So by the time I reached Gobind Sadan, Maharaj ji had already gone to His room to pray.

I used to cry when I could not see Him. Sometimes He would come to me in my dreams and bless me. This made me feel very good. Sometimes I would miss the bus in the morning too. I would have to walk three miles to catch the bus, and all the way I would pray and time would go by very fast. It was very difficult.

The days that I had to walk, I would be late for work. This was another test for me, and the girls would tease me. They said I went to Gobind Sadan to see a boy I liked not because I was religious. I knew they were wrong, so their teasing didn't bother me at all.

Gurcharan and I both had jobs away from Gobind Sadan. I was a senior draftsperson in an architect's office. We had to go to work every day. I was tested once again. Maharaj ji arranged a ride to take Gurcharan to work and back every day. There was no ride for me. I had to take the bus both ways. He then directed the women in the *Langar* (kitchen) to give Gurcharan a special breakfast in the morning and pack her a lunch. For me, there was no similar Hukam (order). I had to pack the leftovers from the previous night for my lunch. I knew Maharaj ji was testing my faith. But I was in love with Maharaj ji's mission.

At home, my parents did not want me to go to Gobind Sadan. People at work teased me. People at Gobind Sadan would ask me why I stayed there. But I had seen the Light, and I would never leave it.

323

Sometimes people used to come from the city to see Maharaj ji. They would bring boxes of sweets for Maharaj ji, and Maharaj ji would distribute the sweets to all of us. One day as he was giving sweets to everyone, I had my eyes on a particular piece in the box. I wanted to have that piece of candy. When my turn came, Maharaj ji gave that exact piece to me. I felt so embarrassed. He always knew what was in our minds. Those were very good days. We used to work all day and see Maharaj ji all day long.

We used to eat very simple food, but it was full of blessings. On rainy days, we couldn't make bread. We had to wait until the rain stopped before a fire could be built so that they could make Khichri (a mixture of rice and lentils).

Maharaj ji's birthday gift and my blessing

Once on Maharaj ji's birthday, I bought a Kirpan (sword) for a gift. I wrapped it and put a ribbon all around it. After work, on my way to Gobind Sadan, I missed the last bus, and again had to walk. It was raining very hard that day. Luckily, I had a plastic bag all around the gift. Even though I was all wet, I kept singing all the way.

I didn't care that it was raining. I was going to see my Guru. When I reached Gobind Sadan, everyone was cleaning the floors and Maharaj ji was standing there. I bowed down to Him and gave him His gift.

In the evening when Gurbaksh Singh (who served Maharaj ji) came out, he told me that Maharaj ji unwrapped the gift with great love. He had opened every piece of wrapping and ribbons with much love, as much love as I had put in wrapping it. Gurbaksh Singh told me that I was very lucky.

One morning I was just about to leave for work when Maharaj ji called me into the kitchen. He told me that I was blessed and that from today on, grain would be grown in the fields for me, too. He then told the women in the kitchen to pack me a lunch every morning before I left for work.

That didn't matter so much. I was just happy that He had blessed me. While I knew that all along He had been testing my faith, I was so glad that He had passed me and had not let me fail the test.

No one can kill you

My parents used to worry about me a lot. One day my father told me that I traveled so far away on the lonely roads that someday, someone would kill me and throw my body away. He said that they would never know where I was.

At Gobind Sadan that night, after my duties I had a dream. In my dream, I saw a lot of people sitting with Maharaj ji. Out of the whole crowd, Maharaj ji told Gurbaksh Singh to call me. I went to Maharaj ji. He then told Gurbaksh Singh to bring the sword. Maharaj ji pulled the sword out and slashed through my neck. He cut through my neck three times back and forth, but I was still standing there with my head intact. Nothing had happened to me at all.

In the morning when I told this dream to Gurbaksh Singh, he told me that my father should stop worrying that someone would kill me. He told me that if the sword had not hurt me in my dreams, that no one would harm me. We come into the world with God's order and we will go out of this world with God's order. We will only go when He wants us to go. No one can ever kill us without God's order.

My family vs. Maharaj ji again

But my uncles and aunts were also talking about me, and asking my father why he would allow me to live at Gobind Sadan. One day they all got together and called Gobind Sadan, asking me to come home so they could talk to me. I had to leave to catch the bus, but I wanted to see Maharaj ji before I left. Maharaj ji was up on the hill. I was praying that I wanted to see Him, but I didn't want to go and disturb Him on the hill. I started to leave. When I left the gate, Maharaj ji was standing in front of me. "Your prayers brought me," he said. I told Him that I had to go home, and He blessed me.

When I arrived home, all my uncles and aunts and my parents were waiting. They all tried their best to convince me not to go to Gobind Sadan anymore, but they could not. I felt so sorry for them that they had not experienced the light as I had.

The darkest night

During the war between India and Pakistan, we had blackouts at night time.

One day, after work when I reached Mehrauli, it was totally dark. There were no lights and the buses were not running. I was stuck there. I was very scared. I knew some people who lived in Mehrauli, but I did not know exactly where their house was. I just stood there and prayed.

Now it was quite late, and I was getting very worried. One man came to me and said that they were going to take a taxi and if I wanted to, I could go with them. These people traveled with me every day on the bus and they knew me. I didn't have any choice. I decided to go with them. I was the only woman in the taxi.

They put me in the front seat and the four men sat in back. Though I was sitting in the taxi, I was still very scared. All of a sudden, one man told everyone that I was their sister, and no one should say anything to me at all. They dropped me off at Gobind Sadan's front gate. When I reached there, everyone told me that Maharaj ji was so worried about me. They were all very happy that I had made it home safely.

Buses

People used to worry about me when I would come so late at night. I still had a mile to walk from the bus stop to Gobind Sadan. It was very dark and there were no lights or houses along the way.

One day they felt so sorry for me that they sent Jagjeet Singh to the bus stop to bring me back. When I got off the bus, Jagjeet Singh was standing there with a sword in his hand. He told me that he came to take me back to Gobind Sadan.

When we reached Gobind Sadan, Maharaj ji was serving dinner to everyone. When he saw Jagjeet Singh with me, he asked him where he had been. Jagjeet replied, "I went to the bus stop to pick up Joginder." Maharaj ji got mad at him. "Why did you go there? She is equal to two men. Give her a two-foot sword and nobody will ever dare to touch her." Everyone was very happy. They told me that I was blessed to be equal to two men.

Sometimes Maharaj ji would leave Gobind Sadan in the morning to go to His other farms in Uttar Pradesh. If I knew He was going, I would purposely miss my bus and start walking on the road. Then when Maharaj ji passed me, He would tell the driver to stop and give me a ride. It was wonderful. Maharaj ji himself would drop me at work. One day Gurmukh Singh and Maharaj ji even came to the bus stop in the evening after work to take me back to Gobind Sadan. I felt so lucky that Maharaj ji had come to pick me up.

Take your head in your hands if you want to meet God

One night Maharaj ji was sitting in the prayer room, singing. People were playing the harmonium, drums, and bells, and we all sang along. Maharaj ji was singing:

"If you want to meet God, first put your head on your palm, and then approach Him."

So I began to think that since I wanted to meet God, I should give him my head. As Maharaj ji kept repeating these lines, the thought kept revolving in my mind. While I was singing, I kept saying to myself, "I should give my head." Then Maharaj ji sang: "Words alone are not acceptable." I thought that he was saying that to me.

So finally I got up, picked up a sword that was lying in front of Guru Granth Sahib, went to Maharaj ji, and asked him to take my head. Maharaj ji had his eyes closed. When he opened his eyes, there I was, sitting with a sword in my hand. I told him again, "Please take my head. I want to meet God."

He laughed very hard and blessed me. Afterwards people told me that now that I had given my head. My life was for the mission, and I can't take it back.

Sleepwalking

I used to get only two and a half to three hours of sleep at night. I used to be tired all the time. Sometimes on the way to work, I would fall asleep on the bus and miss my bus stop. Then I would have to take another bus to go back to my stop. At night when I was working at Gobind Sadan, I was up all night long. Sometimes I would be walking towards the *havan* and while walking, I would fall asleep. When I opened my eyes, I had turned around and was walking back from where I came. One evening we were all singing and they were playing harmonium, drums, and bells very loudly. In the middle of all that, I was sitting there fast asleep. Maharaj ji looked at me and said, "How can she sleep in all this noise?" Then he would say, "God is with those people whose eyes are sleepy."

Decorating the dera
On Maharaj ji's birthday, we used to get truckloads of flowers and all the women would take needles and threads and make garlands. We used to decorate the whole complex. Then we would take some rose petals and put them on the path where Maharaj ji would walk. There was never a dull moment. There was always something to do.

Cleanliness next to Godliness
Maharaj ji loved cleanliness. Every morning He would go to all of the rooms and would check to see if the beds were made and if the rooms were clean.

The Pir of Bareilly and Guru Gobind Singh ji's relics
While Maharaj ji was visiting a devotee in Bareilly, he saw that a certain Pir had a sky-blue *chola* (gown) of Guru Gobind Singh ji, the Tenth Sikh Guru. Now it so happened that a devotee of the Pir was at the gathering and heard Maharaj ji speak about the chola. He hurried back to tell his Master. The Pir was stunned. He had hidden the relics safely and had told no one about them. When he heard of Maharaj ji's vision, the Pir insisted on meeting Maharaj ji and invited Him to see the *chola,* the walking stick of Pir Budha Shah, who had served Guru Gobind Singh, and another blood stained *chola* of one of Guru Gobind Singh ji's sons who had been killed in battle.

After Maharaj ji left, Guru Gobind Singh ji appeared to the Pir and ordered him to deliver the relics to Maharaj ji at Gobind Sadan. So he and his entourage came to Delhi with the chola and other things. Maharaj ji sent people from Gobind Sadan to receive them. When they arrived at Gobind Sadan, they were welcomed and Maharaj ji carried the robe on his head. He brought it to the prayer room where Pir Sahib and Maharaj ji sat. There was singing, and it was a very special occasion. After a few months, Pir Sahib invited Maharaj ji to Bareilly and we all went with Maharaj ji, too. It was a wonderful experience. The Pir Sahib and his followers all sang for us and it was very nice.

Respect for Women

There was a woman who used to come to Gobind Sadan to serve Maharaj ji. When she went home, her husband used to beat her. We have always heard that Guru Gobind Singh ji's spiritual army patrols the area. One day the husband came to Gobind Sadan and Guru Gobind Singh ji's Sikhs beat him up. We couldn't see anyone at all beating him, but he was moving his hands to protect himself. He was crying out in pain, but no one was there. Later on, he apologized to Maharaj ji that he was beating his wife and he promised that he would not do it anymore.

Digging the well by hand

Because of the growing community, we needed more water. So we dug a 50-foot well by hand. Men dug, and all the women carried away the dirt in bowls. We used to stand in lines and pass the big bowls of dirt from one to another. The well was so deep that we had to put ladders down the well so that the men could stand on the bottom and send bowls of dirt upwards to the people above. By evening, our arms would be black and blue, but we never felt any pain at all. The next morning, we would be ready to work again. We finished the well in one month. We all worked very hard to complete this. After the well was completed and water began to flow, Maharaj ji blessed us all.

Brig. Sahib, Gurnam Singh Randhawa at Maharaj ji's feet

Epilogue-II

Famous Alumni – The Pillars of Gobind Sadan

Good universities invite famous graduates back to mingle with the students and share their real life experiences applying the lessons they have learnt. Those listed below are perhaps the most decorated of Gobind Sadan's graduates who have passed on. It has been a privilege having known them, and they all contributed something special to my life. They are the pillars of Gobind Sadan. The one's on whose shoulders we all stand on.

Brig Sahib – I.G. Gurnam Singh Randhawa

To date there is no more 'decorated' a graduate of Gobind Sadan than I.G. (Inspector General of Police) Gurnam Singh Randhawa, a true saint and soldier who devoted his life to Maharaj ji's mission of spreading *Nam*, of healing people's illnesses, and bringing peace wherever he went. His spiritual power was unbelievable and the miracles that Maharaj ji worked through him could fill volumes. And for a child of the 60's and the Vietnam era of American history this was a revelation indeed.

If there was ever a present day Arjun and Lord Krishna it was Brig Sahib and Maharaj ji. He was also my first translator and he would often ask Maharaj ji to show me things. After we would sit together in Baba Siri Chand's *havan* in the mornings for meditation, when he was on leave and he would tell me story after story of how Maharaj ji helped him. They were inseparable. He had so much faith that Maharaj ji would answer His every prayer, from curing his dog, to providing boots and provisions for his men, curing the sick and bringing peace to war torn areas. He had total confidence in Maharaj ji's ability to solve every problem. I never saw him without a *mala* in his hand. *Nam* was on every breath. And yet he was the humblest of men. When I first asked him what he did, he simply replied, "I'm a soldier."

Brig Sahib once told me, "The difference between you and me is that you pray to everyone, and I only pray to Sarawan wale." It has taken me many years to understand the full impact of this statement. Maharaj ji had taught me to love everyone (all the prophets and saints) as my family and I was in the habit of asking all their blessings. Maharaj ji commented to me that Brig Sahib was so firm in his loyalty, that once Guru Gobind Singh ji himself appeared before him and Brig Sahib didn't bow until Maharaj ji also appeared, as if to prove the often quoted line from Mira Bai enshrined in Guru Granth Sahib,

Guru Gobind dono kare – kis ko lago paiy.
Balihari Guru aapni, Sadgur diyo milai.

When the Guru and God both stand before me who should I
bow to first.

I'll bow to my Guru who brought me to God's feet.

I'll just share some of my favorites – I'm sure at some point Brig Sahib's life stories will be published:

Before Brig Sahib sat for meditation or reciting Jaap Sahib, he would always stand in prayer to Maharaj ji, fold his hands and ask very simply and humbly that Maharaj ji allow him to recite *Nam* or give him the blessings to sing His praises. Watching him it was obvious that he was literally standing in Maharaj ji's presence and asking for permission to carry out orders as a soldier would of his commanding officer.

He shared his stories of how Maharaj ji took care of him and his troops in the midst of battle. How he would sit in meditation in the morning and then tell his troops according to what Maharaj ji had showed him – he joked that they often wondered which HQ he was getting his orders from.

Bandipur on the Pakistan Border

The '71 war broke out shortly after my arrival and Brig Sahib was posted to Bandipur.

He used to walk unseen across enemy lines and was shown the names of all the opposing generals and all the opposing troop positions. He said they captured more of enemy territory than any other position though they had the least number of men. He had the women take over all the desk jobs and took every man into the field.

One Sikh soldier refused to recite *Ek onkar satnam siri waheguru*, claiming that waheguru was the only true *Nam* for a Sikh to recite and he was the only one of all the troops to be wounded. A similar episode happened when troops had to cross a raging river. Brig Sahib called out, anyone who recites *Nam* will cross without a problem and the men rushed into the water and were coming out unharmed on the other side. One Sikh was caught in the torrent and close to going under, when Brig Sahib called him. "Recite *Nam*," he shouted to the man. "I am, *Waheguru Waheguru*," he was sputtering. As soon as he recited *Ek onkar satnam siri Waheguru* he stopped bobbing and was able to make it safely across. Brig Sahib smiled. "It is the power of the Guru that kept you alive."

At one point Maharaj ji was jokingly considering sending me to the front to get over any fears I had. Being in battle under Brig Sahib's command, I'm sure would have been a great experience, however being an American it just wasn't possible.

Mizoram

Then when a rebel leader killed all the high command in a daring attack in Mizoram –Brig Sahib was moved from BSF to I G of Police, almost unprecedented for an army officer to be made head of civil police. He said when he arrived to address his command he told the Police Forces directly that he brings Maharaj ji's power of *Nam*.

The Christmas present

One of the most touching stories he shared with me was that of the paralyzed little boy who wanted nothing more than to ride a bike. He couldn't even walk, but had asked his parent to get him the bike for Christmas. The boy kept praying for the bike and his prayers reached Maharaj ji. Now Brig. Sahib had never met the family and didn't know about the boy. But when he sat in meditation Maharaj ji told Brig Sahib about his prayer.

The next day he drove to the boy's house and introduced himself to the astounded parents. After all the I.G. of police doesn't pull up to your house every day. And he certainly doesn't ask, "Do you have a disabled son?"

"Yes, but how did you know?"

Brig Sahib then asked to see the boy. "Son did you pray for a bike?" "Yes," the boy replied.

Then he turned back to the parents with a stern smile. "What's there to think about, get him the bike."

"Son, the One who heard your prayer, will also give you the strength to ride. Just thank him and recite, 'Ek Onkar Satnam Siri Waheguru.'"

The next morning the frantic parents couldn't find the boy. He wasn't in his bed. Then they looked out the window and saw he was riding his new bike. They called Brig Sahib who came right over. He went out to the boy and asked him, "Son, How is it you don't fall?" With a big smile on his face, he replied, "Whenever I start to wobble and feel I might fall, I just recite *Nam* and this hand comes and holds me up."

Capture of Lalia the rebel leader in Mizoram

As in Vietnam there was no real way of knowing your friends from your enemies. The rebel leader was so evasive no one had a clue. So Brig Sahib just prayed: Maharaj ji whenever I stop my jeep I should catch a key leader. So that day as he was driving around Maharaj ji told him to stop next to a man. The person he escorted into his jeep turned out to be the chief of rebel intelligence. Through that lead, Brig Sahib and his men were finally able to lay a trap for the rebel leader. The officer who finally captured and killed him in a hand to hand struggle came to Gobind Sadan to present half of his reward to Maharaj ji – for saving his life. We have Baba Inder Singh on tape interviewing him in Maharaj ji's presence. He was reciting *Nam* and when Lalia came on top of him and put his gun to his head to kill him – the bullet broke in the chamber and he was able to regain control from the shocked leader and dispatch him.

334

Brig Sahib spoke of the power of Jaap Sahib to protect his officers. They were posted in a house right in the center of a clearing surrounded by woods infested by rebels. They recited Jaap sahib all night and no attack came.

He asked the missionaries who would Christ like more, the rebels or his troops? The rebels have no respect for the women, they take labor and materials without paying and snatch your food, whereas my men respect your women and always pay for everything we take. He told them we don't want to kill your children, and instead let's find a peaceful solution. He would use his men and helicopters to help them rebuild their churches or schools.

Nagaland

He told how once he had asked Maharaj ji to accompany him on a mission in the jungle and forgot to ask Maharaj ji to sit in the jeep. Meanwhile back in Gobind Sadan – Maharaj ji's feet began to bleed.

Basketball and mountain climbing

Brig Sahib told me that the power of *Nam* was not limited to "serious matters". In a basketball game he would toss the ball from mid court to watch the astonished looks on his troops' faces as it would go effortlessly through the hoop. In mountain exercises he would challenge the younger soldiers to race him up a steep slope and he would never lose.

Maharaj ji will always keep a place for me

There used to be a small red stool in Baba Siri Chand ji's shrine. One day Brig Sahib pointed to it and said, "Maharaj ji will always keep a place for me by His side." So whenever you are in Maharaj ji's presence, respect the areas closest to Maharaj ji. For those seats may already be taken.

Sardarni Nirlep Kaur – Bibi ji

If you ever wanted to meet a fearless leader, Bibi Nirlep Kaur was it. A regally beautiful woman for whom politics was literally her lifeblood. She was daughter of the famed Gyan Singh Rarewala the first Chief Minister of Pepsu, the state preceding Punjab following partition, and Mata Rarewala whose will was equally indomitable. (I had the pleasure of almost grandchild status with both of them).

While Nirlep became a key mentor and very strict mother to me. She saw that I was comfortably settled and made sure whatever I needed I could get, often making forays to Wengers for special treats for me. But once I was in her residence she became a tough taskmaster. She was a Member of Parliament and had turned her 9 Teen Murti house into Maharaj ji's residence where early *sangat* came to see him while GS was being built. It was her 7 acres which she donated to for the original Gobind Sadan.

She was a tireless worker shuttling back and forth between Gobind Sadan, Delhi and Chandigarh. She was instrumental in the Sis Ganj settlement and the formation of the Delhi Gurdwara Parbandak Committee, the Pheruman Akali Dal, and President of the Takhat Patna Sahib Management Committee- all male dominated positions. Not only did she hold her own, she dominated. With Nirlep, there was no other way. She would cut her way through the toughest opposition. We at Gobind Sadan owe her our lives. She paved the way with hers. Giving up whatever free time she had to raise the name and image of Maharaj ji and Gobind Sadan.

Laughing in the face of death

At the height of the Punjab terrorist movement, Bibi ji was near the top of the hit list. She was outspoken against Bindranwale and his crusade. She told me this story with a chuckle. "I was sitting at home on Curzon Road (now KG Marg) when the phone rang. I picked it up and said hello. The voice on the other end was thick and muffled, 'This is death. Your time has come.' The poor boy sounded so funny I simply laughed." That was the quintessential Bibi ji. No one could dare attack her.

While there was much blustering among the Sikh leadership, Bibi ji had supported Darshan Singh Pheruman. This stalwart had declared a hunger strike in protest against corruption and abuses and while his opponent Sant Fateh Singh, backed out on his vow, Pheruman firmly maintained his strike till death.

During the emergency, there came a point when Bibi ji was seriously considering committing to a hunger strike. She had consulted with doctors, had her blood pressure checked and was totally prepared. But fortunately for all of us, the issue passed and she was spared the necessity.

Sergey Bermeniev May 2004

Longman Studio

Driving during the blackout

During the Indo-Pak war, I was in the car with Bibi ji outside of Chandigarh when the sirens went off. It was getting dark and we still had quite a ways to go. But stubbornly and fearlessly she maintained her composure and drove the almost deserted road without lights to deliver us safely home.

Translating in America

Bibi ji accompanied Maharaj ji on his first visit to the U.S. in 1986. She was immediately welcomed and served as his translator at all functions, most notably at Sandy Reyes' house where she lit up the room of Syracuse dignitaries. Sandy still keeps the space 'sacred' where they both sat.

Gyani ji – Gyani Gurdev Singh

When I first arrived at Gobind Sadan, Gyani ji was my constant companion. He was my first room-mate and Maharaj ji had him tie my first turban (a very significant event for he was accepting responsibility for mentoring me). Gyani Gurdev Singh, farmer from the neighboring village, retired soldier, but best known for being Maharaj ji's earliest disciple since Maharaj ji's youth in Sarawan. First blessed with vision and healing, Maharaj ji developed Gyani ji into the Chaplain for his flock and sent people to Gyani ji to offer prayers for them.

It was Gyani ji whom Maharaj ji had recite Sukhmani Sahib to revive a boy brought dead before them. It was Gyani ji who was not only witness to the early miracles but who participated and to whom Maharaj ji passed the gift of vision and healing.

Gyani ji and the election

While Gyani ji's visions were infallible, they were often extremely humorous. Nirlep was sitting on the porch with M and asked about the upcoming elections. Maharaj ji called Gyani ji and posed the question. Gyani ji touched Maharaj ji's feet and closed his eyes. "A spinning wheel is beating a rooster, jumping all over it," he began totally seriously. It was hard to imagine a cartoon of an animated spinning wheel in a "cockfight." But when Nirlep explained that they were the symbols of 2 parties in the election it became clear.

Syracuse basketball

One much closer to home literally occurred when the boys were with us at the Shiv Sadan guesthouse. Totally out of range of any electronic media or even newspapers, Chetan was trying to figure out how his home team SU had done against Notre Dame. "Just ask Gyani ji," I suggested. "Dad?" "Seriously." So we did. Gyani ji took Chetan on his lap, closed his eyes and described the scene. A small green man was throwing oranges against the wall and they were splattering. ND had beaten SU. Chetan was stunned. Impossible. SU was nationally ranked and it was a home game. He must be wrong.

Soon I had the chance of going to Delhi and found a copy of USA Today. "ND beats SU," blazed across the top of the sports section. I brought it back to confirm Chetan's fears. And from then on Chetan was very comfortable asking Gyani ji any question.

Day or night, this kind soul would take calls from people all over the world from people in senior positions of power to villagers answering their questions and passing on Maharaj ji's blessings. The man in the red dress (as ordered by Maharaj ji) continued to counsel and spread the greatness of Maharaj ji's blessings until his death.

Baba Inder Singh

Senior Superintendent of Railway Police Inder Singh was a hulking man with nothing but kindness for me. But in command of his men he cut a fearsome figure. Maharaj ji blessed him early on to do ardas and he was always present at any community function I can remember. He figures prominently throughout Gobind Sadan's early history. He helped preside over our wedding, helped bring the *chola* from Bareilly, accompanied Maharaj ji to Simla and Chandigarh just to name a few major events. Following his retirement he applied to the Sikh Management Committee to serve in any of the historic Gurdwaras. He was appointed administrator at Patna Sahib the birthplace of Guru Gobind Singh ji and in no time had cleaned up some of the less than moral practices that he uncovered including selling wheat from the *langar* on the market. He had invited me to speak at Patna Sahib, so I had the pleasure of spending 5 days with him. He was always so gracious. The last I saw him was at the Jaap Sahib Seminar, when he had aged to the point where he needed a cane.

Dr. Gurcharan Singh Randhawa

Younger brother of Brig. Sahib, Dr. Sahib, was also greatly blessed with spiritual power.

Educated both in India and abroad (at Cornell), he was a senior scientist at the Pusa Institute in Delhi when he met Maharaj ji and later retired as the Director of the Horticultural Institute in Bangalore where his family still lives.

Once he told me, that Maharaj ji had created such a spiritual connection between him and his wife, that when he would return from a business trip he would never need to call her, she would automatically arrive at the airport at the appointed time to receive him.

The Mullicks of Corning, among others, owe their children to his prayers. His vision was so precise that it was fabled. Two stories stand out:

A young friend had gone to see a movie. When Dr. Randhawa spoke to him on the phone shortly thereafter, the man shared that he'd just returned from the movie hall. "I know," replied Dr. Sahib, and proceeded to describe each scene to the delight and amazement of his friend.

Maharaj ji himself likes to tell the next story:

Shortly before a major meeting, Dr. Sahib shared with his colleagues the entire agenda and even gave the answers to the questions that would be raised. As the meeting commenced. The entire order of business proceeded exactly as he had foretold, down to the details of the answers. Following the meeting his colleagues wanted to meet Maharaj ji as soon as possible, to ask that they be given the same power he had blessed Dr. Randhawa with.

Swaranjit Singh

If there was anyone in the *sangat* who Maharaj ji trusted as an advisor, it was Swaranjit. Son of one of the few Indians knighted by the

339

British, Sardar Bahadur Gurbax Singh, OBE, he had lost everything during partition but maintained his childhood love. Always a maverick and decisive risk taker, he put his family's position on the line and married his sweetheart, Prem. He rebuilt himself into one of the most respected business leaders in India, but unlike some whose greed dominated their decisions, he was motivated by generosity and the well-being of humanity. Swaranjit was a mentor, a friend, the one I'd turn to in difficult times. And he was the one who could always get his points across to Maharaj ji.

Maharaj ji brought Swaranjit with him to try to turn the old dairy farm at Gobind Sadan, USA into a viable business model. He spent countless hours running numbers, tramping through fields looking at cows and equipment, reviewing plans, and looking for funding. In the end without a huge infusion of cash, we just couldn't make it work.

In my eulogy to him I wrote:

He led the Institute with great dedication and wisdom since its inception. He had been a pillar of Gobind Sadan from the beginning, donating the first tractor in 1971, and an ever-faithful devotee of Baba Virsa Singh since he first met him in 1968. He was Gobind Sadan's leading 'Ambassador.' Much of the groundwork for the success of Babaji's recent trip to Russia we owe to him – for he sowed the seeds for Babaji's mission when he single-handedly escorted Babaji to Russia in 1989. He was a world-renowned engineer and retired as a Founder-Director of Escorts Ltd., one of the largest industries in North India. Gobind Sadan will miss him greatly …

Speaking to his family, Baba Virsa Singh said, "Thank God that He sent such a good person, into such a good family, and then took him so peacefully. We made him President of our Societies, and he always gave the welcoming speeches. He was the one who opened the door to Russia, and now they welcome us with so much love. We really miss him. We always felt that he was the elder of our house."

Surendra Nath

In Surendra Nath's own words in tribute to Maharaj ji, he described himself as a skeptical scientist with the cynicism of a professional policeman who came from a Hindu fundamentalist family. But while serving as Chief Secretary of Mizoram at the time of the insurrection, he was brought to Maharaj ji by I.G. Randhawa, and there at his feet vented his feelings, exhausted his life long questions, and found himself totally in love with and bound to Maharaj ji from that time on. I can see him sitting at Maharaj ji's feet in the green room, behind the Darbar Sahib room, asking for clarification of the passages of Jaap Sahib that he was in the midst of translating. His cap always cocked smartly, his sharp eyes both pierced and embraced you, Surendra Nath was a force both within Gobind Sadan and in India. Before his unfortunate accident, he served as Governor of Punjab during the 80's, a time of extreme turmoil, and terrorist outbreaks. With Maharaj ji's blessings and guidance he quelled the fires of extremism, mitigated to whatever extent he could the killing of the youth of Punjab who were often caught up in police or army encounters. In the Governor's mansion, for the first time, he placed a life-sized portrait of Guru Gobind Singh, had *parkash* of Guru Granth Sahib and a *havan* that was tended continuously. Jaap Sahib was always recited there and at one point it is said that the leaders of the movement had seen their defeat was near and declared, "The governor has taken all our source of power (spiritual)." Whatever be said about this man in history books, I can only say that he was a leader of great vision for the future of his country, decisive in his actions, and completely loyal to his Guru.

Harvinder Singh

Each community has its colorful characters, the ones without whom life just wouldn't be the same. Harvinder, or for Maharaj ji his 'malang,' was one of a kind. He was a cut above any of the other residents having retired from a senior post with a major company, he left the comfort of his family home to live simply in Gobind Sadan. In dealing with the various Indians who had set up spiritual shops abroad, he loved to say, "Frawd and Gawd (Fraud and God) can't go together."

One day when Maharaj ji was planning a trip to Sarawan, he caught up with me in the fields, looked me straight in the eyes and with a very serious look on his face said, "Maharaj ji is going to

341

recharge his batteries." I couldn't help smiling. "What do you mean, Harvinder?" "From time to time Maharaj ji returns to his village to recharge his batteries, that's where the original energy came from." While this would have intrigued the science fiction lover in me, Maharaj ji's power was far too pervasive to require plugging in to a specific spot to recharge. "Harvinder," I retorted, "if Maharaj ji can appear to me in the US then why would he need to go to a specific place to recharge?" Seeing that he was not getting the kind of desired response, his gaze fell a bit beneath his spectacles. But I gave him a hug anyway and said it was an interesting idea.

Harvinder loved to sing *Nam* at gatherings and in his high-pitched voice would often lead the *sangat* after Maharaj ji's talks. But this to his mind made him sort of an expert on the subject. His small book, "The science of the mind," tucked safely in his pocket would be passed unsurreptitiously to those he felt would benefit. He had hoped to pass out of the world without leaving his body behind, and when extremely angered because one of the villagers would pull his leg or not show him his due respect, he often would let them know it. But Maharaj ji (so far) has not allowed any of us to so distinguish ourselves. But God bless Harvinder for all that he did to make me and many others feel at home in Gobind Sadan.

Balwant Singh

farm manager, Maharaj ji's driver, and constant companion. Bant died suddenly in 2006. His broad shoulders had supported so much work that it took the Gobind Sadan community almost a year to recover. My memories of Bant are countless but just to get a flavor of the man I'll share a few.

Friends of ours from Syracuse, the Spitzers loved Maharaj ji very much and happened to visit India while Maharaj ji was with us in America. Bant was put in charge of their stay and he looked after their every need. But what sticks with them the most is the time he took them to see the Red Fort chauffeuring them comfortably in the old Mercedes. After the tour they returned to the parking lot to find the Mercedes totally packed in with smaller cars. They were tired and the way it looked it would be hours before the lot cleared. But Bant saw it differently. He picked up the car behind by the front wheels and pushed it back. Then went to the car in front and did the same providing enough room to maneuver out of the tight situation. To this day they remind me about it.

Bant was an expert on getting out of tough situations. As long as he was in control things would go smoothly. He was a master organizer. The larger the function the easier the logistics were for him. Aside from managing the farm, he was a father to much of the dera making sure each person had what they needed.

Most importantly, he never left his Guru's side. When needed he was on duty 24 hours a day sacrificing his personal comfort and family for the well-being of the One he loved and served until death took him away.

Baba Gurbaksh Singh

There was no more humble and faithful servant than Gurbaksh Singh. Always by Maharaj ji's side, carrying a towel and water pot from which Maharaj ji could turn water to *jal* (holy water) simply by dipping his fingers in and then blessing people. He was Maharaj ji's cook, and companion until his death.

Introduction to a pressure cooker

Bibi Nirlep Kaur was always looking for ways to upgrade the service around Maharaj ji and Gobind Sadan. So in order to make Baba Gurbaksh Singh's life as a cook easier she brought him a pressure cooker. She briefly showed him how it would cut down on time for making dal and gave him a crash course in opening and closing it. But apparently either she had forgotten to caution him not to open it under pressure or he didn't get the message. Anyway, the first day he used it he was quite happy. The steam was shooting out of the top and he figured it was time to open it. Unfortunately it had not cooled properly and it exploded. Fortunately, with Maharaj ji's blessings he escaped serious injury. His face was more red from embarrassment than from burns. Needless to say, the pressure cooker was left under the counter from then on.

An eagle eye

When Maharaj ji came to the U.S. the second time, he brought Baba Gurbaksh Singh along. Standing behind our home looking out over the field, he asked me how many acres we had. I said about 20. Gurbaksh Singh became very angry. "Call the town clerk. He has cheated you. There are no more than 16 acres here." Rather than calling the clerk, I went to my files and pulled out an old tax record. Sure enough the total acreage was in fact 16 plus.

Baba Dayal Singh

The tank where Geeta and his wife Sushil live today was home to Baba Dayal Singh, the first person, other the His sister Amarjit, to proclaim Maharaj ji a Saint. Prominent in all the early photos, Dayal Singh ji, would spend his time tending his garden and meditating at the havan.

Dr. Bhai Mohun Singh

He is a legend in the Sikh community. His is one of the most successful business stories in modern India. He had grown from a small chemist shop that he bought into one of the world's foremost Pharmaceuticals, Ranbaxy. Despite his success in business, his reverence for Guru Granth Sahib and his love of kirtan were fabled. He was the model of a Sikh gentleman. But after he came to Maharaj ji late in life, he never left his side. At any major function, he was pictured with his blanket sitting nearby. For us, it was public love and devotion to Maharaj ji and his mission, that distinguished him. Taking over as head of the Institute, he was asked to make VIP arrangements for Maharaj ji on a trip to the U.S. during his transit in London. He called his friend, the then British High Commissioner, and when asked to describe Maharaj ji, he replied: "As Jesus is to you, Maharaj ji is to me." The accommodation was immediately made.

Glossary

Achar – home made fruit or vegetable pickle

Aachar – character

Akhand Path – continuous reading of Guru Granth Sahib's 1430 pages in 48 hours –

Ardas – supplication before God - individual or communal often offered before Guru Granth Sahib (Holy scripture)

Chauri Sahib – fly which waved reverently over scripture or other sacred places

Dana – grain mixture

Darbar Sahib – King's court - used to refer to room where Guru Granth Sahib "reigns"

Darvish – saint

Datri – sickle

Dera – the community compound

Fauj – army

Gaddi – ceremonial seat

Gur – jaggery

Gurbani – the Guru's teachings as enshrined in Guru Granth Sahib

Guru Granth Sahib – Holy Scripture containing revelations of Guru Nanak and successive Gurus and saints born in both Hindu and Muslim families

Gyan – Enlightenment

Havan – sacred fire

Jaap Sahib – Guru Gobind Singh's empowering cosmic hymn in praise of God

Japji Sahib – Guru Nanak's 'preamble' to the Guru Granth Sahib – the essence of the Gurus' teachings

Jot – oil lamp

Kafir – impure one

Kalam – holy words

Keertan – hymns of praise - singing God's praises

Khalsa – a defender of Faith; the modern templar knight; one who embodies the Truth and light of God

Khassi or khai – a spade - used in a axe like motion

Khoya – milk based sweet

Langar – community kitchen and meal - established by Gurus to eliminate caste

Lavan – the sacred rounds in a marriage ceremony

Mutka – clay pot

Nam – God's holy name - Ek Onkar Satnam Siri Waheguru

Papita – papaya

Parantha – fried pan bread often stuffed with potatoes or vegetables

Parshad – blessed offering - can be sweets or in Sikh communities - a pudding of flour butter and sugar - as brought back from heaven by Guru Nanak - food for the Gods

Path – spiritual lessons - passages of scripture

Prakash – the spreading of light - refers to the ceremonial opening of Guru Granth Sahib

Rhumbi – a straight bladed trowel-like tool for digging and weeding

Sangat – the congregation or community members - those who have shared values

Seva – selfless service to humanity

Shwara – the engagement ceremony named after the dried date placed in grooms mouth

Sikh – a disciple of God - one in search of Truth

Smagari – loose incense made of dried flowers, bark, fruits, herbs and spices

Toka – chopping machine for fodder

Vuts – a ridge of dirt dividing fields for irrigation purposes

Note: If the transliterations of quotes from Guru Granth Sahib or Guru Gobind Singh Ji's Dasam Granth may not be 100% accurate, please forgive me. There is still much debate about standardizing transliteration of *Gurmukhi* script into English or other languages where the phonetics of the vowels and consonants may vary.

Notes of Thanks

To my family

To my loving lifelong companion Joginder and our wonderful children Chetan and Tegbir and our new daughter Sukhpreet, and Granddaughter Budhivali – and to my mother Anne who used to correct my school papers, my father Nathan who made every sacrifice to help me, and my grandmother Bessie who spared nothing for her only grandchild, and the Rakieten clan for showering love on me throughout my youth.

And to Gagan and the future of Gobind Sadan.

To my classmates

Of my class, many have already graduated. My dear friends and mentors, translators and tutors, those who cared for me in my early years here, I now have no way to repay them but pass the gifts of kindness and warmth that they shared with me on to the countless others who will come after me. For I was a child in a new family, and while I knew my Father, I came to know and love all my brothers and sisters. To those who are still here I love dearly and constantly learn from sharing new and old perspectives on our life and lessons together.

To Gobind Sadan's current class, all our friends in America and across the globe who share our love of Babaji, our Russian family, and all those across the Republics who will bring forth His vision.

To my childhood friends who had to put up with me while I was searching.

To my teachers and mentors in Syracuse and Islip, at the Gunnery, University of Rochester and Columbia.

To my clients who trusted me with their business.

To all our friends in the Interfaith movement, pioneers in a new world order

To my friends who read and helped me through this effort and were very much part of the story: Jeff Shaw, Arnold Kotler, Joe O'Brien, Jean Polly, Dick Breyer, Major Kirpal Singh, Mary Pat Fisher, Bob Serafini, Fred Fiske, Jay and Sherry Sidhu, Kuldip Nayar, Masooma Ali, S.K. Ghai and the Sterling Family.

Gur Sikh Sikh Guru
Eko Guru Updesh Chalaya

The Guru and His Sikh spread the Same Message

Appendix

Bar Mitzvah Talk
Ralph Neal Rakieten
27 May, 1961

In my Torah portion, it tells how the families of the children of Israel all took part in the building of their "tent of meeting", their ark, and the rest of the furnishings. Not just one family contributed-every family gave what they could and did what they could. This working together is called cooperation.

You can apply cooperation to almost anything in this world. I'm sure that many freedoms we have in our United States would not have come about unless many people had cooperated.

A game of baseball is a prime example of cooperation. If just one of the outfielders played by the rules and really played a hard game I doubt that the team would win. However, if the whole team abided by the rules and tried their best, the team would have a good chance of winning.

Teamwork is necessary also in the operation of a factory. You need a person to design the machines, people to build them and people to run them If there was only the designer, there would be a plan for the machine, but no builder, and no worker.

Our congregation today is faced with a problem similar to the one described in the Torah,

We need to build a new Temple. It would be a simple job if everyone would contribute in some way , like our forefathers did: And we even have an advantage not available to our ancestors-in the building of the ancient "tent of meeting", only the sons from 30 to 50 years of age were assigned any task. In our modern times, We can ask not only the sons – not only those of a special age- but the daughters, the mothers, and yes even the grandparents.

If everybody in this world would contribute to our world's welfare we would have a better place to live. Cooperation is the key to success without it we would be lost. Cooperation is not just important on a team, in a factory, or building our temple, it's important to the whole world.

A Tribute

I had prepared this poem long in advance of Maharaj ji's birthday in 2008 and put it away, much like a Christmas present hidden in the cupboard until the awaited day. Now it is only fitting to share it with you:

I'm sure the Gurus turned to poetry because no ordinary words can describe You
In the language of the heart words come pouring out,
Gushing in a fountain of light.
Trying to illuminate what is already Light.
But the words can't stop so you pour in the Light and the words come out.
Illuminating the mind and the world of those who read them.

You are the One

8-30-07

Yours is the sweetest song - the hand that holds the universe
The hand that spins all time, on which the threads of creation are spun
You are the One of Divine Love
The One of Divine Glory, the One of Divine Creation
Let us always sing your praises

You are the One, in whose hands the world revolves
You are the One from whose eyes the Light to vanquish darkness shines

You are the One
You are the one whose eyes shower blessings,
Rays of hope on those in need
Your eyes pour salve on our wounds and heal the sick
You are the One with whose every breath the oceans swell
and the wind moves clouds across the sky.
You are the one - No one else.
You are the One whose feet create the path for us to follow
You are the One.
You are the One whose very touch is beyond description.
Moving every molecule, every atom to love.
How can hate stand before You? Every particle bows
and sings Your praises or vanishes before Thee.
You are the One
You are the One
You are the One whom we have dreamed of.
There is No Other, You are the One.
You have finally come, how lucky we are.
You are the One for whom we have cried for ages
You are the One for whom we have died for ages
You are the One whose praises have been sung for ages
You are the One
No one else can take Your place. You are the One
The time is near when you will appear to all near and far. You are the
One.
What else need we say? It is just your divine play
And we must act according to your will - You are the One
The Hands of time, the smile that spreads across the Cosmos
Bringing joy as angels' songs descend from heaven
You are the One. No words can describe You, No way to praise
You.
Yet I must sing Your praises for You are the One - Sarawan wale
You are the One, Sarawan wale, You are the One.

•••